EVERYTHING
YOU NEED TO KNOW ABOUT...

Playing
Piano
and Keyboards

EVERYTHING

YOU NEED TO KNOW ABOUT...

Playing Piano
and Keyboards

BROOKE HALPIN

David & Charles

A DAVID & CHARLES BOOK

David & Charles is a subsidiary of F+W (UK) Ltd.,

an F+W Publications Inc. company

First published in the UK in 2004

First published in the USA as
The Everything® Playing Piano and Keyboards Book,
by Adams Media Corporation in 2002

Updates and amendments copyright © 2004 David & Charles
Copyright © 2002 Adams Media Corporation

Project Manager Ian Kearey
Cover Design Ali Myer

A catalogue record for this book is available from the British Library.

ISBN 0 7153 2064 5

Printed in Great Britain by CPI Bath
for David & Charles
Brunel House   Newton Abbot   Devon

Visit our website at www.davidandcharles.co.uk

David & Charles books are available from all good bookshops;
alternatively you can contact our Orderline on (0)1626 334555 or
write to us at FREEPOST EX2110, David & Charles Direct,
Newton Abbot, TQ12 4ZZ (no stamp required UK mainland).

Contents

ACKNOWLEDGMENTS ix
INTRODUCTION xi

CHAPTER 1 History of the Piano 1

The First Piano 2
The Square Piano 3
The Sustain Pedal 4
The Iron Frame 4
Upright Pianos 5
Piano Manufacturers 5
The Family of Keyboard
        Instruments 6

CHAPTER 2 Classical Repertoire
        for the Piano 9

Piano Sonatas 10
Piano Sonata Composers 11
Romantic Composition Styles 16
Piano Concertos 16

CHAPTER 3 Jazz and Pop Repertoire
        for the Piano 19

Well-Known Jazz Pianists 20
Rock and Roll Piano 20
The Beatles and the Piano 21
The Year of Piano Pop 23
Piano in the 1970s 24
Since the 1980s 26

CHAPTER 4 Famous Classical
        Pianists 27

The Classical Composers 28
Recordings of the Classics 28
Victor Borge 30
Alfred Brendel 31
Glenn Gould 33

CHAPTER 5 Famous Romantic
        Pianists 35

Fryderyk François Chopin 36
Van Cliburn 37
Vladimir Horowitz 39
Franz Liszt 40
Ignacy Jan Paderewski 43
Arthur Rubinstein 47
Rudolf Serkin 48

CHAPTER 6 Famous Pop and
        Jazz Pianists 51

Jazz Piano 52
Ray Charles 53
Scott Joplin 54
Oscar Peterson 55
Art Tatum 58
Pop Piano 59
Billy Joel 59
Elton John 61

CHAPTER 7 Types of Pianos 63

Vertical Pianos 64
Horizontal Pianos 65
Exterior Parts of a Piano 66
Interior Parts of a Piano 69
Famous Models 74

CHAPTER 8 Electronic Keyboards 75

Electric Pianos 76
Electric Piano Versus Acoustic Piano . . 76
Digital Pianos 78
Digital Piano Versus Acoustic Piano . . . 79
Synthesizers 81
Synthesizer Versus Acoustic Piano 84

CHAPTER 9 Finding the Right Piano 87

Decide on a Location 88
Determine a Price Range 88
Settle on a Size 89
Choose an Appropriate Style 89
Take Your Time 90
New Pianos 91
Used Pianos 92

CHAPTER 10 Taking Care of
Your Piano 95

The Importance of Humidity Control . . 96
Effects of the Sun 97
Keeping Your Piano in Tune 98
Restoration and Piano Repairs 99
How to Sell Your Piano 99

CHAPTER 11 Practising 101

When to Start Taking Piano Lessons . . . 102
Piano Teachers for Children 103
Piano Teachers for Adults 104
How Often Should I Practise? 105
Keeping Your Concentration 106
Physical Position 107

CHAPTER 12 Recording the Piano or Keyboard . . . 109

Recording Studios 110
Home Recording Studios 110
Recording Equipment 111
Preparing to Record 118
Recording an Acoustic Piano 119
Recording a Non-acoustic Piano 120
Recording Techniques 121
The Mix 122
Pros and Cons of Digital Decks 123

CHAPTER 13 Learning to Play
the Piano 125

Music Terms and Definitions 126
Learning the Names of the Notes . . . 128
Applying Your Fingers to the Keys . . . 129
Noting the Symbols 131
Moving Up the Keyboard 133
Introducing Octaves 136
Playing a Simple Melody 136
Minims and Semibreves 138
Adding the Fourth and Fifth Fingers . . . 139

CHAPTER 14 Adding Your Left Hand 141

Playing a Bass Line 142
Playing Octaves With the Left Hand . . 146
Learning Quavers 146
Practising Techniques When
    Playing With Both Hands 148
The Thumb Goes Under the Fingers . 150
Leaping Over the Thumb 151
Putting It All Together 151

CHAPTER 15 Learning Sharp Key Signatures 155

C Major 156
The Circle of Fifths 160
G Major 161
D Major 166
A Major 170
E Major 171
B Major 172
F Sharp Major 174
Continuing the Circle of Fifths 176

CHAPTER 16 Learning Flat Key
    Signatures 177

The Circle of Fourths 178
F Major 178
B Flat Major 180
E Flat Major 183
A Flat Major 188
D Flat Major 191
Enharmonic Equivalents 192
G Flat Major 193

CHAPTER 17 Learning Chords 195

What Is Harmony? 196
Major Chords 196
Minor Chords 198
Chords in a Major Key 199
Diminished Chords 201
Augmented Chords 201
Root Position and First- and
    Second-Inversion Chords 203
Chords in a Minor Key 204
A Harmonic Relationship 209
The Use of Chords in the
    Right Hand 210
The Use of Chords in the
    Left Hand 211

CHAPTER 18 Listening and Basic
    Music Theory 217

Listen to the Music 218
Analyze the Piece of Music 218
Four-Note Chords 219
Four-Note-Chord Exercises 223
Breaking It Down 227
Pulling It All Together 229

CHAPTER 19 Advanced Chord
        Structures 233

    Major Sevenths 234
    Minor Seventh Chords 237
    Harmonic Minor Sevenths 239
    Dominant Seventh Chords 240
    Seventh-Chord Inversions 241
    Ninth Chords 245
    Suspended Chords 250
    Diminished Chords 250
    Augmented Chords 251
    Arpeggio Chords
        (Broken Chords) 252

CHAPTER 20 Applying Music Theory
        to Playing the Piano 257

    Abbreviated Chord Symbols 258
    Improvisation 261
    Chord Formulas 262
    Tied Rhythm 263
    Suspensions and Resolutions 266
    Staccato 268
    Syncopated Rhythm 272

APPENDIX Quiz Answers 277

INDEX 281

Acknowledgments

I would like to acknowledge the following who have, in one way or another, contributed to my writing this book.

- ♪ Thanks to my mother, who consistently supports my creativity and individuality.

- ♪ Thanks to the Beatles, who are a constant source of inspiration. Without them, I would not have become a musician or have written this book.

- ♪ Thanks to my music teachers, who gave me encouragement and direction.

- ♪ Thanks to my friend Bob Auletta for his resourceful information.

- ♪ Thanks to my agent Wendy Keller, who offered me this writing opportunity and made it happen.

- ♪ And thanks to Bethany Brown at Adams for her support and for believing in me.

Introduction

Music is a universal language that anyone from anywhere in the world can understand, and the piano is a universal instrument that anyone can play and appeals to a wide variety of people. It doesn't matter what language you speak, where you come from, what your ethnic background is, what income bracket you're in or what your religious beliefs are, you can play the piano.

The next time you attend a piano recital or performance, take a look around you at the people sitting in the audience. You'll see a wide variety of people from different walks of life, all gathered together to listen to the pianist and the instrument.

Musical expression has the ability to communicate a variety of human emotions, from sadness and longing to happiness and exuberance. Some people feel more comfortable expressing themselves through music, as opposed to the spoken word. Music is less confrontational than speaking, and is open to personal interpretation. That's part of the magic of music – you have your own personal interpretation of the music you're hearing and what it means to you. A gifted pianist knows how to communicate with an audience through his or her piano playing.

Some people are natural performers – they have a personality that puts them at ease in front of a group of people. Natural performers play the piano because they have a strong desire to shine in the spotlight and want to give the best performance they possibly can. They love an audience. They also want the audience to love them. The natural performer doesn't need to be asked to play the piano. If there's a piano in the room, he or she will sit down and start playing. While this action may have a tendency to raise a few eyebrows, once the piano playing begins, the performer almost always wins the ears and hearts of those in the room.

Other people play the piano solely for themselves – they dread the thought of having to play for others. They tend to be shy, and do not aspire to be a performer. And that's perfectly acceptable, too – it can be a big mistake to push someone into performing when he or she has no interest or desire to do so.

Playing the piano for yourself can be very gratifying. How wonderful it is to be able to play the piano and release some of your emotions. Afterwards, you might feel relieved, having released an emotion (or two or three) by playing the piano. And that in itself is a gift to yourself – having the ability to get something off your chest, perhaps an abstract or deep feeling that you find it difficult to talk about.

Everyone who plays the piano wants to sound good. It is far better to play a simple piece of music well than to play a complicated piece poorly. And, believe me, the listener will agree. There's nothing wrong with wanting to play a challenging piece of music. Just be sure of yourself before you perform it. Practise, practise, practise, and eventually you'll be prepared to give a good performance. And what a good feeling it is to have conquered a complicated piece of music. Knowing you have succeeded is very satisfying, but you have to know when to put a piece of music away and acknowledge that it's not your cup of tea. Because there's such an abundance of piano music written for varying levels of technical proficiency, you can select pieces that you're attracted to, that match your level and that you enjoy playing. After all, playing the piano should feel good and not be an uncomfortable task.

Everyone has his or her own natural style of playing. Find out what your style and preferences are. Some pianists play fast effortlessly, running their fingers up and down the keyboard like smooth lightning, but have difficulty keeping even time when playing slow tempos. Some pianists are naturally inclined to play slow and moderately paced music, but struggle with fast demisemiquaver passages. And that's why there are piano teachers in the world, to strengthen a player's weak spots.

The musical expression through playing the piano is a powerful, wonderful gift for the audience and yourself. I know, because I play for myself and for others.

CHAPTER 1

History of
the Piano

f you are interested in learning to play
the piano or keyboard, it is interesting
to have a little background information.
This chapter provides you a brief history
of the piano, as well as introducing you to
the instruments of the keyboard family.

The First Piano

We have pianos today because of Bartolomeo Cristofori. In the evolution of keyboard instruments, the harpsichord preceded the piano, and Bartolomeo Cristofori built harpsichords in Italy during the late 1600s. As an inventor, however, he was determined to create a keyboard that went beyond the dynamic range and mechanisms possible with the harpsichord. With that in mind, in 1698, he started to build a keyboard that would eventually be called the piano.

Cristofori wanted to create a keyboard that could be played both soft and loud, giving the player a wider range of dynamic expression than that available from the harpsichord. In Italian, the word for soft is *piano*, and the word for loud is *forte*. The original name in Italian for this new keyboard was *gravicembalo col piano e forte*. Translated into English, this means 'harpsichord with soft and loud'. Even though Cristofori had created a new instrument, he still referred to it as a harpsichord, but with modifications. In 1709, he completed the new keyboard, dropped the word *harpsichord*, and renamed it the *pianoforte*.

It's interesting to note the ways in which Cristofori's new instrument influenced composers at the time. The Italian composer Lodovico Giustini was one of the first to compose music for the new instrument. He composed 12 sonatas for the pianoforte, and wrote the words *piano* and *forte* on the music to indicate where he wanted the music to be played soft and loud.

As happens in the creation of anything new, Cristofori's pianoforte had a few problems. Unlike the harpsichord, which creates its sound by plucking the strings with a plectrum, the piano strikes the strings with a device called a hammer. One of the problems Cristofori encountered was that once the hammer hit the strings, it would bounce back and hit the strings again. To prevent this bounce, Cristofori created a device called an escapement. This device succeeds in preventing the hammer from bouncing on the strings a second time.

Another challenge he faced was how to make the new instrument produce a soft sound. To achieve this, Cristofori created a device that shifted the keyboard's action to strike fewer strings, thus reducing the instrument's volume output. On today's pianos, this shift device is activated by pressing down on the soft pedal.

Even with the improvements Cristofori made with his new instrument, the pianoforte was not accepted in Italy. Keyboard players, who were accustomed to harpsichords, complained that the pianoforte was difficult to play, and they didn't like the instrument's tone. As Cristofori continued to refine his instrument, a German organ builder named Gottfried Silberman discovered Cristofori's pianoforte and used it as a model from which to create his own piano.

Silberman was looking for a composer to endorse his new instrument, and arranged a meeting with the famous German composer Johann Sebastian Bach. But Bach was not impressed with Silberman's piano and complained that the upper register sounded weak and the keys were too heavy, making the instrument difficult to play. Soon afterwards, Silberman was able to see a more detailed account of the action (the mechanism that connects the keys to the strings) created by Cristofori. As a result of incorporating the principles of Cristofori's action, Silberman made modifications to his piano and met Bach a second time – and Bach's response to the revised piano was much more positive.

With time and improvements, the piano was gradually accepted by composers and keyboardists alike, and eventually became the standard keyboard. The action of pianos that are built today uses the same basic principles that Cristofori created with his first piano.

Without Cristofori pianos wouldn't exist, and without composers piano music wouldn't exist. Contemporary composers contributed greatly to the popularization of the piano – after all, without composers to write music for the relatively new instrument, there would be no music for pianists to play.

The Square Piano

During the later part of the 1700s, the popularity of the piano spread throughout Europe. The pianos made during this time were grand pianos; they were large and occupied a lot of space. Piano manufacturers experimented with making smaller pianos, and from this experimentation the square piano was born.

Johannes Zumpe, who had studied piano making with Silberman in Germany, moved to London, and soon his square piano was very popular in England – because of its smaller size, it could fit comfortably into parlours and living rooms. Zumpe's square pianos were so popular that many were exported throughout Europe and to the United States.

The Sustain Pedal

Thanks to Zumpe's influence and the growing demand for pianos, London was a major centre for piano manufacture by the late 1700s. The London-based piano-manufacturing company Broadwood added the sustain pedal to its line of pianos, and this new device set a precedent that other manufacturers followed. Soon thereafter, the soft pedal was added, which is based on Cristofori's shift device and designed to soften the sound of the piano.

What is a sustain pedal?
A sustain pedal releases the damper pads, allowing the strings being played to sustain their sounds and resonate until the sounds naturally dissipate or until you take your foot off the pedal.

The Iron Frame

As the overall piano evolved, so did its parts. Today's iron frame is a very important part, located inside the piano – it's a harp-shaped object over which the strings are stretched and attached at both ends.

The very first piano frames were made of wood and supported with metal braces. Wooden frames cause problems for pianos because wood expands and contracts according to changes in climatic conditions. The expansion and contraction of wooden frames has a direct impact on the strings, making the piano go out of tune.

An American piano maker named Alpheus Babcock came up with the idea of replacing the wooden frame with a metal one, and in 1825 his company made the first metal-frame piano. It was a big success, as the metal frame greatly improved the tuning stability of the instrument. Other piano manufacturers were quick to make use of Babcock's metal frame to the extent that it became an industry standard.

 In grand pianos, the iron frame is critical in its structural ability to support tons of tension created by more than 200 stretched strings.

Upright Pianos

Although the square piano was a success, piano manufacturers wanted to build a smaller instrument without compromising sound quality. Piano makers conducted numerous experiments, including the repositioning of the placement of the strings and action. They moved them from a horizontal position to a vertical position, making the piano very tall.

One of the first vertical pianos to emerge was called the giraffe piano, but this bizarre-looking instrument was not very popular. Robert Wornum, a London-based piano maker, redesigned the giraffe piano to make it much shorter and smaller, and thus the upright piano was born.

Piano Manufacturers

The popularity of the piano created a strong supply and demand for the instrument, and, as a result, piano manufacturing flourished. By the early 1900s, there were over 350 piano manufacturers in Europe and the United States. At that time, the piano was often the single source of entertainment in the home – unlike today, there were no radios, televisions, cassette players, CD players or VCRs and DVDs.

With the advent of radio and television, the piano began to lose its popularity. It's startling to note that only a handful of piano makers exist today. The following is a necessarily incomplete list of piano manufacturers in existence at the time of writing.

Bechstein (Germany)	Seiler (Germany)
Blutner (Germany)	Steinmayer (South Korea
Gors & Kallmann (South Korea)	Steinway (Germany/USA)
Grotrian (Germany)	Weber (USA)
Kawai (Japan)	Yamaha (Japan)
Kemble (UK)	Young & Chang (South Korea)
Samick (South Korea/Indonesia)	Zimmerman (Germany)
Schimmel (Germany)	

The Family of Keyboard Instruments

There are three distinct categories of keyboard instruments:

1. Stringed keyboards: clavichords, harpsichords, virginals, spinets and pianos.
2. Wind keyboards: organs, harmoniums and accordions.
3. Electronic keyboards: electric pianos, electric organs, digital pianos and synthesizers.

In a separate category of keyboards is the celeste or celesta, which has metal bars instead of strings. This relatively small instrument is commonly found in the percussion section of orchestras.

Stringed Keyboard Instruments

The clavichord is the oldest and most primitive keyboard instrument. It was a very popular instrument during the 17th and 18th centuries. Unlike the plucked harpsichord, the strings of the clavichord are struck, producing a percussive sound. Because of its light tone, the clavichord was ideal for practising and playing solo.

During the 16th, 17th and 18th centuries, the harpsichord was a very popular keyboard instrument throughout much of central and southern Europe, especially in Italy, Germany and France. This instrument produces a very distinctive plucked sound. When a key is pressed down, a jack containing a small plectrum is lifted and actually plucks the corresponding string. The harpsichord is more versatile than the clavichord, with some models having as many as three keyboards. It also has levers that determine the number of strings that are played. When only one string per note is selected, the sound is soft, warm and expressive; when two or three strings per note are plucked, the sound is rich, full and relatively louder.

The spinet is a smaller version of the harpsichord, having only one string per note in most cases. Spinets were popular because of their size, light weight and easy mobility.

The virginal is also a smaller variation of the harpsichord. During the 16th and early 17th centuries, the virginal was more popular than the harpsichord in northern Europe.

Wind Keyboard Instruments

Organs are comprised of four basic parts: pipes that produce sounds; a wind chamber; mechanically generated pressure; and a keyboard that accesses and directs wind to designated pipes.

Ktesibios, a 3rd-century Greek engineer, is credited with creating the first organ. He named this very primitive instrument the hydraulis. Over the course of time, the basic principles of the hydraulis were developed and were utilized in many different types of organs. All today's organs use the same four basic characteristics incorporated by Ktesibios into his hydraulis.

The organ is considered to be the most complex of all the keyboard instruments. Organs produce sounds by applying pressurized air into the organ's pipes. The size of the pipes ranges from very small to very large, and they are made of metal or wood. Devices called stops open and close individual pipes, resulting in a specific sound or combination of sounds. Apart from using pipes instead of strings, one of the biggest differences between the piano and the organ is the way the keys are played – to produce sound from the organ, you have to keep the keys depressed, and the longer you keep the keys depressed, the longer the sound lasts.

The harmonium, or parlour organ, is a reed organ that uses reeds instead of pipes. The sound of the harmonium is produced pumping air into the body of the instrument by foot pedals. During the 19th century, harmonium manufacturers in France, Germany and England developed and refined the instrument, and harmoniums became very popular because they were relatively inexpensive yet produced rich, colourful sounds. Due to their small size, harmoniums have shorter keyboards than other organs.

The accordion is comprised of three main parts: the right-hand keyboard for playing melodies; the bellows, which produce the pressurized air; and the left-hand buttons for playing chords and harmony. At the beginning of the 20th century, the accordion gained popularity worldwide. But it wasn't until 1953 that the accordion peaked in production due to demand – in that year alone, Italian and German manufacturers each exported 200,000 instruments.

The electronic keyboards category includes electric pianos, electric organs, synthesizers and digital keyboards. These are explored in detail in Chapter 8.

CHAPTER 2

Classical Repertoire for the Piano

Any classical piano student will gain a superior knowledge of the piano by studying some of the piano compositions listed in this chapter, and repeated listening of recordings of these works is highly recommended. If you're taking piano lessons or writing music for keyboards, these piano compositions and performances can be a great source of inspiration.

Piano Sonatas

One of the earliest forms of music written for the piano is the piano sonata – the Italian word *sonata* is translated as 'something sounded'. Prior to the classical period, the sonata form was comprised of a series of dances, which included gigues, sarabands, minuets and marches. During the classical period, composers restructured the sonata form so that it was comprised of three sections and two principle themes of music. Most sonatas follow the A-B-A form. The A section states the first theme, followed by the B section, which states the second theme. The third section, which is also called the A section, returns to the first theme, and in doing so is also called the recapitulation. These three sections constitute .

Many of the most famous pieces of music written for the piano are by composers who were also proficient pianists. For example, Beethoven, Brahms, Chopin, Clementi, Haydn, Liszt, Mozart, Prokofiev, Rachmaninov, Schumann and Tchaikovsky represent the classical repertoire for the piano, and all of them played the piano as well.

The two themes used in the sonata form are heard with some variation throughout the piece. The variations can be changes in key, rhythm, tempo and/or harmony. For instance, if the sonata is in the key of C major, the first and third section will be in that key, while the second section is in the key of C major's relative minor, A minor. Piano sonatas written during the classical and romantic periods typically use a moderate tempo for the first section, a slow tempo for the second section, and a fast tempo for the third section. In musical terms, these corresponding tempos are called *moderato*; *adagio* or *andante*; and *allegro* or *presto*.

In some instances, composers such as Beethoven wrote sonatas that contained four sections. The third section was a minuet, scherzo or march, incorporating dance music from the earlier sonata form. Four-section sonatas by Beethoven are mostly encountered in his earlier works.

The piano sonata provides a platform for aspiring composers and performers who want to gain the public's attention. The format of the piano sonata was originally, and still is, ideally suited for teaching purposes, giving the student a cohesive musical structure to follow. During the classical period, it also played an important role in church music and was the favoured format of church musicians.

Piano Sonata Composers

The great composers Haydn, Mozart, Clementi, Beethoven and Schubert all played a significant role in the development of the piano sonata.

Haydn

Austrian composer Franz Joseph Haydn (1732–1809) was one of the first composers to develop the piano sonata form. Haydn's earlier piano sonatas were written primarily for teaching purposes. In total, Haydn composed 62 piano sonatas, ranging from his early divertimento-like, baroque-styled sonatas to the masterpieces written in his later years. One of his most popular sonatas is his last one, Piano Sonata no. 52 in E flat Major.

Here's a list of some of Haydn's sonatas:

Piano Sonata no. 11 in B flat Major	Piano Sonata no. 28 in D Major
Piano Sonata no. 12 in A Major	Piano Sonata no. 29 in E flat Major
Piano Sonata no. 13 in G Major	Piano Sonata no. 30 in B Minor
Piano Sonata no. 14 in C Major	Piano Sonata no. 31 in A flat Major
Piano Sonata no. 15 in E Major	Piano Sonata no. 32 in D Major
Piano Sonata no. 16 in D Major	Piano Sonata no. 33 in D Major
Piano Sonata no. 17 in E flat Major	Piano Sonata no. 34 in D Major
Piano Sonata no. 18 in E flat Major	Piano Sonata no. 35 in A flat Major
Piano Sonata no. 19 in E Minor	Piano Sonata no. 36 in C Major
Piano Sonata no. 20 in B flat Major	Piano Sonata no. 37 in E Major
Piano Sonata no. 24 in A Major	Piano Sonata no. 38 in F Major

Piano Sonata no. 39 in D Major
Piano Sonata no. 40 in E flat Major
Piano Sonata no. 41 in A Major
Piano Sonata no. 42 in G Major
Piano Sonata no. 43 in E flat Major
Piano Sonata no. 44 in E flat Major
Piano Sonata no. 45 in A Major
Piano Sonata no. 46 in E Major
Piano Sonata no. 47 in B Minor
Piano Sonata no. 48 in C Major
Piano Sonata no. 49 in E flat Major
Piano Sonata no. 50 in D Major

Piano Sonata no. 51 in D Major
Piano Sonata no. 52 in E flat Major
Piano Sonata no. 53 in E Minor
Piano Sonata no. 54 in G Major
Piano Sonata no. 55 in B flat Major
Piano Sonata no. 56 in D Major
Piano Sonata no. 58 in C Major
Piano Sonata no. 59 in E flat Major
Piano Sonata no. 60 in C Major
Piano Sonata no. 61 in D Major
Piano Sonata no. 62 in E flat Major

Mozart

Wolfgang Amadeus Mozart (1756–91) is one of the greatest composers to use the piano sonata form. His first sonatas, written when he was a young boy, were short, somewhat mechanical-like pieces for the piano. Mozart's second group of sonatas was written while he was in London, and some music critics believe that they were influenced by Johann Sebastian Bach.

Here's a list of some of Mozart's piano sonatas. The numbers following the letter *K* represent catalogue listings (the K stands for 'Köchel', the scholar who first catalogued Mozart's works) and the chronological order of the compositions.

Sonata no. 1 in C Major, K. 279
Sonata no. 2 in F Major, K. 280
Sonata no. 3 in B flat Major, K. 281
Sonata no. 4 in E flat Major, K. 282
Sonata no. 5 in G Major, K. 283
Sonata no. 6 in D Major, K. 284
Sonata no. 7 in C Major, K. 309
Sonata no. 8 in D Major, K. 311
Sonata no. 9 in A Minor, K. 310
Sonata no. 10 in C Major, K. 330

Sonata no. 11 in A Major, K. 331
Sonata no. 12 in F Major, K. 332
Sonata no. 13 in B flat Major, K. 333
Sonata no. 14 in C Minor, K. 457
Sonata no. 15 in F Major, K. 533
Sonata no. 16 in F Major, K. 547
Sonata no. 17 in C Major, K. 545
Sonata no. 18 in B flat Major, K. 570
Sonata no. 19 in D Major, K. 576

Clementi

The Italian composer Muzio Clementi (1752–1832) also contributed to the development of the piano sonata. Clementi was born in Rome and moved to England when he was a young boy. He was a popular composer in his day and was highly acclaimed for his numerous piano compositions. His piano sonatas became very popular as a result of his frequent public performances.

Clementi composed an extraordinary number of pieces for the piano, which included more than 100 piano sonatas. His early sonatas are very dynamic and contain sweeping melodies that run up and down the keyboard, somewhat characteristic of Beethoven's early piano works. Clementi's piano sonatas exemplify his mastery of the instrument and structure of the piano sonata form. Some of his sonatas contain highly virtuoso passages that are technically demanding. His later sonatas are known for their modern qualities, experimental and extended form, and technical mastery.

f@ct

Due to his tremendous creative output, Clementi gained the reputation of being the father of the piano sonata. Clementi influenced other great composers of the piano sonata form, including Beethoven.

Here's a list of some of Clementi's sonatas:

Piano Sonata in G Minor, op. 7, no. 3
Piano Sonata in F Minor, op. 13, no. 6
Piano Sonata in B flat Major, op. 24, no. 2
Piano Sonata in F sharp Minor, op. 25, no. 5
Piano Sonata in D Major, op. 25, no. 6
Piano Sonata in A Major, op. 33, no. 1
Piano Sonata in B Minor, op. 40, no. 2
Piano Sonata in D Major, op. 40, no. 3
Piano Sonata in G Minor, op. 50, no. 3

Beethoven

Ludwig van Beethoven (1770–1827) is one of the greatest composers of all time. His musical genius contributed to the continuing development of the piano sonata. When Beethoven was young, he earned the reputation of being both a great pianist and a great composer for the piano.

As a pianist, Beethoven was intense, fiery and emotional. His compositions embodied his emotions and gave birth to a new style of music, called romanticism. Beethoven's music went beyond the formality and structure of the classical period and is filled with a variety of human emotions and innovation. As a result of his musical innovations, he is regarded as the father of romanticism.

Here's the complete list of Beethoven's piano sonatas:

Piano Sonata no. 1 in F Minor, op. 2
Piano Sonata no. 2 in A Major, op. 2, no. 2
Piano Sonata no. 3 in C Major, op. 2, no. 3
Piano Sonata no. 4 in E flat Major, op. 7
Piano Sonata no. 5 in C Minor, op. 10, no. 1
Piano Sonata no. 6 in F Major, op. 10, no. 2
Piano Sonata no. 7 in D Major, op. 10, no. 3
Piano Sonata no. 8 in C Minor, op. 13; 'Pathetique'
Piano Sonata no. 9 in E Major, op. 14, no. 1
Piano Sonata no. 10 in G Major, op. 14, no. 2
Piano Sonata no. 11 in B flat Major, op. 22
Piano Sonata no. 12 in A Major, op. 26
Piano Sonata no. 13 in E flat Major, op. 27
Piano Sonata no. 14 in C sharp Minor, op. 27, no. 2; 'Moonlight'
Piano Sonata no. 15 in D Major, op. 28; 'Pastoral'
Piano Sonata no. 16 in G Major, op. 31, no. 1
Piano Sonata no. 17 in D Minor, op. 31, no. 2; 'Tempest'
Piano Sonata no. 18 in E flat Major, op. 31, no. 3
Piano Sonata no. 19 in G Minor, op. 49, no. 1
Piano Sonata no. 20 in G Major, op. 49, no. 2
Piano Sonata no. 21 in C Major, op. 53; 'Waldstein'
Piano Sonata no. 22 in F Major, op. 54
Piano Sonata no. 23 in F Minor, op. 57; 'Appassionata'

Piano Sonata no. 24 in F sharp Major, op. 78
Piano Sonata no. 25 in G Major, op. 79
Piano Sonata no. 26 in E flat Major, op. 81a; 'Les Adieux'
Piano Sonata no. 27 in E Minor, op. 90
Piano Sonata no. 28 in A Major, op. 101
Piano Sonata no. 29 in B flat Major, op. 106; 'Hammerklavier'
Piano Sonata no. 30 in E Major, op. 109
Piano Sonata no. 31 in A flat Major, op. 110
Piano Sonata no. 32 in C Minor, op. 111

Schubert

Following in Beethoven's shadow, Franz Peter Schubert was a successful composer who lived his short life in Vienna (1797–1828). Even though he was a gifted composer, Schubert didn't possess the personality of Beethoven and didn't experience the same level of popularity and success. Nonetheless, his compositions contain sublime melodies and compositional mastery, as demonstrated in his piano sonatas.

Schubert composed 21 piano sonatas. Here's an incomplete list of some of his popular sonatas. The letter *D* stands for the Deutsch catalogue listing.

Piano Sonata in E flat Major, D. 568
Piano Sonata in C Major, D. 613 (unfinished)
Piano Sonata in F Minor, D. 625 (unfinished)
Piano Sonata in A Major, D. 664
Piano Sonata in A Minor, D. 784
Piano Sonata in G Major, D. 894
Piano Sonata in B flat Major, D. 960

f@ct

As musical styles developed and as time progressed, the piano sonata form was expanded further. With the advent of impressionist and atonal music, the sonata form was transformed to the extent that the classical A-B-A form was no longer easily recognizable. Some composers still used the term *piano sonata* without following or being restricted to its original classical form.

Romantic Composition Styles

Romantic piano composition styles went beyond the classical confines of the piano sonata form. These styles included scherzos, rondos, etudes, tone poems, nocturnes and preludes. Composers such as Chopin wrote dance pieces for the piano, including polonaises, mazurkas and waltzes. Here is an incomplete list of Chopin's most famous pieces.

Rondo for Piano in C Minor, op. 1
Piano Sonata no. 1, op. 4
Rondo for Piano in F Major, op. 5; 'La Mazur'
Scherzo no. 1 in B Minor, op. 20
Etude in F sharp Minor, op. 25, no. 7
Scherzo no. 2 in B flat Minor, op. 31
Scherzo no. 3 in C sharp Minor, op. 39
Waltz in F Major, op. 34, no. 3
Piano Sonata no. 2, op. 35
Impromptu in F sharp, op. 36
Impromptu in G flat, op. 51
Scherzo no. 4 in E Major, op. 54
Piano Sonata no. 3, op. 58
Barcarolle, op. 60
Polonaise-Fantaisie in A flat Major, op. 61
Mazurka in C sharp Minor, op. 63, no. 3
Mazurka in C Major, op. 67, no. 3
Mazurka in F Major, op. 68, no. 3
Waltz in D flat Minor, op. 70, no. 3

Piano Concertos

A concerto is a musical composition form that features a solo instrument with an orchestra, so piano concertos feature the piano as that solo instrument. Unlike a piano sonata, a piano concerto contains passages in which the piano is completely silent while the orchestra continues to play.

The most famous piano concertos have solo piano passages in which the orchestra is completely silent. During these solo passages, sometimes known as cadenzas, the pianist demonstrates virtuoso playing and technical prowess.

Typical piano concertos have three movements. The tempos of the movements are usually *allegro* (fast) for the first movement, *adagio* (slow) for the second movement and *allegro* or *presto* (fast) for the third movement.

During the late 17th and early 18th centuries, composers Arcangelo Corelli and George Friedrich Handel composed orchestral works that featured a particular group of instruments within the orchestra. Johann Sebastian Bach took this concept one step further with concertos in which he featured solo instruments with orchestral accompaniment.

Following Bach's model, Antonio Vivaldi and Handel composed concertos featuring solo instruments with an orchestra using a three-movement form. Mozart expanded on the concerto form with his 27 piano concertos, making them more expressive, longer and more complex than Bach's, Vivaldi's and Handel's concertos.

Beethoven is credited with developing the piano concerto format further by introducing complex, emotional passages that set the precedent for the early romantic style of writing. His five piano concertos embody the evolution of the piano concerto form.

During the romantic period, the concerto became more virtuoso in character. German composers Robert Schumann and Johannes Brahms added virtuoso passages for the piano and expanded the orchestral sections. Fryderyk Chopin, Franz Liszt and Felix Mendelssohn further developed the role of the soloist. The concertos of Edvard Grieg, Sergei Rachmaninov and Peter Tchaikovsky exemplify the style of great romantic piano compositions.

Franz Liszt, the famous Hungarian composer, is credited with introducing the tone poem, a descriptive style of writing for the piano, an example of which is his Piano Sonata in B Minor.

As the styles of the late romantic period evolved into more abstract, modern styles, the concerto went far beyond its classical roots. In some instances, the writing is more percussive and less melodic or lyrical. These changes are inherent in compositions by Bela Bartok, Sergei Prokofiev and Dimitri Shostakovich.

Famous Piano Concertos

- Bela Bartok
  - No. 1 in A Major
  - No. 2 in G Major
  - No. 3 in E Major
- Ludwig van Beethoven
  - No. 1 in C Major, op. 15
  - No. 2 in B flat Major, op. 19
  - No. 3 in C Minor, op. 37
  - No. 4 in G Major, op. 58
  - No. 5 in E flat Major, op. 73;
    'The Emperor'
- Johannes Brahms
  - No. 1 in D Minor, op. 15
  - No. 2 in B flat Major, op. 83
- Fryderyk Chopin
  - No. 1 in E Minor, op. 11
  - No. 2 in F Major, op. 21
- Joseph Haydn
  - No. 3 in F Major
  - No. 4 in G Major
  - No. 11 in D Major
- Franz Liszt
  - No. 1 in E flat Major
  - No. 2 in A Major
  - No. 3 in E flat Major
- Felix Mendelssohn
  - No. 1 in G Minor, op. 25
  - No. 2 in D Minor, op. 40
- Wolfgang Amadeus Mozart
  - No. 9 in E flat Major
  - No. 15 in B flat Major
  - No. 17 in G Major
  - No. 20 in D Minor
  - No. 21 in C Major

- No. 22 in E flat Major
- No. 23 in A Major
- No. 24 in C Minor
- No. 25 in C Major
- No. 26 in D Major
- No. 27 in B flat Major
- Sergei Prokofiev
  - No. 1 in D flat Major, op. 10
  - No. 2 in C Minor, op. 16
  - No. 3 in C Major, op. 26
  - No. 4 in B flat Major, op. 53
  - No. 5 in G Major, op. 55
- Sergei Rachmaninov
  - No. 1 in F sharp Minor, op. 1
  - No. 2 in C Minor, op. 18
  - No. 3 in D Minor, op. 30
  - No. 4 in G Minor, op. 40
- Maurice Ravel
  - No. 1 in G Major
  - No. 2 in C Major (for the left hand)
- Camille Saint-Saens
  - No. 1 in D Major, op. 17
  - No. 2 in G Minor, op. 22
  - No. 3 in E flat Major, op. 29
  - No. 4 in C Minor, op. 44
  - No. 5 in F Major, op. 108
- Dimitri Shostakovich
  - No. 1 in C Minor, op. 35
  - No. 2 in F Major, op. 102
- Peter Tchaikovsky
  - No. 1 in B flat Minor, op. 23
  - No. 2 in G Major, op. 44
  - No. 3 in E flat Major, op. 75 (published
    posthumously)

CHAPTER 3

Jazz and Pop Repertoire for the Piano

There is an extensive amount of music written for the piano. The styles of the pieces reflect the artistic trends of different time periods. The last chapter introduced classical styles; this chapter jumps ahead to modern times and concentrates on jazz and pop styles.

Well-Known Jazz Pianists

Because the number of jazz pieces that use the piano is so extensive, the following examples represent only a very small number of pieces that crossed over to mainstream popularity. The piano is a primary instrument in jazz.

George Gershwin wrote piano music in the jazz idiom, his most famous piano composition being his 'Rhapsody in Blue'. This piece of music, written for piano and orchestra, is a landmark piece of American music – it is a wonderful mixture of styles, incorporating jazz, blues and classical elements. In terms of song standards played on the piano, Gershwin's 'Summertime', from his opera *Porgy and Bess*, is one of the most performed and recorded songs of all time.

Duke Ellington was one of the greatest jazz pianists and band leaders. One of his most famous songs is 'It Don't Mean a Thing (If It Ain't Got That Swing)', with lyrics written by Bob Russell. Other Ellington songs include 'Satin Doll', 'Mood Indigo', and 'Sophisticated Lady'.

Jazz pianist Dave Brubeck is credited with reawakening the public's interest in jazz after World War Two. Hailing from California, his style of music was called 'West Coast Cool Jazz', and had a great influence on jazz in the 1950s and 1960s. His hit instrumental recording 'Take Five' (released in 1959) sold over one million copies.

The Ramsey Lewis Trio, led by Ramsey Lewis on piano, was very popular in the 1960s. Their biggest hit was 'The In Crowd', a light jazz instrumental that was recorded and released in 1965.

Rock and Roll Piano

In piano sonatas and piano concertos, the piano is the featured solo instrument. In rock and roll songs, the piano is used primarily as an accompaniment instrument to a singing voice. Some songs also contain piano introductions and piano solos, while others use the piano only as a rhythm instrument. The following, necessarily short, material on rock and roll piano music refers to the piano in all of these roles.

In 1955, with his pounding rhythm-and-blues-style piano playing, Fats Domino put the piano in rock and roll history with his hit single 'Ain't

That a Shame'. Other hits included 'I'm Walkin' and his biggest hit single, 'Blueberry Hill', which was released in 1956.

Another rock and roll song that featured the piano is 'Great Balls of Fire' by Jerry Lee Lewis. This single was a big hit in 1957 and inspired hundreds of future rock and roll piano players. 'Whole Lotta Shakin' Goin' On' is another of Lewis's piano rockers, made up of the same powerful ingredients as 'Great Balls of Fire'.

Little Richard's uninhibited piano playing, allied with a wild stage act and full-throttle vocals, brought him many hits in the 1950s, including 'Tutti Frutti', 'Lucille' and 'Long Tall Sally'.

The Beatles and the Piano

When The Beatles used any instrument, it became a music industry standard by dint of the band's tremendous popularity and influence. As they used more keyboards and pianos in their recordings, so the piano gained popularity.

When The Beatles came along, everything changed. During their first tours as headliners after 1962, they performed using guitars, bass and drums – not a piano was in sight. However, when they were in the recording studio, piano tracks were added to some of their songs. As early as their *With The Beatles* LP, recorded in 1963, a piano solo (played by their record producer George Martin, a classically trained musician) was overdubbed in the song 'Not A Second Time', and as their music developed, so did the band's arrangements and instrumentation. On the same album, you can hear a driving piano track in 'Money', and a rhythm-and-blues-styled piano in 'You've Really Got a Hold on Me'. Once again, George Martin played the piano tracks.

The rather obscure George Harrison song 'You Like Me Too Much', released on the 1965 LP *Help* (although not featured in the film itself), has two piano tracks: electric piano played by Lennon and acoustic grand piano played by Paul McCartney and George Martin.

In performance scenes from The Beatles's second film, *Help*, we see Lennon playing electric piano in the song 'The Night Before' as a background rhythmic accompaniment to McCartney's lead vocal. In the following year, 1965, with the release of the LP *Rubber Soul*, the piano is prominent in 'You Won't See Me', and a very classical-sounding piano solo, played by George Martin, is the centrepiece of Lennon's moving ballad 'In My Life'.

f(a)*ct*

The Beatles's use of the piano in the studio eventually carried over into their live performances. During their last tour in 1966, Lennon put his guitar down for a few songs and played organ in the screaming 'I'm Down'. Lennon's keyboard technique was very much influenced by rockers such as Jerry Lee Lewis and Little Richard, as he played glissandos up and down the keys using his elbow.

On The Beatles's *Revolver* LP, released in 1966, the piano takes centre stage in McCartney's ballad 'For No One'; adding to its central piano sound, McCartney overdubbed a clavichord. The *Revolver* LP features the piano again in the honky-tonk-styled piano solo in 'Good Day Sunshine', played by George Martin. Another *Revolver* song that uses the piano prominently is Harrison's 'I Want to Tell You'.

The opening chords of 'Strawberry Fields Forever', played by McCartney on a mellotron, a precursor to the synthesizer, is another example of keyboard use with The Beatles' songs. On the other side of the single is McCartney's 'Penny Lane', with the piano as the centrepiece of the song.

The critically and publicly acclaimed masterpiece *Sgt. Pepper's Lonely Hearts Club Band* LP uses piano in 'A Day in a Life', 'Lovely Rita Meter Maid' and 'When I'm Sixty-Four'. The use of the piano increased with the songs 'The Fool on the Hill', 'Your Mother Should Know', 'Hello Goodbye', and the amazing 'I Am The Walrus' on the *Magical Mystery Tour* LP, released in 1967.

The combination of these songs and the use of keyboards had a strong influence on thousands of guitar players and songwriters. Other bands followed The Beatles' lead, and keyboards were used more prominently in rock and pop songs, probably most famously by Procol Harum in 'A Whiter Shade of Pale', with its much-imitated Bach-and-blues mix of piano and organ.

While The Beatles are generally classified as a rock or pop musical group, many of their songs incorporate baroque, classical, romantic and electronic styles and elements. To a large extent, this was the result of George Martin's influence combined with the creative musical talent and open-mindedness of The Beatles.

The Year of Piano Pop

1968 was probably the first year when pianos and keyboards became standard instruments in pop music.

The Beatles returned to the top of the charts in February 1968 with the driving, rhythmic piano sounds of 'Lady Madonna'. Soon afterwards, McCartney's piano playing took centre stage with 'Hey Jude', which is almost entirely a piano song accompanied by rhythm acoustic guitar, lead electric guitar, bass and drums.

If there is one pop song that elevated the status and role of the piano to a primary instrument, it's 'Hey Jude'.

Prior to the release of 'Hey Jude', a sophisticated, astonishing piece of music called 'MacArthur Park', sung by Richard Harris and written by Jimmy Webb, dominated the airwaves and remained in the charts for almost two months during the summer of 1968. This epic piece of music uses the harpsichord as its primary instrument, with added orchestration, bass and drums. Opening with the main theme heard on the harpsichord, 'MacArthur Park' takes the listener on a melodramatic ride through key changes, a driving up-tempo instrumental section, and a soaring vocal ending complete with full orchestra. With its seven minutes 20 seconds of music, it continued the demise of the three-minute formula pop song, which had been started by Bob Dylan's five-minute-plus, organ-dominated 'Like a Rolling Stone' three years earlier.

During that same summer of 1968, The Moody Blues released their *Days of Future Passed* LP. This thought-provoking classic rock recording features the piano as a lead instrument on 'Tuesday Afternoon'. *Days of Future Passed* was recorded with the London Festival Orchestra, which provided orchestral accompaniment and thematic passages throughout the recording. The mellotron was also used on this recording.

The Beatles ended this piano year with the release of *The Beatles*, otherwise known as the 'White Album'. This double-record set features the piano on McCartney's upbeat 'Ob-La-Di, Ob-La-Da', 'Martha My Dear', 'Honey Pie' and 'Back in the USSR', Lennon's 'Sexy Sadie,' Harrison's 'While My Guitar Gently Weeps', and harpsichord on 'Piggies'.

Piano in the 1970s

When it comes to the 1970s and piano music, the list is long and includes several superstars. This decade is filled with examples of piano and keyboard in the pop music culture. A few of the prime players are highlighted below.

As early as 1970, Elton John brought the piano into the spotlight as part of his many hits, including 'Bennie and the Jets', 'Daniel', 'Don't Let the Sun Go Down on Me', 'Goodbye Yellow Brick Road', 'Honky Cat', 'Sorry Seems To Be the Hardest Word', 'Saturday Night's Alright for Fighting' and 'Your Song'.

Billy Joel didn't reach mass commercial success until the release of *The Stranger* LP. Produced by Phil Ramone, *The Stranger* contained the top-selling keyboard single 'Just the Way You Are'. Joel's earlier recording, the *Piano Man* LP, contains some of his greatest songs, such as 'Ain't No Crime', 'Piano Man', 'The Ballad of Billy the Kid' and 'Travellin' Prayer'.

Carole King released a series of hit songs with the piano on her *Tapestry* LP, including 'It's Too Late', 'I Feel the Earth Move', 'You've Got a Friend' and 'So Far Away'.

Barry Manilow is another 1970s piano man with hit songs including 'Mandy', 'Could It Be Magic', 'I Write the Songs', 'Weekend in New England' and 'Tryin' to Get the Feeling Again'.

The amazing Stevie Wonder released his *Songs in the Key of Life* LP in 1976, containing such keyboard gems as 'Knocks Me Off My Feet' and 'Summer Soft'. Other Wonder keyboard hits include the syncopated clavinet sounds of 'Superstition' and 'Higher Ground', and Wonder's smash hit song, 'You Are the Sunshine of My Life'.

The 1970s also produced keyboard-dominated groups such as Electric Light Orchestra; Emerson, Lake and Palmer; and Supertramp. In addition to the songs already mentioned above, the following are some well-known keyboard songs from the 1970s.

'1985' by Paul McCartney (Wings)
'All By Myself' by Eric Carmen
'Angie' by The Rolling Stones
'Breakfast in America' by Supertramp
'Child of Vision' by Supertramp
'Desperado' by The Eagles
'Evergreen' by Barbara Streisand
'Evil Woman' by Electric Light Orchestra
'God' by John Lennon
'Imagine' by John Lennon
'Layla' by Derek and the Dominos
'Love Will Keep Us Together' by Captain and Tennille
'Maybe I'm Amazed' by Paul McCartney
'Morning Has Broken' by Cat Stevens
'My Little Town' by Paul Simon
'Oh My Love' by John Lennon
'Our House' by Crosby, Stills, Nash and Young
'Photograph' by Ringo Starr
'Ride Like the Wind' by Christopher Cross
'Saturday in the Park' by Chicago
'Still Crazy After All These Years' by Paul Simon
'Take the Long Way Home' by Supertramp
'The Low Spark of High-Heeled Boys' by Traffic
'Warm and Beautiful' by Paul McCartney
'Without You' by Harry Nilsson
'You Light Up My Life' by Debby Boone

Since the 1980s

Following the impact of the musicians mentioned above – and many, many more, including Joni Mitchell, John Cale, Mike Barson of Madness and The Band's Garth Hudson – a large number of piano and keyboard musicians have made a significant impact on the music industry. A small sample of these since the 1980s is provided below.

Ben Folds Five
Sting
Alanis Morissette
Belle and Sebastian
Chemical Brothers
Asian Dub Foundation
Lamb
Stereolab
Broadcast
Goldfrapp
Spiritualized
Air
Massive Attack
Radiohead
Pulp
Luscious Jackson
Mercury Rev
Happy Mondays
Muse
Cocteau Twins
Jools Holland
Coldplay
Tindersticks
St Germain
Elbow
Zero 7

Famous Classical Pianists

Classical music reflects a specific period in the history of music and the fine arts. The classical period was approximately from 1750 to 1820. Unlike music and art created during the preceding baroque period, which is ornamental and decorative, the style of the classical period is clean and precise.

The Classical Composers

Some of the finest examples of classical music for the piano are piano sonatas composed by Wolfgang Amadeus Mozart, whose music reaches a fine degree of harmonic perfection. The form and structure of his piano sonatas and concertos are very precise, logical and accessible, and this makes Mozart's music very appealing to pianists and a pleasure to listen to.

Another great classical composer was Franz Joseph Haydn, who wrote 62 piano sonatas. His earlier sonatas reflect the baroque style that was beginning to wane as the classical style was gaining popularity. (As is the case with most styles and periods, there is no fine line when one style ends and another one begins, so the terms are not precise.)

Slightly less known is Muzio Clementi. As mentioned earlier, Clementi contributed greatly to the development of the piano sonata.

Recordings of the Classics

The works of these composers have been played (and sometimes recorded) extensively by both amateur and professional pianists. It's fascinating to listen to the same piano piece played by different pianists – even though the music is exactly the same, each pianist makes it his or her own by marking it with individual personality and interpretation. With fine-tuned listening, one can hear the differences from pianist to pianist.

Because of Mozart's brilliant compositional structure and clearly defined form, most pianists have a strong desire to play his music. Murray Perahia has recorded several of Mozart's piano sonatas, including Sonata no. 13 in B flat Major, K. 333, and Sonata no. 15 in F Major, K. 533. Perahia has also recorded all of Mozart's piano concertos with the English Chamber Orchestra, and a ten-box CD set is available on the Sony Classical label.

Rudolph Buchbinder has recorded Haydn's piano sonatas from number 17 through to 62. This comprehensive recording is available on the Teldec Classics International record label.

At time of writing, Jeno Jando has recorded nearly all of Haydn's piano sonatas, with the exception of his very early pieces. These recordings include sonatas 11 through to 62 and are available on the NAXOS Classical label.

The Russian pianist Nikolai Demidenko has recorded Clementi's Sonata in D Major, op. 40, no. 3, Sonata in F sharp Minor, op. 25, no. 5 and Sonata in B Minor, op. 40, no. 2. Demidenko's recordings are available on Hyperion Records.

f@ct

Among the many sonata recordings available on the NAXOS Classical label are Clementi's Piano Sonata in G Major, op. 40, no. 1; Sonata in B Minor, op. 40, no. 2; and Sonata in D Major, op. 40, no. 3, all recorded by pianist Pietro De Maria.

Peter Katin has recorded more of Clementi's sonatas, including F sharp Minor, op. 25, no. 5, B flat Major, op. 24, G Minor, op. 7, no. 3, D Major, op. 25, no. 6 and F Minor, op. 13, no. 6. For these sonatas, Katin played a square piano, an instrument that was very popular during the time Clementi composed these piano pieces. Not only did Clementi compose volumes of piano music, he was also a piano manufacturer, and the square piano that Katin played on is a Clementi piano, built in 1832. This recording is available on the Athene label.

Michael Leuschner has recorded Clementi's Piano Sonata in D Major, op. 40, no. 3, Piano Sonata in G Minor, op. 7, no. 3 and Piano Sonata in D Minor, op. 50, no. 2. This recording is available on the Brioso label.

For the NAXOS Classical label, Balazs Szokolay has recorded the following Clementi piano pieces:

Piano Sonata in B flat Major, op. 24, no. 2
Piano Sonata in G Major, op. 25, no. 2
Piano Sonata in F sharp Minor, op. 25, no. 5
Sonatina no. 1 in C Major, op. 36
Sonatina no. 2 in G Major, op. 36
Sonatina no. 3 in C Major, op. 36
Sonatina no. 4 in F Major, op. 36
Sonatina no. 5 in G Major, op. 36
Sonatina no. 6 in D Major, op. 36
Piano Sonatina in D Major, op. 37, no. 2

Victor Borge

Victor Borge was certainly a very unique pianist, and combined his musical talents with original humour to become a one-of-a-kind entertainer.

Borge was born in Copenhagen, Denmark, in 1909. At the young age of three, his mother introduced him to the piano. The Royal Danish Music Conservatory recognized the young boy's talent and awarded him with a scholarship. Continuing with his studies, Borge studied with Frederic Lamond and Egon Petri. As he grew into his twenties, Borge's unique sense of humour and skill as a pianist earned him leading film roles and stage appearances throughout the Scandinavian countries.

When it came to humour, Borge's satirical style did not count in his favour when the Nazi invasion spread across Europe. During his performances at that time, Borge made cutting remarks about Hitler. The Nazis found out about this and put Borge on their blacklist. Fortunately, Borge was able to escape from Finland on what turned out to be the last passenger ship to sail from Europe before the outbreak of World War Two.

Borge was considered an ambassador of goodwill for both his native Denmark and his adopted new homeland, America. As a result, many people throughout the world referred to him as the 'Great Dane'. In recognition of his goodwill towards the USA, Borge received the Medal of Honor from the Statue of Liberty Centennial Committee at a gala ceremony in New York. Borge also received the honour of being knighted by the five Scandinavian countries – Denmark, Finland, Iceland, Norway and Sweden.

Now living in the USA, Borge performed extensively. He played on radio and television stations, put on concerts in opera houses and sports arenas, made several film appearances and performed at the White House. Borge was also active on Broadway, giving 849 performances of his one-man show entitled 'Comedy in Music', which still holds the record in the *Guinness Book of Records* for being the longest running one-man show in the world.

As a pianist, Borge performed with the New York Philharmonic, London Philharmonic, Royal Danish Philharmonic and the Cleveland, Philadelphia, San Francisco and Chicago Symphony Orchestras.

Borge worked on a number of televised specials, including one hosted by Itzhak Perlman and the Chicago Symphony Orchestra. For this special,

Borge performed his popular 'Borgeism' treatment of Mozart's music and teamed up with Perlman for a violin/piano duet. Other specials included 'Bernstein' (which took place in Tanglewood, Massachusetts, and featured Borge performing with the Boston Symphony Orchestra) and the 'Victor Borge: Then and Now' fundraising series. Borge also created and released a successful videotape designed specifically for children, entitled *Victor Borge Tells Hans Christian Andersen Stories*.

As a testament to his commitment to education, Borge established scholarship funds at a number of American colleges and universities. In 1963, he created the multimillion-dollar Thanks To Scandinavia Scholarship Fund, which acknowledged the Scandinavians who risked their lives while saving thousands of people who were potential victims of the Holocaust.

Victor Borge died on 23 December 2000. On that day, the world lost an individual who had the gift of bringing millions of people together through his musicianship and original humour.

Alfred Brendel

Alfred Brendel was born in Wiesenberg, Moravia on 5 January 1931; his background is multi-ethnic, with a mixture of Austrian, German, Italian and Slav roots. Soon after Brendel was born, his family moved to Yugoslavia, where his father owned and operated a hotel. Brendel started playing the piano when he was six years old. To round out his music studies and satisfy his interests, he began formal studies in piano, music composition and conducting.

In 1948, Brendel made his concert debut and performed keyboard compositions by Bach, Brahms and Liszt. For this debut, he also performed an original composition – a double fugue for piano.

While Brendel was in Vienna at this time, he had the opportunity to attend concerts given by Alfred Cortot, Wilhelm Kempff and Arthur

Schnabel. From these fine performers, he gained keyboard insights and applied them to his piano-playing technique.

Brendel's international career was launched when he won the coveted Busoni Piano Competition in 1949. For the next several years, he performed solo piano recitals across Europe and in the USA. He also performed piano concertos with some of the world's best orchestras.

In recognition of his talents, Brendel has received several professional and academic honours, which include the Grand Prix of the Liszt Society, the Prix Mondial du Disque, the Edison Award, the Grand Prix de l'Académie Charles Cros, the Japanese Record Academy Award and the Gramophone Award. He also holds honorary degrees from Oxford and Yale Universities.

Brendel's creative interests are not limited to music. In his late teens, he studied literature and began painting. Some of his early watercolour paintings were exhibited at an art gallery in Graz, Austria.

Brendel is known for his performances and recordings of Beethoven's piano music, and is credited with being the first pianist to record all the Beethoven piano sonatas. The first time he did this was for the VOX record label in the 1960s, but Brendel wasn't satisfied with his playing, so he recorded all of the sonatas a second time for Philips Records in 1970.

As a performer, Brendel has sustained a remarkable output. For instance, he performed 77 recitals throughout the world during the 1982–83 performance season. He played the Beethoven piano sonatas on this tour and attracted sell-out crowds everywhere he went. He replicated the same Beethoven programme for his 1990 world tour. Illustrating his unrelenting passion for Beethoven's piano music, in 1996 Brendel recorded the complete Beethoven piano sonatas again for Philips Records. This second recording for the label captures Brendel's years of playing the sonatas and his evolved interpretations and insights into Beethoven's piano music. It's a fascinating and unique experience to be able to listen to and study three different recordings of the same piano music covering the span and maturity of over 30 years of Brendel's playing the Beethoven piano sonatas.

When he's not playing Beethoven's piano music, Brendel performs compositions by Bach, Brahms, Haydn, Liszt, Mozart, Mussorgsky, Schoenberg, Schubert, Schumann and Weber.

When he takes time away from his busy performing and recording schedules, Brendel writes books about music. He has published *Musical Thoughts and Afterthoughts* (Robson Books, 1976) and *Music Sounded Out* (Robson Books, 1990), both of which exemplify the sly wit found in his piano playing.

It's interesting to note that despite his world acclaim as a fine pianist, Brendel claims that he is not a good sight reader, doesn't have a photographic memory and doesn't consider himself to be a fast piano player.

Alfred Brendel currently resides in London with his wife, Irene.

Glenn Gould

Glenn Gould was born in Toronto, Canada, on 25 September 1932. From the very beginning of his life, Gould was exposed to music, as his mother played the piano, and his father played the violin.

His parents noticed Gould's extraordinary musical gifts when he was very young – when he was five years old, he was composing music and playing the piano for friends and family members. Gould began formal piano lessons when he was ten and studied at the Royal Conservatory of Music in Toronto. Two years later, he entered the Kiwanis Music Festival Competition and won a trophy in the piano category. This was the only competition Gould performed in, as he decided not to compete in any capacity from then on. At the age of 14, he received a diploma with highest honours from the Royal Conservatory of Music. During his time as a teenager, Gould listened to and was very influenced by Arthur Schnabel, Rosalyn Tureck and Leopold Stokowski.

Surprisingly, at his first public performance, Gould didn't play the piano – instead, he played the organ at a recital in Toronto in 1945. The following year, he made his formal Canadian debut as a soloist and performed Beethoven's Fourth Piano Concerto at the Royal Conservatory of

Music. Gould made his first broadcast with the Canadian Broadcast Company in 1950, and went on to develop a long career with the company.

When Gould was 22, he gave his United States debut performance in New York City in January 1955. Because of his piano artistry, Gould was offered a recording contract with Columbia Masterworks the day after his debut, and five months later, his first recording, of the Goldberg Variations by Johann Sebastian Bach, was released. This recording was such a big success that it made the bestsellers list. This was the beginning of an extensive recording career with Columbia Masterworks, for whom he produced over 60 recordings.

In 1957, Gould embarked on his first European tour, starting with a performance in the Soviet Union, the first by a Canadian. His concerts were very successful, and part of the tour included a performance with Herbert von Karajan and the Berlin Philharmonic, in which Gould performed Beethoven's Third Piano Concerto.

Three years later, Gould collaborated with Leonard Bernstein and the New York Philharmonic and made his first American television appearance. However, by the mid-1960s, Gould was losing interest in performing. He made his last public performance in Los Angeles, California, in April 1964, when he acknowledged his preference for the recording studio over the concert hall. Through his recordings and televised broadcasts, he was able to reach his audience worldwide.

Glenn Gould was a strong individualist who touched and inspired the lives of many people throughout the world with his extraordinary piano playing. At the age of 50, Gould passed away on 4 October 1982, the victim of a stroke.

Famous
Romantic Pianists

The romantic period in music began in the early 1800s and lasted into the early 20th century. Several pianists left their mark on the music of this period, and modern pianists enjoy recapturing the essence of this genre of music. This chapter highlights a few of the most popular romantic pianists.

Fryderyk François Chopin

Fryderyk François Chopin was born in Zelazowa Wola, Poland. Some musicologists argue that his exact birth date is not known, but the general consensus is that it was 22 February 1810.

At the age of six, Chopin began his piano studies with the Czech teacher Wojciech Zywny. In 1822, he completed his piano studies with Zywny and began private composition lessons with Josef Elsner. A year later, Chopin became a student at the Warsaw Lyceum, studying classical literature, singing, drawing, music theory and harmony. Chopin finished his studies at the Warsaw Lyceum in July 1826, and later that year he entered the Fine Arts Department of the Warsaw University. His first piano composition, Polonaise in B flat Major, was written when he was 17 years old. Two years later, Chopin began to perform for the aristocracy in Warsaw.

His first visit to Vienna took place in 1829, and there he played several concerts, which were well received by both critics and audiences alike. In March 1830, the premiere performance of his Concerto in F Minor took place at Warsaw's National Theatre.

The difference between classical and romantic music is the form and content. Some composers wanted to be more expressive and infuse their emotions into their compositions and go beyond the confines of the classical form. In doing so, the tightly knit A-B-A classical form was expanded to accommodate their expression.

While Chopin was in Vienna, he led a very active social life and was a familiar face among the local musical community. In the summer of 1830, he left Vienna and travelled to Salzburg, Munich and Stuttgart, before eventually settling down in Paris. Later that year, however, signs of his failing health began to appear.

In February 1832, Chopin gave his first performance in Paris at the Salle Pleyel and played his Concerto in E Minor; the noted composers Franz Liszt and Felix Mendelssohn were in the audience. In Paris, Chopin's popularity grew, and he became a well-known teacher. He regularly frequented the best Parisian aristocratic, social and political circles. During this period, Chopin met Liszt and was very impressed with Liszt's musical interpretation of his Etudes op. 10 – so much so that he dedicated the entire set to Liszt.

For the next three years, Chopin was very productive. In addition to performing on a regular basis and teaching piano to the Parisian aristocracy, he composed several of his piano compositions. However, in 1836, due to his deteriorating health from TB, Chopin made a first draft of his will and testament.

For the next ten years, Chopin continued to perform and received rave reviews in Paris. His growing successes and popularity spread throughout Europe and reached his homeland, Poland.

On 16 February 1848, Chopin played his final concert in Paris at the Pleyel Salon, and soon after became so ill that he had to stop teaching. In 1849, he sketched his last piano piece, Mazurka in F Minor, and burned all his unpublished and uncompleted compositions. On 17 October 1849, Chopin died.

Van Cliburn

Van Cliburn, whose complete name is Harvey Lavan Cliburn Jr., was born on 12 July 1934, in Shreveport, Louisiana, USA. He started playing the piano when he was three years old, and his piano teacher at that time was his mother, Rildia Bee O'Bryan Cliburn. Rildia studied piano with Arthur Friedheim, who himself had been a pupil of the famous Franz Liszt. Cliburn's first public performance took place when he was only four years old. By the time he was six years old, it was obvious both to him and his parents that he was destined to be a concert pianist. At the age of 12, Cliburn made his orchestral debut with the Houston Symphony Orchestra, thanks to his winning first prize in a statewide piano competition for young Texan pianists. His mother continued to be his piano teacher until he was 17 years old, at which time he left home to study at the Juilliard School in New York City, where he furthered his piano studies with Mme Rosina Lhevinne.

In 1958, when the Cold War was at its height, Cliburn, at the age of 23, won the hearts of the Russian people when he was awarded first prize at the first International Tchaikovsky Competition in Moscow. By winning this coveted prize his career was launched, and Cliburn made front-page news worldwide. In New York City, he was given a ticker-tape parade, which was unheard of for a classical musician. Despite the Cold War, Nikita Khrushchev invited Cliburn to return to the Soviet Union several times for an extended number of concerts. When he recorded Tchaikovsky's Piano Concerto no. 1, it was the first classical recording to reach platinum status, and since then has sold over three million copies.

 Van Cliburn's worldwide fame is due to his outstanding musical accomplishments, particularly his interpretation of piano works by romantic composers.

Because of Cliburn's outstanding achievement in winning the competition in Moscow, he was at the very hub of the classical music world. His international concert tours were always met with sold-out crowds, and his recordings went to the top of record sales charts. For the next 20 years, Cliburn performed with every major orchestra and leading conductor at concert halls throughout the world. During this same time, Cliburn was in high demand for formal performances with presidents, royalty, dignitaries and heads of state from countries in Europe, South America and Asia. Despite his demanding performance schedule, Cliburn made time to establish the Van Cliburn International Piano Competition in 1962 as a testament to his commitment to support and develop young talent.

Reflecting his continued commitment to the needs of aspiring young pianists, Cliburn has provided scholarships at the Juilliard School, the Cincinnati Conservatory, the Franz Liszt Academy, Louisiana State University, the Moscow Conservatory and the Leningrad Conservatory. In addition, he has established scholarships at the Interlochen Arts Academy, where the Van Cliburn Scholarship Lodge is located.

Vladimir Horowitz

Vladimir Horowitz was born in the Ukraine on 1 October 1903. He began playing the piano at the age of five, and was taught by his mother. He studied with her until 1912, when he entered the Kiev Conservatory to further his piano studies. Two years later, he met and played for the famous Russian composer Alexander Scriabin. He graduated from the Conservatory in 1919, performing Rachmaninov's Piano Concerto no. 3 at his graduation.

In 1920 Horowitz made his solo debut performance in Kiev. By 1922 he was performing throughout Russia. In 1925 he left Russia and went to Germany, a year later making his first solo Western European performance in Berlin. With only 90 minutes' prior notice, he performed Tchaikovsky's Piano Concerto no. 1 with the Hamburg Philharmonic in 1926. Horowitz received a standing ovation for this performance, which launched his career as a concert pianist, first in Germany and then throughout Europe.

In 1928 Horowitz travelled to New York and performed Tchaikovsky's Piano Concerto no. 1 with the New York Philharmonic orchestra. Following the success of this performance, he embarked on an extensive tour of the USA.

Soon after meeting the Russian composer Sergei Rachmaninov, Horowitz recorded Rachmaninov's Piano Concerto no. 3 with the London Symphony Orchestra, which received great reviews and sold very well. These two great musicians remained close friends until Rachmaninov's death in 1943.

During the early 1930s, Horowitz performed with the world's greatest orchestras and conductors. In 1932, the great conductor Arturo Toscanini, hearing of Horowitz's extraordinary talents, asked him to perform with the New York Philharmonic at Carnegie Hall. The fiery Italian conductor took a strong liking to Horowitz, which was the beginning of a long-lasting artistic relationship between the two. As fate would have it, Horowitz married Toscanini's daughter Wanda in December 1933.

When World War Two began in 1939, the Horowitz and Toscanini families fled Europe and came to the USA. In 1943, at the height of the war, Horowitz and Toscanini performed Tchaikovsky's Piano Concerto no. 1 at Carnegie Hall and raised over $10 million to help victims of the war. In 1945, Horowitz took out American citizenship.

Horowitz performed regularly in the USA and Europe, and gave the American premiere performances of Sergei Prokofiev's Sixth, Seventh and Eighth Piano Concertos. After years of performing, he decided to retire from the concert stage in 1953.

Horowitz was the recipient of 15 Grammy Awards, including one for his recording of Chopin's piano music for Sony Classical, which won the best solo classical album category in 1991.

During the 1950s and 1960s, Horowitz recorded for both CBS Masterworks and RCA Records. In 1965 he returned to the concert hall with his 'Historic Return' performance series. He also performed a one-hour concert for CBS television in 1968.

Honouring the Golden Jubilee of his American debut, in 1978 Horowitz performed Rachmaninov's Piano Concerto no. 3 with Eugene Ormandy and the New York Philharmonic Orchestra. Later that year, he performed at the White House for President and Mrs Carter. In 1982, at the invitation of Prince Charles, Horowitz performed a televised broadcast in London for the Royal Family.

After an absence of 60 years, Horowitz returned to Russia and performed for sold-out audiences in Moscow and Leningrad. While at home on 5 November 1989, Vladimir Horowitz died of a heart attack.

Franz Liszt

Franz Liszt, regarded by many as the greatest pianist of all time, was certainly one of the most awe-inspiring and influential pianists of the 19th century. He was born Ferencz Liszt on 22 October 1811, in Raiding, Hungary. At the age of six, Liszt was a child prodigy. He received his early piano instruction from his father, Adam, who was a professional cellist. Recognizing his son's amazing talents, Adam arranged a series of public exhibitions for his son, in hopes of getting backers to help finance Liszt's musical education. He succeeded, and a group of Hungarian noblemen set up a fund allowing the Liszt family to move to Austria. When Liszt was 11 years old, he and his family relocated to the thriving musical capital of Vienna, where he studied piano with Carl Czerny, who had studied with Ludwig van Beethoven. Allegedly, Czerny was so impressed with Liszt's innate talents that he offered to teach him at no cost.

By 1823 Liszt was astonishing audiences, musicians and kings with his superb musicianship and his wonderful ability to improvise on the spot. Soon afterwards, the Liszt family travelled to Paris with the intention of admitting Franz in the Paris Conservatory of Music, but the Conservatory rejected him on the grounds that he was considered a foreigner, not being a French citizen.

When Liszt was 15 years old, his father died, and Liszt was left with the responsibility of having to take care of his mother. He tried to make a living by teaching piano, but the young pianist was plagued with depression and disillusionment, to the point of beginning to lose interest in music. Liszt's newfound interest was reading, and he immersed himself in the subjects of literature and religion.

In 1830, with the outbreak of the French Revolution, Liszt returned with a new commitment to music. During this time he heard the Italian violinist Nicolò Paganini, who inspired Liszt to develop the same virtuoso technique for the piano that Paganini had done with the violin. Liszt is credited with exploring, developing and expanding piano playing and technique to its fullest potential, achieving this at the expense of breaking strings and even piano legs by performing with a powerful technique, passion, drama and force.

After becoming a virtuoso pianist, Liszt embarked on whirlwind tours throughout Europe, conquering wildly enthusiastic audiences by storm. By 1844, 'Lisztomania' was in full force, and Liszt reached a level of fame unprecedented by any other performing artist. His command of the instrument and dazzling showmanship resulted in sold-out audiences everywhere he performed.

Anyone who creates innovative changes and does something new and different from the norm is going to be met with resistance from the status quo. Music critics did not accept Liszt's dramatic theatrics, and the famous German composer Johannes Brahms went so far as to publish a manifesto against Liszt. The critics and the intellectuals of the day didn't take Liszt's crowd-pleasing pieces seriously – and some critics also didn't approve of his playing for the general mass audience instead of catering only to the kings, queens and aristocracy. But in time the older classical traditions eventually faded, giving way to the new musical movement led by Liszt, known as the Late Romantics. (It should be noted that Liszt did win the approval of a group of composers including Berlioz and Schumann, who acknowledged his superb musicianship and ingenious compositions.)

Liszt was also a humanitarian and philanthropist. For example, he raised money from his performances to aid Hungarian victims of the 1838 Danube flood, and to underwrite the cost of erecting a Beethoven memorial statue in 1839.

Liszt knew how to cater to the public and win their high approval with his brilliant showpieces. He could play from memory for hours. Women often threw themselves at the famed virtuoso.

In 1847, much to the surprise of the European music community, Liszt stopped performing and retired at the age of 36. That same year, Liszt met the Russian princess Carolyne Sayn-Wittgenstein, who became his companion for the rest of his life. The following year, Liszt and Carolyne moved to Weimar, where he held the esteemed position of Court Kapellmeister in Altenberg. In 1860, Liszt and Carolyne attempted to get married in Rome, but their plans were unsuccessful because Carolyne had difficulty in obtaining the necessary divorce papers.

After 13 years in Weimar giving numerous performances of music by Berlioz, Debussy and Wagner, and of his own compositions, Liszt resigned the post of Kapellmeister after repeated attacks from conservatives who were threatened by his musical innovations.

Liszt studied theology in Rome, and in 1866 was granted the religious title of Abbé by Pope Pius IX. After 1867, Liszt divided his time between Rome, Weimar and Budapest, conducting, teaching, composing and promoting the music of Richard Wagner. In Budapest he established the Conservatory of Music and was elected to be the school's first president.

In addition to his accomplishments as a virtuoso pianist, Liszt taught more than 350 students, composed over 400 pieces of music, and was responsible for creating today's popular solo piano recital. He repositioned the piano sideways on to the audience for visual and acoustic effect.

At every stage of his pioneering life, Liszt attracted two opposing groups of people: jealous cynics and open-minded, enlightened followers.

On 31 July 1886 Franz Liszt died of pneumonia in Bayreuth, Germany.

Ignacy Jan Paderewski

Ignacy Jan Paderewski was born in November 1860 in the small village of Kurylowka in Padolia, Poland. Paderewski's childhood was very unsettling – soon after he was born his mother died, a victim of Russian pogroms, and his father, the administrator of several large estates and a member of the minor nobility, was sent to prison. Luckily for Paderewski, an aunt was able to take care of him.

When he was three years old, Paderewski started to play the piano, but unlike some of his contemporaries, Paderewski had a late start with formal piano studies. His first piano lesson took place during his early teenage years at the Warsaw Conservatoire, and much to his dismay, his first piano teacher told him he didn't have the hands required to be a pianist. Crushed, Paderewski wanted to discontinue studying the piano, but fortunately another piano teacher told him he had a natural gift to be a pianist, and he resumed his lessons.

When he was 16, Paderewski went on a tour of Poland with a violinist and cellist, and performed at a variety of venues. Some had inadequate pianos or no piano at all, so Paderewski approached wealthy local residents and begged to borrow their pianos for his performances.

In 1878 he graduated from the Warsaw Conservatoire and accepted an offer to be one of its piano teachers. Two years later, he married a student named Antonia Korsak, but she died while giving birth to a baby boy the following year. Soon afterwards, Paderewski left his son with his mother-in-law, resigned from the Warsaw Conservatoire and went to Berlin.

While continuing his musical studies in Berlin, he met the pianist Anton Rubinstein, who assured Paderewski that he had a great future as a pianist. With these encouraging words, Paderewski moved to Vienna to study piano with Leschetizky, reputed to be one of the best piano teachers. Early on, Leschetizky told Paderewski that he could have been a great pianist if he had taken piano lessons at an earlier age. However, after a period of teaching his eager pupil, Leschetizky was amazed at Paderewski's remarkable progress and acknowledged the prowess he commanded at the keyboard.

A Great Career Begins

Paderewski accepted a teaching position at the Strasbourg Conservatoire in 1885, and also performed frequently, attracting a strong following and quickly rising to fame. Because of a dispute with the directors over his not being allowed two months' holiday pay, Paderewski resigned from the Strasbourg Conservatoire, returned to Berlin and continued his studies with Leschetizky.

In Berlin, Leschetizky arranged to have Paderewski perform at an important concert, which turned out to be a big success. He then travelled to Paris and made his debut at the Salle Erard in 1888. In the audience were local celebrities, including Tchaikovsky and the famous conductor Lamoureux. Paderewski was so well received by the audience that he played for an additional hour after the concert had officially ended. Lamoureux, very impressed with Paderewski's performance, made arrangements to have Paderewski appear at his concerts. After another successful performance in Paris, he returned to Vienna. With the success of his Paris performances under his belt, Paderewski was acclaimed by the audiences in Vienna.

His next trip was to London, where Paderewski gave a series of recitals at the St James's Hall. He then embarked on a successful tour of Germany and Romania. On his return to Berlin, Paderewski rehearsed with the Berlin Philharmonic Orchestra, conducted by Hans Von Bulow. After the rehearsal, a successful booking agent named Wolff (who had previously refused to work with Paderewski) approached him, asking to manage his career. Paderewski declined Wolff's offer. At the performance, when Paderewski was playing the concerto the orchestra played out of tune and played wrong notes, souring Paderewski's performance. To add insult to the injured performer, Von Bulow walked off the stage during Paderewski's solo.

Injured at the Peak of His Career

In 1891, Paderewski travelled to the USA for an extensive tour. His performances attracted the largest crowds in concert history. At his New York City performance, while playing Beethoven's 'Appassionata' piano sonata, Paderewski tore some of the tendons in his right arm and injured one of his fingers. He was advised by a doctor to stop playing for several months, but he did not take the doctor's advice. Despite this critical handicap, he continued with the tour.

Because of the injuries, Paderewski could only use three fingers on his right hand and required medical attention before each concert. After this strenuous tour, and with little rest, Paderewski went back to England for two concert performances. By this time, his injured finger had become completely dysfunctional, and medical specialists told Paderewski that there was no chance of a complete recovery. In time he regained the full strength of his right arm, but his finger remained useless until Paderewski developed his own physical therapy and finger exercises. As a result, the damaged finger became somewhat functional, but remained much weaker than his others.

During his second tour of the USA, Paderewski's finger became infected. Despite this, he continued with the tour. Sometimes while playing, his finger bled and covered the keyboard with blood. After this tour, he continued playing and gave performances in Warsaw, Moscow and St Petersburg. Paderewski finally returned to his home near Lake Geneva in Switzerland, and married Baroness Helena Gorska.

While performing in the USA, Paderewski became attracted to the climate and beauty of California, particularly the area of Paso Robles. He also liked the sulphur bath waters, which relieved his rheumatism. During World War One, Paderewski purchased 2,800 acres of sprawling hills in Paso Robles, and at the same time he raised more than £40,000 to help free Poland recover from the hardships and destruction of the war.

In response to his commitment to the people of Poland, Paderewski was made the country's prime minister in 1919. He restored civil order and helped to shape a new future for Poland by taking part in the historical signing of the Versailles Peace Treaty. A year later, Paderewski resigned the premiership and returned to Paso Robles to give his full attention to his music. He also returned to the concert stage and continued to attract large audiences wherever he played.

fact

Despite his overwhelming popularity with the mass of concertgoers, some critics complained that Paderewski played using too much rubato – taking the liberty of slowing down and speeding up passages of music that were actually written to be played evenly or in strict time. This style of personal interpretation is popular with pianists who take a dramatic, romantic approach.

When Germany invaded Poland at the beginning of World War Two, Paderewski was living in Switzerland and his health was failing. The people of Poland once more turned to Paderewski, seeking his leadership. In 1940 he became president of the new Polish parliament in exile. A year later, despite his ill health, Paderewski travelled to New York in his continuing efforts to help Poland, but shortly after became extremely ill, and died at the age of 80.

His funeral was held at St Patrick's Cathedral in New York and was attended by 4,500 people, including statesmen, political leaders and famous musicians from all over the world. Another 35,000 people stood outside the cathedral to pay tribute.

President Roosevelt made a declaration that Paderewski's remains were to be temporarily laid to rest at the *USS Maine* Monument in the Arlington National Cemetery, Virginia. In 1992, when Poland was once again a free country, Paderewski's remains were transported to his homeland and finally laid to rest in a crypt at St John's Cathedral in Warsaw, except for his heart – following his wishes, his heart is encased in a bronze sculpture at the Church of the Black Madonna in the predominately Polish-American community of Doylestown, Pennsylvania.

Arthur Rubinstein

Arthur Rubinstein was born in Lodz, Poland, on 28 January 1887. He began to study the piano at the age of three, and gave his first public performance when he was eight years old. Two years later, Rubinstein and his mother travelled to Berlin to audition for the famous violinist Joseph Joachim. The young Rubinstein made a strong impression on Joachim, who agreed to take Rubinstein under his wing and be responsible for his overall musical education.

Soon afterwards, Joachim introduced Rubinstein to a prominent piano teacher in Berlin named Heinrich Barth. After three years of studying with Barth, Rubinstein made his debut performance with the Berlin Philharmonic, performing pieces by Chopin, Mozart, Schumann and Saint-Saens. Local critics were very impressed with Rubinstein's performance, and as a result, his concert pianist career was launched. Rubinstein went on to perform throughout Europe, receiving the highest public and critical acclaim.

Rubinstein travelled to New York in 1906, where he performed at Carnegie Hall for the first time. Although he received a lukewarm reception, he continued touring and performing throughout the USA.

When Rubinstein returned to Paris, he became friends with the conductor Serge Koussevitzky and the composer Igor Stravinsky. In 1914 World War One began, and Rubinstein left Paris for on a concert tour of Spain. The audiences of Spain responded to his playing with enthusiasm and approval. His playing had matured and he played with more passion – not like the controlled, sedate playing of traditional pianists, but with an intense, freewheeling style. Rubinstein's new charismatic, passionate performance style attracted a large body of listeners in Spain, and he then went on an extended tour of South America.

When he returned to Paris, Rubinstein felt that his piano playing had become stale, but this all changed when he met his future wife, Nela Mlynarski, who was nearly 20 years younger than him. They married in London in 1932. Soon after the birth of their first child, Rubinstein felt the need to return to the discipline of piano studies and began to practise the piano for 12–16 hours a day.

Rubinstein made his return to Carnegie Hall in 1937, performing a ground-breaking interpretation of Chopin's piano music, and this time he was hailed as a musical genius – the critics called him a master musician. With the growing threat of the Nazi occupation of France, Rubinstein quickly relocated his family to the USA and settled in Los Angeles, California. He became an American citizen in 1946, but spent most of his later years in Europe. After World War Two and the loss of his entire family in Poland, Rubinstein's performances supported the new state of Israel.

Despite his failing health, Rubinstein continued to perform during his seventies and eighties. Even after he lost his eyesight, he travelled the world, teaching and lecturing. He died in Geneva, Switzerland, in 1982; his ashes are buried in a forest in Israll that bears his name.

Rudolf Serkin

Rudolf Serkin was born in Eger, Bohemia, on 28 March 1903. His parents, Mordko and Augusta, were Russian Jews who had fled Russia for Bohemia to escape Russian pogroms.

At the age of four, Serkin was playing the piano and reading music. The celebrated Viennese pianist Alfred Grunfield heard young Serkin play, and encouraged his parents to send him to Vienna to study piano with renowned teacher Richard Robert. Taking Grunfield's advice, the Serkin family relocated to Vienna, where Rudolf studied piano with Robert and composition with Arnold Schoenberg.

When Serkin was only 12 years old, he made his concert debut with the Vienna Symphony Orchestra, playing Mendelssohn's Piano Concerto in G Minor. Serkin performed so well that he was invited to tour throughout Europe, but he turned down the opportunity in order to continue his studies in Vienna.

Serkin began his professional career as a pianist when he was 17 years old, performing solo recitals and playing with chamber orchestras. At this time, he also played a series of violin sonatas with the violinist Adolf Busch. During the next two years, Serkin toured Europe, dazzling audiences with his intense style of playing.

In 1935, Serkin made his first American appearance at the Coolidge Festival, performing with Busch. His solo concert career was launched in 1936 when he performed Beethoven's Piano Concerto no. 4 and Mozart's Piano Concerto no. 27 with the New York Philharmonic. Serkin received praise from the New York critics, who acknowledged his unusual and impressive talents and powerful technique. That same year, Serkin married Irene Busch, the daughter of his violin partner.

Serkin performed his first New York solo recital in 1937 at Carnegie Hall. Again, the New York critics hailed him as a pianist possessing magnificent control and the keen ability to focus on each individual piano composition. The following year, Serkin and Busch played a series of concerts in New York, performing violin sonatas composed by Beethoven and Schubert.

Serkin became an American citizen in 1939 and moved to Philadelphia, where he soon became the head of the piano department at the Curtis Institute of Music. He taught piano there for 30 years before becoming the institute's director in 1968. During this time, Serkin continued making tours of the USA, performing Beethoven and Schubert piano sonatas.

Throughout the years, Serkin continued to teach at the Curtis Institute, until his failing health forced him to stop. He retired from touring in 1987, and died at his home in Guilford, Vermont, on 9 May 1991, a victim of cancer.

CHAPTER 6

Famous Pop
and Jazz Pianists

Because there are so many famous pianists, there is not the space here to include them all. With that in mind, the following are some of the most well-known pianists representing the musical styles of jazz, pop and rock and roll.

Jazz Piano

Jazz is a broad term representing many different styles of music, including ragtime, Dixieland, stride, big band, blues, swing, bebop and fusion. There is also a category of popular songs called standards, which include songs written by the likes of Irving Berlin, Duke Ellington, George Gershwin, Jerome Kern and Cole Porter.

Some of the best examples of stride piano playing can be heard in the recordings of Fats Waller and Dick Hyman. In the 1930s and 1940s, Fats Waller was largely responsible for putting the stride piano style on the music map. When playing stride, the left hand does a good deal of jumping octaves in the lower register, up and down the keyboard, playing the root note and leaping up an octave to play the corresponding chord. Dick Hyman is a modern exponent of stride.

Some up-tempo Dixieland and ragtime music has a stride feel to it. In simple terms, the stride sound is sometimes referred to as 'ump-ah-ump-ah' (root-chord-root-chord), which gives it a very bouncy sound.

The styles of Duke Ellington and Count Basie are examples of big band and swing with pianists as leaders of the band. There are many other examples of big band music, usually led by clarinettists and brass players including the Tommy Dorsey Band, the Benny Goodman Band, the Harry James Band and the Glen Miller Orchestra.

Bebop music is fast-paced, with complex harmonies and intricate melodies. A good example of bebop is the music of the pianists Thelonious Monk and Bud Powell.

Fusion is a term representing a combination of musical styles – one could say that George Gershwin's music is fusion. The contemporary pianist Keith Jarrett plays so many different types and styles of music, from standards to classical to pure improvisation, that he is not limited to any one category. Chic Corea and Herbie Hancock also play multiple styles of music.

Ray Charles

Ray Charles created a new genre of music called soul, which is a mixture of rhythm and blues, gospel, and light jazz. In doing so, he pioneered a new style of piano playing incorporating these different styles of music.

In 1930, Ray Charles Robinson was born in Albany, Georgia. When Charles was 3 years old, he started to lose his eyesight due to a glaucoma condition.

At the age of 15, Charles was off on his own, performing in bands in Florida. Three years later, he moved to Seattle, where he formed the Maxim Trio, which was modelled on the sound of Nat King Cole. In 1949 the Maxim Trio had a hit single called 'Confession Blues', which was released on the Downbeat record label.

In 1952, Atlantic Records bought Charles's recording contract from Swingtime for $2,500. Charles decided to move on from the Nat King Cole style and started to mix gospel music with blues lyrics. Charles's next hit single, 'I've Got A Woman', crossed from the rhythm and blues to the pop music charts and gave Charles a broad-based listening audience.

During the 1950s, Charles gained popularity with jazz fans, and performed at the 1959 Newport Jazz Festival. His next hit single, 'What'd I Say, Parts 1 and 2', was a huge hit single that clearly established Charles as a popular recording artist.

tips

In 1982 Charles was inducted into the Blues Foundation's Hall of Fame, and in 1986 he received the same honour from the Rock and Roll Hall of Fame. From his early days, Ray Charles inspired people throughout the world with his singing and soulful piano playing.

In 1959, Charles left Atlantic Records and began to record for the ABC-Paramount label. In the early 1960s he had a run of top hit singles, including 'Georgia on My Mind', 'Hit the Road, Jack', 'Ruby' and 'Unchain My Heart'. He also had a hit instrumental single, 'One Mint Julep', which was very popular with his growing number of jazz fans.

Wanting to have more control with his music, Charles formed Ray Charles Enterprises, comprising record labels and sheet music companies. He opened the RCE recording studios and offices in Los Angeles in 1963.

At this time, Charles was using a 40-piece orchestra and full chorus with his recordings. With this full commercial sound, he had huge hit records, including 'I Can't Stop Loving You' and 'You Don't Know Me'. He continued to tour and record until his death in June 2004, aged 73.

Scott Joplin

Scott Joplin was born in 1867, in the vicinity of Linden, Texas, into a very musical family, where everyone played an instrument or sang – his father, Jiles, played the violin, and his mother, Florence, played the banjo.

In 1872, the Joplin family moved to Texarkana, Texas, where Joplin's mother worked as a housekeeper. Some of the homes she worked in had pianos, and that's where Joplin practised the piano. Ten years after moving, Florence bought a piano for her son.

Towards the end of the 1880s, Joplin left home and performed with various musical groups that travelled around the Midwestern states. He is believed to have attended the Chicago World's Fair in 1893, playing the cornet in one of these bands. In 1895 his travels took him to Syracuse, New York, where he sold two original songs, 'Please Say You Will' and 'A Picture of Her Face'.

Joplin finally settled in Sedalia, Missouri, where he worked as a pianist at the Maple Leaf and Black 400 Clubs, which were social clubs for black gentlemen. At this time, he reportedly attended George R. Smith College.

Original Rags was Joplin's first ragtime book of music, which he sold to a publisher in 1898. John Stark & Sons published his ragtime composition, 'Maple Leaf Rag', in 1899; he received a 1-cent royalty for each copy sold, plus ten free copies. This was a better-than-average publishing deal at the time for a black composer; more often than not, white publishers took advantage of black composers, paying them a one-off flat fee of $10–20 per piece, with no royalties. For 'Maple Leaf Rag', Joplin earned approximately $360 a year for the duration of his lifetime.

At the beginning of the 20th century, Joplin continued his creative output and wrote his first opera, *A Guest of Honor*. This was a fully fledged production, consisting of a touring company of over 24 performers. After a five-state tour, *A Guest of Honor* failed because someone stole the box office receipts, seriously impairing the financial affairs of the company. Unfortunately, this opera is lost because a copy was never registered with the copyright office at the Library of Congress.

No one could possibly have known that nearly 60 years after Joplin's death, his ragtime tune 'The Entertainer' would be such a huge success as the theme song to the feature film *The Sting*, played by Joshua Rifkin. As a result, ragtime music was revitalized and appreciated by millions worldwide.

Joplin moved to New York City in 1907 and lived there for the remainder of his life. New York was inspiring for Joplin – there he wrote and published several new songs, as well as his second opera, *Treemonisha*, in 1910. This opera contained the gems 'Overture', 'Aunt Dinah Has Blown De Horn' and 'A Real Slow Drag'. Despite the wonderful music, *Treemonisha* was not a success because the lyrics were not easily understood.

The failure of *Treemonisha* hit Joplin hard and slowed his creative output. In the next six years, only three of his songs were published: 'Felicity Rag', 'Kismet Rag' and 'Magnetic Rag'.

Joplin was also terminally ill, suffering from syphilis. By 1916, he was attacked by dementia, paranoia, paralyzation and other syphilis-related symptoms. In January 1917, he was admitted to Manhattan State Hospital, dying there on 1 April.

At the time of his death, ragtime had begun to lose its popularity, and the wilder sounds of jazz had begun to take over. Joplin is buried in St Michael's Cemetery in Astoria, Queens, New York.

Oscar Peterson

Oscar Peterson was born in Montreal, Canada, on 15 August 1925. His father, Daniel, played the piano and was Peterson's first piano teacher. When

Peterson was at high school , he studied piano with an accomplished classical pianist named Paul de Marky, who developed Peterson's technique and overall keyboard proficiency. He also recognized Peterson's talent and convinced him to share his musical gift with the rest of the world.

When Peterson was a teenager, his father played him recordings by Art Tatum. Allegedly, Peterson was so intimidated by Tatum's superb playing that he didn't play the piano for over a month. Fortunately, the intimidation soon turned into inspiration, and Peterson was once again playing the piano.

Peterson met Tatum during the early 1950s. They eventually became close friends; however, it took Peterson some time before he felt comfortable enough to play the piano with Tatum in the same room.

Peterson went to Montreal High School, where he played piano in a band called the Serenaders. During that time, his older sister Daisy arranged an audition and entered him in a national amateur contest sponsored by the Canadian Broadcasting Company. Peterson won, and as a result became a regular performer on a weekly Montreal radio programme and performed on a national television show. This media exposure launched his musical career.

By 1942, Peterson was playing piano with the Johnny Holmes Orchestra in the greater metropolitan area of Montreal; Maynard Ferguson played trumpet in the same group.

Eventually, Peterson went out on his own and formed a trio with Ozzie Roberts on bass and Clarence Jones on drums. They performed regularly at the Alberta Lounge in Montreal. Soon afterwards, a local radio station began to broadcast live from the Alberta, sending Peterson's music across the airwaves. Norman Granz, the producer of Jazz at the Philharmonic, heard one of the radio broadcasts and went to hear Peterson and his trio live at the Alberta.

Impressed with what he heard, Granz arranged for Peterson to play with Jazz at the Philharmonic as a surprise guest at a Carnegie Hall performance in New York. The audience and critics were thrilled by Peterson's playing, and he joined the Jazz at the Philharmonic ensemble and toured North America.

For two years, Peterson played with just Ray Brown on bass. In the third year, Granz suggested that Peterson played in a trio, and Charlie Smith joined him on drums. Peterson soon replaced drums with guitar, and Irving Ashby joined as guitarist. Ashby and Barney Kessel played guitar with Peterson for about a year, and then, at the suggestion of Ray Brown, Herb Ellis became their guitar player. This line-up of the Oscar Peterson Trio became one of the best in the business.

For five consecutive years (1950–55), Peterson was voted best pianist in the *Down Beat Magazine* reader polls. He went on to receive this same award again for five years in a row from 1959 to 1963.

During the 1950s, the Oscar Peterson Trio toured Europe with the Jazz Philharmonic and made their debut performance in Japan in 1953. In addition to a rigorous touring schedule, the trio recorded extensively, producing dozens of albums, both live and in the studio, and became known as one of the greatest jazz trios. In 1958, Herb Ellis reluctantly retired and was replaced with Ed Thigpen on drums. With Thigpen on drums, a new trio was born.

fact

In the early 1990s, a joyous reunion took place between Peterson, Brown and Ellis, which resulted in four new album releases and confirmed Peterson's status as one of the greatest jazz pianists of all time.

In just one year, 1962, the Oscar Peterson Trio recorded seven studio albums and four live albums. Two years later, Peterson accepted an invitation to play from a German millionaire/audio engineer named Hans Gerg Brunner-Schwer. This was the beginning of a long and prosperous relationship, which resulted in Brunner-Schwer capturing some of Peterson's finest playing. In 1965, Thigpen, tired of life on the road, left the trio, and the following year, Brown did the same.

During the remainder of the 1960s, Peterson continued to record with Brunner-Schwer, who had formed his own record label. Together they produced 15 albums.

In 1972, Peterson was recognized by his country for his outstanding achievements and was honoured as an Officer of the Order of Canada. At around the same time, Granz launched a new record company and recorded Peterson's newly formed trio, with Joe Pass on guitar and Niels Pederson on bass. This trio toured North America extensively for the best part of eight years.

In the early 1980s, Peterson played more solo recitals and did less touring. He developed arthritis, which made it difficult for him to walk, and he sometimes had to cancel performances because of the excessive pain in his hands.

Peterson has been presented with numerous awards and honours from institutions and organizations in Canada and the USA. As a recording artist, he has received eight Grammy Awards, including the 1997 Lifetime Achievement Award.

Art Tatum

Art Tatum was born on 13 October 1909, in Toledo, Ohio. Despite being blind in one eye and partially blind in the other, Tatum established himself to be one of the most amazing pianists of the 20th century.

His ears and hands made up for any inadequacy he had with his eyes. Apart from learning to read music with the aid of glasses and Braille, Tatum was for the most part self-taught, learning from playing piano rolls and listening to records. He was greatly influenced by the stride pianist Fats Waller.

Tatum moved to New York in 1932 and recorded his first solo recording for the Brunswick label. During this time, he performed regularly at the fashionable New York jazz clubs of the day, including the Three Deuces. For the majority of the time he performed as a soloist, but in the mid-1940s he formed a successful trio with Tiny Grimes on guitar and Slam Stewart on bass.

Tatum's solo recordings are a testament to his musical genius. He recorded a series of solo recordings for Verve Records that captured his technical abilities, his full command of the keyboard and his unlimited capacity to develop and expand both melody and harmony. Tatum had an unprecedented style of piano playing that astonished and amazed his fellow jazz pianists, as well as the great classical pianist Vladimir Horowitz. The world lost this great pianist when he died in Los Angeles, California, on 4 November 1956.

Piano in Pop

In many rock and pop songs you can hear a variety of keyboards, from organs to harpsichords to synthesizers, instead of, or in addition to, the piano. The piano and/or keyboard play different roles in these songs, including background, repeated rhythmic patterns, single minimal phrases, introductions and full-blown solos in the foreground. Some recording artists use the piano sparingly, bringing it in and out of the song or only for the introduction or solo, while other artists use the keyboard throughout the entire song as a rhythm instrument, with or without drums and bass. All these different uses of pianos and keyboards demonstrate how versatile the keyboard is.

Although there are numerous examples of pianists in pop and rock and roll, there isn't time or space to go into detail of each of them here. The next sections highlight two of the more famous pianists in pop.

Billy Joel

Billy Joel is one of the most proficient popular pianists who emerged in the late 20th century. His early turbulent background set the stage for some memorable pop-rock songs.

Joel was born on 9 May 1949 in Long Island and grew up in a housing development in Levittown, New York. He was a rebellious, anti-social, hell-raising teenager, but fortunately was deeply influenced by The

Beatles and the other bands that made up the powerful 'British Invasion' of the USA in the 1960s.

His father, a classically trained pianist, had encouraged Joel to take piano lessons as a child. With the fever of Beatlemania raging, Joel applied his early piano training to form his first rock and roll band, The Echoes. When he was 18, he joined a popular local band called The Hassles, who recorded two albums that didn't go anywhere and then broke up. Joel then formed a psychedelic band called Attila, which recorded and released an album, but ended up a failure.

His next attempt was a solo album entitled *Cold Spring Harbor*. Plagued with technical recording and mastering errors, it was added to Joel's growing list of failures. Joel and his future wife and manager, Elizabeth Weber, went to Los Angeles. Making a fresh start, Joel used the pseudonym Bill Martin and played in piano bars, which inspired his famous song 'Piano Man'. His talents were finally recognized in 1973, and he signed a recording contract with Columbia Records. As a result, the *Piano Man* album was released, selling over a million copies. But because of the way the deal was structured, Joel made very little money from the album.

His next recording with Columbia was *Streetlife Serenade*, which included his first hit single, 'The Entertainer'. He went on to record *Turnstiles*. However, while Joel appreciated the progress he was making, he was by no means a superstar. That all changed in 1977 when record producer Phil Ramone worked with Joel on *The Stranger*. By the end of 1979, the album had sold more than five million copies, and five songs from it generated top hit singles including the Grammy Award-winning song, 'Just The Way You Are'.

Joel went on to write, record and perform some of his finest work with his subsequent albums *52nd Street* (1979), *Glass Houses* (1980), *Songs in the Attic* (1981), *Nylon Curtain* (1982), *An Innocent Man* (1983), *The Bridge* (1986), *Kohuept* (1987) and *Storm Front* (1989).

Since the critically acclaimed *River of Dreams* (1993), Joel has focused his musical talents on classical music, with the intention of composing and orchestrating instrumental music.

Elton John

Elton John, whose real name is Reginald Kenneth Dwight, was born on 25 March 1947 in Pinner, Middlesex. His father, Stanley Dwight, a squadron leader in the Royal Air Force, wanted John to be a Royal Air Force pilot or a bank clerk, and insisted that his son did not play or listen to the new American music called rock and roll. However, John and his mother listened to the music of Elvis Presley and Buddy Holly, which was easy to do since John's father was away from home most of the time with the Royal Air Force.

John started playing piano at a young age. When he was eleven years old, he won a scholarship to the Royal Academy of Music, where he studied until he was 15. Buddy Holly was a big influence on John. At the same time, he copied Buddy Holly's look and wore dark-rimmed glasses, even though he had perfect vision and didn't need to wear glasses.

In 1960, John formed his first band, called The Corvettes, and eventually renamed the band Bluesology. During the 1960s, John provided piano and back-up vocals for Long John Baldry, The Drifters, The Inkspots, Patti LaBelle and Major Lance. John decided to quit Bluesology in 1967 and teamed up with a lyricist named Bernie Taupin. The two met at Liberty Records in London, responding to an advertisement seeking songwriters, but Liberty turned them both down. At that time, John, who was still known as Reginald or Reggie, changed his name to Elton Hercules John, choosing Elton from his friend Elton Dean's name and John from Long John Baldry. (Hercules sounded good, he claimed.)

In 1970, John and Taupin released their first album, called *Empty Sky*. Later that year, they released a second album, simply called *Elton John*, which gave them their first hit single, 'Your Song'.

During the 1970s, John recorded several top-ten hit singles and award-winning albums, including *Tumbleweed Connection*, *11-17-70*, *Madman Across the Water*, *Cowboy* and *Rock of the Westies*. In 1973 he launched his own record label, called Rocket Records, and in 1974, he succeeded in getting a reclusive John Lennon onstage during a Madison Square Garden concert – Lennon's final public performance.

In 1992, John formed the Elton John AIDS Foundation in honour of his friend Ryan White, who died of the disease. Profits from John's single records are donated to the foundation.

In 1994, John was inducted into the Rock and Roll Hall of Fame. As a gesture of creative appreciation, he later gave the award to Bernie Taupin. In 1995, he was created Commander of the British Empire, and three years later at Buckingham Palace, John was given the honorary title of Knight Bachelor, making him Sir Elton John, CBE.

In 1999 John and Tim Rice released the soundtrack to the Disney stage musical *Aida*. Various recording artists sang the songs, including John, Tina Turner, LeAnn Rimes, Sting, Janet Jackson and the Spice Girls. In July of the same year, John had an operation to install a pacemaker due to an irregular heartbeat. The operation was a success, but the pacemaker activates alarms every time he walks through a security device at airports. Not very tuneful for the melodious Elton John.

CHAPTER 7

Types of Pianos

With a wide variety of sizes, shapes and designs, there really is a piano for everyone. Pianos fall into two basic categories: verticals and horizontals. This chapter will explain the types of pianos in each of these categories, as well as explaining the external and interior parts that make a piano a piano.

Vertical Pianos

Vertical pianos are spinets, consoles, studios and uprights. The next few sections give an overview of each of these types. Let's start with the smallest piano, the spinet, and work our way up to the upright.

Spinet Pianos

Spinet pianos range from 91.5cm to 96.5cm (3ft to 3ft 2in) in height and are approximately wide. Spinets are the smallest pianos made, and due to their size, they are very popular with people in flats. They are also very practical for beginners and fit nicely in a spare bedroom. Spinets are made in a wide variety of furniture styles and finishes.

Although spinets are popular because of their small size, there aren't many on the market to choose from. If you're looking for a new small piano, you'll have far more to choose from if you consider a console.

However, there are very few companies manufacturing new spinet pianos. This is due in part to spinet pianos using what is called an indirect blow action – to make the spinet piano shorter, the keys have to go through more steps before striking the string, and because of this, you get less power and accuracy. This deficiency is referred to as lost motion.

Console Pianos

Console pianos are the next size up, ranging from 1.01m to 1.09m (3ft 4in to 3ft 7in) in height and approximately 1.47m (4ft 10in) wide. These pianos are made with a direct action, which produces a balanced feel in the keys. Consoles have long strings and a larger soundboard than the spinet, which gives the console an enhanced tone. They are made in a variety of furniture styles and finishes.

Studio Pianos

Compared to consoles, studio pianos are built with longer strings and have a larger soundboard. They range in size from 1.14m to 1.22m (3ft 11in to

4ft) in height and approximately 1.47m (4ft 10in) wide. Studio pianos are very popular with teachers, professionals and music schools because of their good tone quality and durability.

Upright Piano

Upright pianos are tall, ranging in size from 1.27m to 1.52m (4ft 2in to 5ft) in height and approximately 1.47m (4ft 10in) wide. Manufacturers still make new uprights, but most on the market are secondhand. Older uprights may have experienced years of playing, resulting in a tired and worn sound. The hard wear on the action also slows down the response. However, when properly restored by a skilled craftsperson, uprights can produce a deep rich tone, and some are very good instruments.

Horizontal Pianos

Grand pianos come in varying lengths. The smallest grand is called the petite grand and ranges in length from 1.34m to 1.47m (4ft 5in to 4ft 10in). The next size up is the popular baby grand, ranging in length from 1.5m to 1.67m (4 ft 11in to 5ft 6in). Next is the medium grand, which is 1.7m (5ft 7in) long.

Baby grands are popular because they sound good, look good in most living rooms, and are more affordable than the larger grands.

The parlour grand piano, also known as the living room grand, ranges in length from 1.75m to 1.85m (5ft 9in to 6ft 1in). Getting even bigger is the ballroom or semiconcert grand, which is 2.13m (7ft) long. And the biggest of all grand pianos is the concert grand, which comes in at a striking 2.74m (9ft) long.

The size, distinctive shape and design make the grand the most prized piano of all. Grand pianos come in a wide variety of styles and finishes, and of all the pianos, grand pianos have the finest piano tone and the most responsive key action.

Exterior Parts of a Piano

The exterior structure of a piano is called the cabinet or casing. This term refers to the wood that makes up the top, front and sides of the piano. Matching mouldings complete the cabinet. The shape of the cabinet is determined by the type or particular model.

Once the wood cabinet has been assembled, a stain is applied to the wood before it is French-polished or varnished. The standard types of finishes are mahogany, walnut (light, medium and dark), oak, cherry and ebony. Rosewood finishes, once popular, have been discontinued.

Fall

The fall or fallboard is the long, horizontal, movable wooden piece located directly where the keys end. When placed in the down position, the fall completely covers the keys, protecting them from dust and other unwanted materials. Some piano manufacturers make falls that incorporate a lock-and-key mechanism – when the fall is locked, there is no access to the keyboard and the instrument cannot be played.

Keys

The keys are the exterior part of the piano action. Older top-of-the-range pianos have ivory white keys – strips of ivory are placed on top of the wooden keys, ebony for the shorter black keys. But due to the scarcity of ivory, thankfully now protected by law, it's more common to find plastic covering on both the white and black keys. All but the smallest acoustic pianos have 88 keys.

Music Stand

The music stand is a movable set of pieces of wood that looks like the top part of a standard music stand. It is located directly above the fall. On grand pianos, the music stand is adjustable and can be moved forward or backward to meet the player's preference. It can also be folded down to a completely flat position. On upright pianos, the music stand can be folded away inside the lid.

Adjustable Lids

All grand piano models have adjustable lids, where the lid can be opened partially, halfway or all the way. When the lid is open, it is supported by the prop stick, which is located inside the piano and is mounted to the right side of the casing. Some grand pianos have three prop sticks, but most have two, which allow the player to set the lid on the short one or the long one. When the lid is closed, the sound is somewhat muted and not very loud. This lid position is ideal when the pianist is accompanying a singer, as the volume of the piano isn't overbearing and doesn't drown out the singer.

On grand pianos, a hinged movable piece called the flyleaf is part of the lid. When the flyleaf is in the down or closed position, the top of the piano is completely closed. The flyleaf must be open if the pianist wants to gain access to the music stand and to set the lid on the prop stick.

The piano will give out more sound and volume when the lid is put on the short prop stick. This position is good when the pianist is accompanying a solo instrumentalist, such as a violinist, cellist, flautist or acoustic guitarist. This lid position also works well when playing with a small group of instrumentalists, such as a string quartet or small chamber group.

When the lid is set on the tall prop stick, the piano resounds with a full sound, and when playing forte, the piano is at its loudest. This lid position is ideal for solo piano playing or work with a full orchestra. If the piano player wants to sing while playing, and doesn't want to be drowned out by the piano, it is suggested that the lid is lowered to the short prop stick position.

The vast majority of console, studio and upright pianos have one prop stick located beneath the top lid. When the lid is opened and set on the prop stick, the piano will resonate more and give out more sound.

Pedals

All pianos have pedals that are located at the bottom of the piano. The first pianos had two pedals: the loud pedal and the soft pedal, also called the damper pedal. The loud pedal is positioned on the right. When depressed, it releases the damper pads, allowing the strings being played to sustain their sounds and resonate until the sounds naturally dissipate or until you take your foot off the pedal. The soft, or damper pedal is positioned on the left on grand pianos. When depressed, it actually shifts the entire keyboard to the right. As a result of this shifted position, the hammers strike fewer strings, making less sound. On smaller piano models, when the soft pedal is depressed it moves the hammers closer to the strings, shortening the striking distance. As a result, when the keys are struck, the hammers produce a smaller sound.

Around the turn of the 20th century, piano manufacturers, influenced by French impressionist composers, such as Debussy, Ravel and Satie, added a third pedal, called the sustain, or sostenuto pedal. This pedal, which is the middle pedal on grand pianos, is designed to create a 'ring-over' effect that sustains the first chord or series of notes played, and sustains common notes among different chords. For example, press down on the middle pedal and leave it depressed. Play a C major chord, followed by an F major chord and an A flat major chord. Release your fingers after playing each chord, and you'll hear the note C ring through.

Pianos sit on castors or wheels made of either steel or rubber. Without castors, it would be extremely difficult to move a piano.

The sustain pedal is similar to the loud pedal, but differs because it sustains only the common notes within chord progressions and not the entire chord. Very few piano players use this pedal unless indicated to use it in piano music. Despite its lack of use, it remains today as one of the three piano pedals found on grand pianos.

The middle pedal on some vertical pianos is called the practice pedal. When this is depressed, a felt device is placed between all of the hammers and the strings, making the sound softer and lighter.

On grand pianos, the pedals are located in a section called the lyre, which extends from the bottom of the wooden casing down to just above the floor. Depending on the style and design of the grand piano, some lyres are very ornate and decorative.

Interior Parts of a Piano

You are familiar with the beautiful sounds that resonate from a piano. But do you know what makes those sounds possible? The next few sections take you on a tour through the inside of a piano.

Strings

The strings are the voice of the piano. Piano strings are made of steel, and the bass strings have copper wrapped around them. Inside the piano, you will find 200 to 230 strings, which are graduated in length and thickness. The number of strings varies according to the manufacturer, and the length of the strings varies according to the model. The longest and thickest strings are located in the bass section, which begins with the lowest note on the piano (A). The strings get shorter and thinner as you move up the keyboard. The shortest string, located in the top of the treble section, is the highest note on the piano (C).

Piano strings last a long time, but eventually they lose their brightness and tone quality and need to be replaced. Generally speaking, if a piano is 20 years old and has its original strings, the strings probably need to be replaced. This can be a rather costly proposition, so be aware of it when buying a piano that is 20 or more years old.

Action

The piano action is an intricate, complex mechanism that is made from up to 10,000 parts. These parts include keys, spoon, bridle, catcher, capstan, back check, rails, wires, hammers, jacks, whippens, dampers, felts, flanges, levers and springs. In simple terms, the action is the mechanism that connects the keys to the strings. When a key is struck, a series of motions occur in the action, resulting in the hammer hitting the string, thus producing sound.

Soundboard

The soundboard is a large piece of wood that stretches across the width and length of the piano. It is located underneath the strings and metal plate. The soundboard, usually made of spruce, acts as a resonator and amplifies the sound of the piano. When the strings are struck, the sound travels through a wooden bridge that is attached to the soundboard (see below).

Piano manufacturers have various methods of making soundboards – some laminate the soundboard, using more than one layer of wood. Laminated soundboards are stronger and more durable than solid soundboards and are less expensive to make.

All soundboards are made with a curvature. This process of curving the soundboard varies from manufacturer to manufacturer. Some companies make solid soundboards with extremely thin laminations added to the upper and under surfaces, while others make soundboards that are tapered in thickness from the centre out to the edges.

Bridge

The bridge is a curved piece of wood that supports the strings. It is located directly under the strings and is the connection between the strings and the soundboard by transmitting the strings' vibrations to the soundboard.

The bridge has to be very strong to support the intensity of downward pressure created by the strings, and yet be very efficient in transmitting the sound vibrations down to the soundboard. Most bridges are made in a series of laminations, making them stronger and more efficient in transmitting sound vibrations.

These laminated thin layers of wood are constructed both horizontally and vertically. Horizontal laminated bridges run parallel to the soundboard, while vertical ones run perpendicular to the soundboard. Vertical laminated bridges are more effective in transmitting a good sound, because the vibrations travel directly down to the soundboard without having to traverse layers of horizontal glue, which is the case with horizontal bridges.

Some bridges are also capped with another layer of wood placed horizontally on top of the bridge. This cap is designed to give more support to the pins that are driven into the bridge, which hold the strings in their designated positions. A vertical, laminated, capped bridge is considered to be the best for producing top-quality sound.

Iron Plate

The plate is the cast-iron frame that holds and supports the tension of the strings. The plate is also known as the harp, as when it is extracted from the piano case, it looks like a harp. The strings are stretched from one end of the plate to its opposite end and held in position by pins at each end. Each string has about 76.5kg (170lb) of tension. The combined total amount of tension from all of the strings is approximately 18,000kg (40,000lb). For this reason, the plate has to be very durable in order to support this tremendous amount of tension, and is securely fastened to the inside of the piano case. Some cheaper upright pianos were made with wooden frames, but few of these have stayed playable.

Hammers

When you press down on piano keys, the hammers are activated to hit the strings and make them resonate. Piano hammers are made of wooden stems, usually hard maple, and have rounded felt heads made of compressed layers of fine wool. The finest hammers are made with two layers of felt. The outer layer is white and the inner layer is green, purple or magenta. Putting the felt onto the hammer is achieved by hammer presses that apply a tremendous amount of pressure from several different angles.

The quality of sound a hammer produces has a lot to do with the hardness of the hammer. Hard hammers produce a bright sound, whereas soft hammers produce a dull sound. New pianos and fully restored pianos have hard hammers, giving the piano a bright sound, while used pianos probably have older hammers, which more than likely have become softened from years of use and need to be voiced, or better yet, replaced with new hammers.

What is voicing?

Voicing a hammer is the process of shaving the felt head and removing the soft edge. When the hammer has been voiced, the felt head is harder and, as a result, the tone of the piano is brighter.

Dampers

Dampers are made of wooden blocks with felt pads attached to each end. When the dampers are resting on the strings, they stop the sound of the strings from resonating. Conversely, when the dampers are lifted off the strings, the strings resonate.

When the piano player presses down on a key, a metal rod attached to the damper raises the damper off the strings, allowing the string to vibrate. Once the key is released, the damper resumes its stopped position, resting on the string. Take a look inside the piano, and you'll see that the highest notes don't have any dampers. That's because the strings are short and don't resonate that much. When you play these high notes without any dampers, you'll hear the notes continue to resonate after you lift your fingers from the keys.

As mentioned in the pedal section of this chapter, the right pedal is called the loud pedal. When depressed, this pedal raises all the dampers off the strings. When the loud pedal is in this position, all notes played will resonate, even after you lift your fingers from the keys. The notes will continue to resonate until the loud pedal is released, which lowers the dampers back onto the strings and stops their sounds.

On grand pianos, the sustain pedal, which is the middle pedal, also activates the dampers. When you play any series of notes and then press down on the sustain pedal, the dampers above those notes are lifted up and stay in that position until the pedal is released, which lowers the dampers back down to the stop position.

Tuning Pins

The tuning pins, which are usually nickel-plated, are located at the front of the piano. This positioning provides easy access to the pins when the piano needs to be tuned. The tuning pins are securely housed in the iron plate and extend down through the plate and into the pin block. Each piano string is wrapped around a separate tuning pin. Keys that have three strings per key need to have a tuning pin for each string – as a result, most pianos have as many as 225 tuning pins, and in some cases there are even more.

The pin block is located underneath the iron plate. It is made of layers of laminated wood, which are bonded or glued together. The pin block has to be strong enough to support approximately 18,000kg (40,000lb) of pressure exerted on the tuning pins by the tightened piano strings.

Backposts

The ribbed soundboard is exposed on the back side of vertical pianos and the underside of grand pianos. Extra-heavy backposts provide support to the soundboard and the rest of the piano. The backposts are made of solid spruce wood.

Famous Models

Now that you know the basic structure of a piano and how it works, below are just a few of the more famous piano models.

- Louis XVI: these models are made in a variety of sizes, including 1.75m and 1.88m (5ft 9in and 6ft 2in) grands. These models incorporate the style of the Louis XVI era (1774–92) with simple lines and classic columns.
- Queen Anne: these models capture the distinctive style of furniture made during the reign of Queen Anne (1702–14), with elegant swan-necked cabriole legs on the piano and matching piano bench.
- French Provincial: this beautiful furniture style began during the latter part of the 17th century. French Provincial pianos reflect this style with decorative music stands, legs and lyre.
- Chippendale: originating in England during the 18th century, this style is characterized by its graceful lines, elaborate ornamentation, detailed music stand, lyre and leg design.

CHAPTER 8

Electronic Keyboards

With the advent of electricity, it was only a matter of time before it was applied to musical instruments. This chapter introduces several electronic instruments, including electric pianos, digital pianos and synthesizers.

Electric Pianos

The basic principle of the electric piano is to imitate the sound of an acoustic piano and amplify the sound through speakers. Electric pianos are very different from acoustic pianos – they are not acoustic pianos that are amplified by attaching a microphone device to them, as they have no strings or soundboard.

In 1927, the first electric piano, called the Superpiano, was made. It was followed by the Neo-Bechstein-Flugel in 1931 and the Elektrochord in 1933. These instruments produce electronic sounds generated by striking reeds or metal bars, creating sound vibrations that are then amplified through speakers.

As the manufacturing of the electric piano developed, the sound and touch of the instrument improved dramatically. When rock and roll exploded onto the music scene in the mid-1950s, however, the acoustic piano was still the preferred keyboard instrument. For example, during that time, Fats Domino, Jerry Lee Lewis and Little Richard always played acoustic pianos.

It wasn't until the 1960s, when rock groups turned up the volume, that electric pianos increased in popularity. This happened for a number of reasons. First, the textural sound of electric pianos blends very well with electric guitars. Second, electric pianos have the ability to have their amplified sound turned up to match the volume level of electric guitars, augmented with external amplifiers and speakers. And, unlike acoustic pianos, electric pianos are lightweight, small, easy to transport and never go out of tune.

Electric Piano Versus Acoustic Piano

When choosing between these two very different keyboards, consider the following before making a decision.

Difference in Sound

The sounds of an acoustic piano and an electric piano are two different, distinct things. The sound quality of an acoustic piano is very difficult to replicate with any electronic keyboard. If you really want the sound of an acoustic piano, don't even bother thinking about buying an electric piano, because you won't be satisfied. On the other hand, if you're open to the sound of electric pianos, then you should familiarize yourself with electric piano products. Another factor regarding sound: most electric pianos can be played using headphones, which is a good option to have when practising.

Difference in Touch

Electric piano keys and actions are easy to play; however, they don't have the range of dynamics that you have when playing an acoustic piano. An electric piano's volume is determined by how you set or adjust the volume level. The sound is then electrically generated through speakers or headphones. If the volume level is set low, even if you play with full force and bash the keys, the sound will be low. If you have the volume level set high and you play the keys lightly, the sound will be loud – and this is the case even with the 'weighted' keys now available on top-end electric pianos. With acoustic pianos, there is much more of a direct relationship between how you play the keys and the corresponding sound you generate.

Difference in Size

Electric pianos are much smaller than acoustic pianos. If you don't have much space in your home and you like the sound of electric pianos, then you should probably buy an electric piano. Given their small size and relatively light weight, electric pianos are very portable and can easily fit in the boot of a car. Even though acoustic pianos are movable, they're not easy to move because of their size and weight. If you are going to move an acoustic piano, it's best to get it moved by a professional piano mover.

Digital Pianos

In terms of electronic keyboard evolution, digital pianos and synthesizers were among the next wave of products. Digital pianos, being less complicated than synthesizers, were first in bringing their delights to the buying public.

Roland made the first digital piano in 1974. Using the same digital technology, many other manufacturers followed with their own line of digital pianos, including Casio, Korg and Yamaha.

Unlike acoustic pianos, digital pianos have no strings or hammers. The sound is generated by prerecorded sampled sounds, which are then amplified through speakers. A digital piano attempts to duplicate the sound and feel of an acoustic piano.

It should be noted that if you play very aggressively and bash on electric piano keys, you could damage a key or two. When this happens, no sound is generated when you press down on the damaged key. It can be pretty costly to have these keys repaired.

Digital pianos are made up of a number of components. The keys have a weighted key action that imitates the action of acoustic pianos. Unlike electric pianos, digital pianos have electronic sensors that detect the rate of velocity when the keys are struck, resulting with the corresponding soft or loud degree of volume. A digital sound bank contains numerous sampled keyboard sounds, including grand piano, electric piano, harpsichord and organ. Digital effects are also available, including reverb, chorus, delay and flanges. The digital sounds are amplified through speakers or headphones.

As with most products, there are pluses and minuses. Here are some pluses regarding digital pianos.

1. They are portable, weighing less than 90kg (200lb), compared with an acoustic vertical piano, which can weigh as much as 225kg (500lb). Digital piano legs can easily be removed, making it even easier to transport the instrument.

2. They don't need to be tuned. The digital sounds, which do not go out of tune, are stored on microprocessing chips.
3. They can be played silently, by using the headphones option. When playing with the headphones on, the sound is diverted from the speakers to the headphones. This allows the player to play as loud as he or she likes without disturbing anyone else in the room.
4. They are, for the most part, maintenance-free.
5. Most digital pianos have a MIDI interface, which provides the technical capability to connect with other MIDI instruments.
6. Digital pianos have multiple built-in sounds stored in sound banks, which can be very quickly accessed by simply pressing a button.

Here are some digital piano minuses.

1. Even with the latest sampling sound technologies, the sound quality does not equal that of acoustic pianos.
2. The recorded sampled sounds are set and cannot be enhanced or coloured by the subtle playing techniques of the player.
3. When there is a problem, because of the complicated technology of the instrument, digital pianos are difficult and expensive to repair.
4. Because digital pianos are a product of the time and incorporate ever-changing digital technology, they become outdated very quickly – and spare parts can be difficult to obtain because of this.

Digital Piano Versus Acoustic Piano

As technology continues to advance, improvements in overall quality occur in the manufacturing of digital keyboards. The sound is better, the action feels better, and the price of digital pianos is more affordable – you can buy a good-quality digital piano, such as a Yamaha or a Korg, for about £550; for the same price, you can also buy a good used acoustic piano. In choosing between the two keyboards, it really depends on your personal taste – what sounds and feels better to you.

Because of the never-ending evolution in technology, digital pianos are constantly being improved and become outdated with each technological advance. With acoustic pianos, the evolution hasn't changed that much over the past 100 years, so you're dealing with an instrument that is relatively constant and timeless.

Polyphony

Another very important distinction between the two keyboards is something called polyphony. With acoustic pianos, you can play as many notes as your fingers are capable of playing all at the same time, but some digital pianos are limited in the number of keys that can be played simultaneously. This is due to certain models having a limited polyphony capability, allowing only a certain number of keys to be played at the same time. This big difference can be the deciding factor between buying a digital or an acoustic piano.

Before you go shopping for a digital piano, it would benefit you to first buy a set of quality headphones. This will allow you to hear what the instrument sounds like when using the headphones option.

To further compound the decision-making process, some acoustic piano manufacturers make acoustic pianos with a digital device attached to the keyboard. With this attachment, digital disks can be inserted into the device and the piano can play by itself, much like the old pianolas or player-pianos. This also gives the player the option to play using headphones. These pianos are more expensive than your average acoustic piano because of the digital addition.

Comparing Models

As you compare the different digital piano manufacturers and models, take account of the difference in the quality of the sampled sounds, the action of the keys, the number of keys (some of the lower-end models have fewer than the standard number of 88 keys), the quality and number of sound speakers, the power and output of the amplifier, and the quality of the sound when using headphones.

Some of the many digital piano manufacturers to choose from include Baldwin, Casio, Kawai, Korg, Kurzweil, Roland, Samick, Suzuki, Technics, Wersi and Yamaha.

If you can't make up your mind between buying a digital or an acoustic piano, alternate between trying out the two types of piano. The differences between the two keyboards should be quite striking and should help you in the decision-making process.

Synthesizers

As advances and improvements were made in applying electronics to keyboard instruments and generating sound, the synthesizer was born. Synthesizers allow the player to produce, control and modify sounds, going far beyond the capabilities of other keyboard instruments.

Analog Synthesizers

The first synthesizers used analog technology made up of voltage-controlled oscillators (VCOs), voltage-controlled filters (VCFs) and voltage-controlled amplifiers (VCAs). Each oscillator produces a waveform, or sound, that can be free of harmonics or overtones. The oscillators can also generate white noise, a somewhat flat, grainy, non-pitched sound that can whisper or roar. The sounds are then processed through filters, which change and modify the shape of the sounds. This filtering process can apply pitch, rhythm and effects to the sounds, and determine the degree of attack and decay, and level of volume. The VCAs generate the sound through speakers.

In 1955, RCA Laboratories introduced its first synthesizer. It looked nothing like the synthesizers we have today – all early models were large, complicated and very expensive. The very first synthesizers were, for the most part, experimental and in the development stage, and were not available to the buying public. These synthesizers were found in the most advanced electronic music studios and educational institutions. They were not very reliable or consistent instruments – they required a long period of time to warm up, and they didn't stay in tune. In order to produce sounds, patch cords had to be connected to sound modules, each of which produced a specific sound. Once a sound was created, you couldn't save it by simply pressing a save button, as we can with today's synthesizers. You had to write down the patch cord configuration and parameter settings in order to reconstruct the sound at a later time. This process had to be done with every sound generated by this early breed of synthesizers. This required a lot of experimentation, time, numerous patch cord changes, writing down each sound configuration – and patience. To a large degree, the first synthesizer players were actually sound programmers.

Hugh Le Caine is credited with building the world's first voltage-controlled music synthesizer, in 1945. This early-stage electronic instrument also incorporated a touch-sensitive keyboard and variable-speed multitrack tape recorder.

During the 1960s, synthesizers became user-friendly with the creation of the Buchla and Moog synthesizers, but they were still large. In the early 1970s, Robert Moog made the MiniMoog, which became quite popular, due in part to its relatively small size and its being the first portable synthesizer. But, typically with synthesizers made at the time, the MiniMoog was a limited monophonic instrument that could only produce one sound at any one given time. If you wanted to play more than one note simultaneously, you had to have additional synthesizers. Another way to produce more than one sound at a time was to laboriously multitrack several notes by recording them individually and then playing them back all together – a recording technique called overdubbing.

The next generation of synthesizers was polyphonic, a huge technological breakthrough that arrived towards the end of the 1970s. The Prophet 5, made by Sequential Circuits, was very popular because, for the first time with synthesizers, you could play more than one note at a time. Because these instruments were highly advanced and new on the market, they were very expensive.

Digital Synthesizers

When digital technology arrived, synthesizer manufacturers began to incorporate this new technology in their latest models. As a result, analog synthesizers were eventually phased out of production and replaced with digital synthesizers, which operate on microprocessing chips called digital circuits. This new breed of synthesizer was smaller, less complicated and more affordable.

Digital synthesizers have a very different sound compared to analog synthesizers. Digital sound is comprised of numbers, which are stored in memory sound banks. When the sounds are activated, the microprocessor retrieves the numbers from the memory and converts them to the highest quality sound. Digital synthesizers sound bright and crisp, and can even have a biting edge to them, compared to analog sounds, which sound warmer and rounder.

fact

The Yamaha DX-7 was one of the first fully digital polyphonic synthesizers to catch on with keyboard players in the early 1980s. This was due in equal parts to its relatively affordable price, many brand-new sounds and easy-to-play functions.

When playing an analog synthesizer in real time, the player was restricted to the preprogrammed sounds. However, there was (and still is) a pitch wheel on analog synthesizers that allows the player to raise or lower the pitch while playing in real time. With digital synthesizers, the player could make several modifications to the sounds in real time and create new sounds on the fly.

With today's synthesizers, the sounds are already programmed and preset in numerous sound banks. These sounds are accessed by scrolling through the sound banks and distributed to the keyboard. For instance, if you pick solo flute, the entire keyboard sounds like a flute; by choosing another sound – string orchestra, for example – the entire keyboard then sounds like a string orchestra. The choice of sounds is very extensive and available with the touch of a button. You also have the option to modify and change the parameters of the preset sounds, and if you do, you can save the modified sounds in the memory bank.

MIDI

Digital synthesizers can interface with each other and other non-keyboard digital equipment such as a drum machine, recording deck, sampling unit or effects unit. This digital connection is possible because of MIDI, which stands for Musical Instrument Digital Interface.

> A MIDI controller is not restricted to only keyboards; digital drum machines, samplers, sequencers and computers can all function as controllers and can trigger all MIDI-connected instruments.

Using MIDI, several synthesizers programmed to play different sounds can be connected together. By playing one note, chord or series of notes on the lead synthesizer, called the controller, all of the connected synthesizers can be activated simultaneously through MIDI. The combined sound possibilities are endless, with a vast number of sounds to choose from on each individual synthesizer, sampler or effects unit.

Synthesizer Versus Acoustic Piano

The differences between these two keyboards are vast, and the two greatest differences are in sound and touch.

Difference in Sound

If you have an ear attuned to pure acoustic piano sounds, you probably shouldn't buy a synthesizer. On the other hand, if you want a wide variety of electronically produced sounds and the option of playing while wearing headphones, you should seriously consider buying a synthesizer. The sounds vary from manufacturer to manufacturer.

The number of synthesizer sounds can be overwhelming. Try to identify what your keyboard needs are and what type or types of sounds you want before trying out the different makes and models.

Even though the digital sampled sounds of an acoustic piano are improving with the latest synthesizers, they will never be able to sound the same as acoustic pianos because of the difference in sound fundamentals. Synthesizer sounds are electronically generated and amplified, while acoustic piano sounds are naturally produced with old-fashioned strings, hammers, soundboards and wooden cases.

Difference in Touch

If you like the feel of a hammer-and-string action and weighted keys, you should probably buy an acoustic piano. If you prefer the feel and light-touch ease of playing synthesizer keys, then you should consider buying a synthesizer. Most synthesizer keys are touch-velocity sensitive – the harder you press the key, the louder the sound; the lighter you press the key, the softer the sound. Aftertouch is another characteristic of synthesizer keys. When you hold down on a synthesizer key, the sound will continue until you release your finger. This aftertouch function can also give the note a variety of expressions, including vibrato, overtones and various sound effects.

Difference in Number of Keys

Another difference between these two keyboards is the number of keys. Nearly all acoustic pianos have 88 keys. Some synthesizers have 88 keys, while others have 76, 61, 48 or as few as 36 keys. If you're used to playing the standard 88 keys, it will probably feel very strange to play a keyboard that has fewer keys. Because of your prior playing experience on the full number of keys, your fingers will probably have the physical expectation of being able to play notes in the upper and lower registers of the keyboard. When playing on 76 keys or less, adjustments have to be made in terms of registration, octave placement and the voicing of chords, bass lines and melodies. In general, synthesizers with 88 keys cost more than models with 76 or fewer keys.

CHAPTER 9

Finding the
Right Piano

A pianist isn't a pianist without a piano. But don't rush into buying one – several factors need to be considered when choosing a piano. You should take your time over making a decision and shop around until you find the piano that is just right for you.

Decide on a Location

Before you go shopping for a piano, work out which room in your home is best suited to accommodate the instrument. Typically, people put their piano in the living room, family room or even dining room, since these are the usual gathering places for family and friends. Make sure you place the piano far away from the television – there will be many times when you want to play the piano while others are glued to the football or *EastEnders* and do not want to be disturbed.

For the professional musician who spends a lot of time playing the piano, it might be best to put the piano in a spare room. This is ideal for everyone – the pianist can concentrate without extraneous sounds and interruptions, while others in the household are undisturbed.

Determine a Price Range

Once you know where you're going to put the piano, you have to work out how much money you are willing to spend. If you have a big flat or house and really want a grand piano but have a small budget, you can make a down payment and pay the remaining balance by credit.

What you're willing to pay for a piano will also determine whether you buy a new or used piano – new pianos are generally more expensive than used or restored ones. The exception to this would be if you were looking for a rare restored piano, when the price could be considerably higher than that of a new piano.

If you're going to buy a used or restored piano, be prepared to ask the vendor a lot of questions. A list of questions should include the following:

1. When was the piano built?
2. What is the condition of the soundboard?
3. Has it been replaced?
4. Have the strings, felts, hammers and action been replaced?
5. Under normal playing conditions, how long will the piano last?
6. Other than the difference in price, why should I buy a used piano instead of a new piano?

Settle on a Size

What you can afford to spend will usually determine the size of the piano. The most affordable pianos are spinets and consoles, which happen to be the smallest acoustic pianos made. Spinets are good for beginners and for people who have space constraints. However, very few manufacturers make new spinets. Consoles are the next size up and cost a little more than spinets, and due to their popularity, most piano manufacturers make new consoles.

Studio pianos are even bigger in size and price. Upright pianos are taller and more expensive than studios. Grand pianos, which are the most expensive, range in size from petite grands to concert grands.

Make sure that the size of the piano you choose is appropriate to the size of the room you're going to put it in. For instance, putting a grand piano in a small studio flat would look very strange!

Choose an Appropriate Style

Pianos come in a variety of finishes, including high-gloss black, satin black, cherry, mahogany, walnut and oak. The style of the casing also has several varieties, including modern, French Provincial, Italian Provincial, Queen Anne and Louis XVI. You want to choose a piano that blends in with the overall style and design of the room you're going to put it in.

If you have wood panelling, wood-beamed ceilings or hardwood floors, a wood finish piano would look good. On the other hand, if the style of your home is modern with white and black tones, a black satin or high-gloss ebony piano would blend in well.

In terms of the casing, again choose a piano that matches your overall decor. For example, if your home is filled with antiques, you might want to choose a Louis XVI or Queen Anne. For the modern home, a contemporary-style black piano would be appropriate.

Take Your Time

Every piano is different. The sound, feel and action of a piano are based on your own subjectivity. Granted, most ears can hear the qualities that are inherent in high-quality pianos, which sound better than pianos of lesser quality, but what sounds or feels good to one person might not be the same for another. Therefore you have to spend some time with each piano you are considering to buy.

Narrow your choices down to two or three pianos. Play the same piece of music on each one and make comparisons. Which one sounds better? Which one is easier to play? Which one feels better? Ask the vendor to tell you the pros and cons of each piano.

If you're still undecided and you have a friend or family member who plays the piano, ask him or her to go to the piano shop with you and play the pianos you are considering. Ask for his or her opinion.

It's always a good idea to shop around and not limit your potential purchase to one piano shop or retail outlet. Visit a big retail outlet that carries a lot of different pianos from a variety of manufacturers; go to a smaller, local piano shop; and visit an exclusive dealership and individual manufacturer's showroom. By doing so, you'll get an excellent education, which will help you in your decision-making process.

> **tips**
>
> Be sure to ask the vendor if the price includes the bench (seat), transport and tuning. When a piano is moved or transported from the warehouse or shop to your home, it invariably goes out of tune and needs to be tuned once it arrives.

Don't feel as though you have to pay the asking price. Every piano shop wants your business, so you can say it's a buyer's market when it comes to pianos. In that respect, negotiate with the vendor or salesperson and make a counter-offer.

Another thing you might wish to consider is choosing a British-made piano, given the reputation of makers such as Broadwood. In the United Kingdom today, however, the only current manufacturers are Kemble, although such makes as Bentley and Cramer can be found secondhand.

New Pianos

With a very wide range of prices that will suit the buyer's budget, there really is a piano for everyone. Keep in mind that the following prices are approximate at the time of writing and reflect the different types of sizes, cabinets and finishes. Shopping around for the best price can also make quite a difference. Regarding new pianos, prices start as low as £1,000 for a small vertical and as high as over £80,000 for a 2.74m (9ft) concert grand. Thanks to Piano Warehouse in London for much of the following information; visit their website at *www.pianowarehouse.co.uk*.

Bechstein pianos are made in Germany. Their vertical piano prices start at £9,000 and go up to £18,000. Bechstein grand pianos start at £22,000 and go as high as £75,000 for a 2.74m (9ft) concert grand.

Blutner pianos are also made in Germany. Their vertical piano prices are similar to those of Bechstein, starting at £9,000 and going up to £18,000. Blutner grand piano prices start at £20,000 and go as high as £70,000 for a 2.74m (9ft) concert grand.

Gors & Kallmann pianos are designed in Germany and made in South Asia. They only make vertical pianos, and their uprights start at £2,500, going up to £3,500.

Grotrian pianos are made in Germany. Their upright pianos are around £6,000. Grand piano prices start at £20,000 and go up to £60,000 for a 2.74m (9ft) concert grand.

Kawai pianos are made in Japan. Vertical piano prices start at £2,300 and go up to £6,000. Kawai grand piano prices start at £7,500 and go as high as £70,000 for a 2.74m (9ft) concert grand.

Kemble pianos are the last British manufacturer still in operation. Vertical piano prices start at £2,700 and go up to £6,500. Kemble make only one model of grand piano, which retails for about £14,000.

Samick pianos are made in South Korea. Vertical piano prices start at £1,900 and go up to £3,000. Their budget grand piano prices start at £5,000 and go up to £8,000.

Schimmel pianos are made in Germany. Vertical piano prices start at £7,000 and go up to £12,000. Grand piano prices start at £20,000 and go as high as £70,000 for a 2.74m (9ft) concert grand.

Seiler pianos are made in Germany. Vertical piano prices start at £5,500 and go up to £12,000. Grand piano prices range from £21,000 to £80,000 for a 2.74m (9ft) concert grand.

Steinmayer pianos are, like Gors & Kallmann, made in South Asia from German design. Their uprights start at £2,500, going up to £3,500. Steinmayer grand pianos start at £10,000 and go up to 20,000 for a 2.74m (9ft) concert grand.

Steinway & Sons pianos are made in the USA, with a limited number made in Germany. Their vertical piano prices start at £9,000 and go up to £18,000. Steinway grand pianos start at £22,000 and go as high as £75,000 for a 2.74m (9ft) concert grand.

Yamaha pianos are made in Japan and China. Vertical piano prices start at £2,300 and go up to £9,000. Yamaha grand piano prices start at £8,000 and go as high as £80,000 for a 2.74m (9ft) concert grand.

Young & Chang pianos are made in China by Weber. Vertical piano prices start at £1,800 and go up to £3,000. Grand piano prices range from £4,500 to £8,000.

Zimmerman pianos are made in Germany, and are the Bechstein 'budget' range. They do not make vertical pianos. Grand pianos start at £8,000 and go up to £20,000.

Used Pianos

Used pianos come in all sizes and models, with the exception of limited custom editions and rare pianos, which are hard to find and are generally quite expensive. There are two basic categories of used pianos: 'as is' and rebuilt or restored. 'As is' pianos, more often than not, need to be rebuilt, at least to some extent. Some 'as is' pianos need to be completely restored, which can be quite costly, and in some cases this can work out even more expensive than buying a new piano.

Piano prices for used verticals at piano shops and dealers can start as low as £250 and go as high as £2,000, depending on the manufacturer, model and condition of the piano. Used grand piano prices can start as low as £1,200 and go as high as you like. Here again, the difference in price depends on the manufacturer, model and condition of the piano.

> **tips**
>
> If you're looking for a used piano, make sure to check your local classified ads. More likely than not, you can get the same piano for less when buying from a private individual as opposed to buying from a used-piano shop. The person selling the piano doesn't have the overheads and expense of running a business that the piano shop has – but you may have no comeback.

Another thing you should do when looking for a used piano is to get in touch with local music schools or the music department of a community college or university. Every so often, these institutions replace their old pianos with new ones, or sometimes have to make cutbacks, both of which present an excellent opportunity to get a used piano at a very good price. Alternatively, they may know of some other institution or organization in the area that wants to sell a piano.

When I was a student at the Hartford Conservatory of Music in the USA, I let my teachers know that I was looking for a used piano. A local convalescent home had contacted the conservatory and said they had an old upright piano that no one was playing; it was stashed away in a corner collecting dust. The convalescent home just wanted to get rid of it. My piano teacher heard about this and gave me the phone number to call.

When I called, I inquired about the asking price of the piano. Now, being a student, I didn't have much of a budget for a piano. When the person replied that it was for sale for the equivalent of £10, I nearly fell over. The only thing I had to do was to arrange for it to be moved to my father's house, where I was living at the time. It just so happened that my father had a sizeable truck that had more than enough room to accommodate the old upright. It didn't cost me a penny to have it moved, thanks to my father and a few strong friends. The piano was in such good condition that the only thing it needed was a tuning once it landed in the living room. I sold the piano two years later for more than £100.

There's no need to rush your decision. Take your time and feel good about your purchase. Whichever piano you choose, you'll be spending a lot of time with it, so be sure it's the one you really want.

CHAPTER 10

Taking Care of Your Piano

Even though the piano is large and produces a strong sound, it is still a delicate instrument and must be treated as such. Regardless of the size and price of your piano, you must protect and take care of it. In doing so, you will maximize the value of your piano and protect your investment.

The Importance of Humidity Control

A piano functions best under consistent climatic conditions – not too moist or too dry. The ideal temperature is 20°C (68°F) with 42 per cent relative humidity.

Pianos are mostly made of wood, and wood is greatly affected by varying degrees of humidity. Changes in humidity cause the wooden parts of a piano to swell and shrink. These changes have a direct impact on the tuning and action of pianos – when extreme swings occur in humidity levels, wood can crack and glue joints can be damaged.

Hundreds of felt and leather parts in the piano's action are also affected by changes in humidity, which can increase friction and make the piano's action feel stiff and resistant to the touch. Under very high humid conditions, condensation can build up on the metal parts of the piano and eventually rust the strings, tuning pins and iron plate.

You might consider it aesthetically pleasing to have a piano in a beach home, but all that moisture from the sea air, surf and low clouds can eventually damage any piano.

The opposite extreme is having a piano in a very dry climate. Apart from potential damage from the sun, a climate that is very arid can dry out the wooden parts of the piano and cause them to crack.

The suggested humidity level for your piano should be a consistent 42 per cent, as recommended by major piano manufacturers and technicians. When your piano is kept at a constant moisture level, shrinking and swelling are minimized, and your piano will stay in tune for a longer period of time.

The best way to maintain a consistent humidity level for your piano (and ultimately to prevent damage from occurring) is to install a humidity control system. This device, which can be attached directly to a piano, has three parts: a humidifier that adds moisture, a dehumidifier that eliminates excessive moisture, and a humidistat that detects the relative humidity of the air within the piano and adds or removes moisture as needed.

Effects of the Sun

Beware of direct sunlight – do not place your piano in front of windows or below skylights. The ultraviolet rays of the sun can damage the finish on your piano. With repeated exposure to the sun, the piano casing will get bleached out, blisters may appear on the finish and the piano may go out of tune.

Aesthetically, it's tempting to place the piano near a window – it's inspiring to look out of the window instead of looking at the wall when playing the piano, particularly when the pianist is playing from memory and not reading music or looking at his or her fingers. But even so, it isn't a good idea to put your piano in harm's way.

If you are tempted to move your piano to a window for inspiration, consider this: would you rather be inspired and play beautifully for a short period of time or find other sources of inspiration and play beautifully for several years?

When I lived in Laguna Beach, California, my patron had an ebony Steinway grand piano placed by the window in her living room. I must admit it was very pleasing to play the piano while looking out of the window and seeing the sun glistening on the Pacific Ocean. Unfortunately, this Steinway fell victim to the exposed sunlight – the colour of the side of the casing turned to a chalky white and the piano suffered from drying out, which adversely affected the action, the hammers and the keys. The exposure to the sun also made the piano go out of tune.

Having seen the damage to this Steinway grand, I made sure not to place my own Knabe grand near a window in my living room. However, I overlooked the fact that a skylight in the living room's vaulted ceiling was beaming sunlight down on the lid of the Knabe. It gets pretty hot during the summer months, and after this happened repeatedly for three years in a row, I noticed blisters popping up on the surface of the lid. I looked up, saw the skylight and realized this was the result of the lid being exposed to the powerful rays of the sun. I had to have the lid refinished. Now during the summer months, I simply place a satin cover over the lid to protect it from the sun. As a result, no blisters have resurfaced.

Keeping Your Piano in Tune

If you protect your piano from direct sunlight, excessive moisture and extreme dryness, the instrument is more likely to stay in tune. These conditions and extreme changes in temperature can cause a piano to go out of tune.

But even under the best climatic conditions, pianos still need to be tuned at least once a year. Depending on how critical your ears are, and the age and condition of your piano, you may need to tune your piano every six months.

If your piano can be moved without much effort and you want to reposition it in your home, it probably won't need to be tuned after moving it. However, when a piano needs to be moved with the help of piano movers and put in a van or truck to be transported to another location, it will more than likely need to be tuned once it reaches its new home.

If you are courageous and have very good ears, you might want to get a tuning hammer and tune a string or two. But beware – you could do more harm than good. Keep in mind that the overall tuning of the piano involves all the strings.

Apart from having your piano tuned on a regular basis, your piano may need to be voiced. This is a process in which the felt heads of the hammers are shaved in order to produce a brighter sound when they strike the string.

In addition, when attempting to tune a note that sounds either sharp or flat, you could be dealing with a note that has two or three strings. You have to be able to isolate the string that sounds out of tune and match it with the other string or strings. This requires the use of a rubber insert to stop the other string or strings from resonating. You also have to compare the string with its upper and lower octaves. I cannot stress too highly that it is far better to have an experienced piano technician tune your piano.

Restoration and Piano Repairs

Restoration is the skilled process of transforming older pianos to their original condition. This process involves restoring or replacing the soundboard; restringing and repinning the frame; restoring, rebuilding and regulating the action, damper assembly and keyboard; stretching the strings and raising the pitch to A-440 tuning (the universal tuning for all musical instruments); overhauling the pedals; and stripping down and refinishing the casing to the original wood grain.

To polish your piano, most manufacturers suggest simply wiping it with a soft damp cloth. If you want to apply furniture polish or lemon oil, it's recommended that you check with your piano tuner or piano salesperson before doing so, to make sure you don't cause any damage to the finish.

A new piano shouldn't require any repairs, but a used piano is an entirely different story. Due to its age and having endured years of playing, a piano's parts may need to be replaced.

Some used pianos may need to be completely restored, with all of the parts having to be replaced. This can take as long as four to six months to complete. A complete restoration can be quite costly and, in some instances, can cost as much as the price of a new piano. If you're going to buy a used piano, it's best to buy one that is already repaired and restored.

Occasionally, piano strings break. When I used to bang away on my Hardman grand, once in a while, I would break a string. It was a very old piano (built around 1909), and I played very aggressively. However, even when playing non-aggressively, strings can break on used pianos because of old age and changes in climatic conditions. Rarely does a string break on a new piano. When a string breaks, it needs to be replaced by a piano tuner.

How to Sell Your Piano

The time may come when you want to sell your piano. You might want to upgrade and get a bigger and better one. Perhaps you or your child has lost interest in the piano and it hasn't been played for an extended period of time. Or maybe you're moving and you'd rather sell it than have it moved to your new home. (Moving is a good time to upgrade and get a new piano for your new home.)

In any case, do some research before selling your piano. Call your local piano shops and ask them how much they're asking for a piano model that is comparable to yours. If possible, contact the manufacturer of your piano and find out what they think your piano is worth. And for comparison's sake, ask the manufacturer what the selling price is for a new piano that is the same as yours. You can also get your piano appraised by a piano tuner or dealer, who can tell you what your piano is worth. The goal is to come up with a fair market price for your piano. Naturally, the age and overall condition of your piano count towards the selling price.

You can trade in your piano to a piano shop and put it towards the purchase price of another piano. However, by selling your piano on your own, you will get more money than what the piano shop offers.

Because some buyers offer you less than your asking price, it's always a good selling practice to ask a little more than what you're willing to settle for. Most things are negotiable, and a used piano falls into that category.

If someone is paying by cheque, be careful. If you don't know who they are (or in some cases, even if you do), it's a good idea to ask the buyer to show a current cheque card to protect yourself.

Run a classified ad in your local newspaper to attract prospective buyers. Based on the response rate of the ad and the number of calls you get, you may not have to take the first offer. Some buyers aren't really serious; they're simply curious and aren't sure that they want to buy a piano – these are the type of people who make an appointment and then don't show up. The serious buyer will be more obvious and straightforward. He or she will set a time to meet and show up with a chequebook, or better still, cash in hand.

CHAPTER 11

Practising

I f you want to become an accomplished pianist, you must practise, practise, practise. It also helps to have a piano teacher who complements you – taking piano lessons with the right teacher builds the technique required to learn how to play the piano proficiently. This chapter helps you to find the right teacher and improve your practising techniques.

When to Start Taking Piano Lessons

There isn't a magic age you need to be to start taking piano lessons. The time to start is when you really want to, and when you can commit yourself to going to lessons and practising on a regular basis. Personal desire and wanting to play the instrument are essential in starting a good working relationship with the piano, while sustained self-motivation and discipline keep the interested going.

Children

Expose your children to the piano from a very young age by playing recordings of piano music. Even though they might be too young to speak, children are very receptive to their immediate surroundings. They are also very impressionable and easily influenced. With that in mind, play a variety of musical styles such as children's songs, Broadway musicals, pop songs and classical music. While driving in your car, play piano music CDs or cassettes. Observe how your child responds and what style of music he or she seems to prefer. In essence, your child will let you know his or her level of interest in the piano.

If possible, take your children to piano recitals. This experience can be very inspiring, not only from the audio perspective, but also from the visual experience of the performance.

If your child is three or four years old and is showing signs of having an interest in the piano, hire a piano for six months to a year. If the child has a natural tendency towards the piano, he or she will start playing it on his or her own. This is the best possible situation. Encourage your child to play the piano, and when he or she finishes playing, clap with approval. This will give your child the confidence he or she is seeking and the encouragement to stay at it and keep playing. When the level of desire becomes more consistent, it's time to find a good piano teacher who has experience in teaching children.

Adults

Adults should start taking piano lessons once they have decided to go to every lesson and make the necessary time to practise each week between the lessons. Here again, the level of desire to play the piano will substantially help in keeping to your commitment. As with any discipline, a routine is good because it sets a condition and habit. That said, try to schedule your practising for the same time each day – you'll find it will become part of your daily and weekly schedules.

There's no point in taking piano lessons if you don't have a piano to practise on. Ideally, you already have a piano sitting in your living room or family room; if not, contact your local piano retailer and inquire about hiring a piano. For the beginner of any age, it's wise to hire a piano before making a purchase. The vast majority of piano shops will put the cost of the hire towards the purchase price – in which case, you're making a small investment while taking time to see how serious you really are about playing the piano.

Piano Teachers for Children

Piano lessons for children should be a positive experience – your child should want to go to piano lessons, so it's very important that he or she likes the piano teacher. To find the right piano teacher for your child, start by asking your friends if their children are taking piano lessons with someone in your local community; friends who already have some experience in this area can be very helpful in starting you off.

Once you've established that the teacher is qualified and has a good reputation for teaching children, ask to meet the teacher and, of course, bring your child. Based on your child's initial reaction to the teacher, you'll probably know early on whether or not this is the right teacher for your child. Because the teacher/child relationship is so important, make sure to take the time to find a teacher to whom your child will have a positive response.

At what age should a child begin piano lessons?
A child could start taking piano lessons as early as the age of four. But please, don't ever force your child to take piano lessons if he or she doesn't want to – by forcing the issue, the parent can actually kill any desire or curiosity the child may have for the piano.

Piano Teachers for Adults

There are a lot of piano teachers to choose from – and some are better than others. Some teachers are faculty members at music conservatories, schools or universities; others teach at local music shops; some teach in their homes where they have set up a home piano studio. Depending on your comfort level, you might prefer the formality and academic setting of studying at a conservatory, music school or university; alternatively, you might prefer the more casual environment of the local music shop, while there are many who prefer the style of a more personal teaching-from-home piano teacher.

Teaching requires giving and nurturing, and the ability to effectively communicate with the student at each lesson. The best piano teachers are the ones who take pride in developing the talents of their students. They know how to motivate and encourage their students and give them the necessary constructive criticism.

In all cases, find out what the teachers' qualifications are and whether or not they are in good standing with professional music teachers' associations. Find out where they studied and what diplomas or degrees they earned. If you haven't already heard them play, ask them to play the piano for you. You should be impressed with the way your piano teacher plays the piano; hopefully, it will be a source of inspiration and something for you to aspire to.

But even the most qualified piano teacher might not be right for you. It depends on how much discipline you want from your teacher. Some teachers are more rigid than others, and some teachers are nicer than others. Once their teaching skills are established, it really boils down to personality. You want to like and admire your teacher. While deciding which teacher to choose, ask your prospective teachers a lot of questions, which should help you choose the teacher who is best suited for you.

1. How long have you been teaching?
2. Why do you teach the piano?
3. How many students do you currently have?
4. What is your method of teaching?
5. How often should I practise?
6. What can I expect to accomplish after six months of lessons?

How Often Should I Practise?

A tourist was visiting New York for the first time and asked a bystander on the street, 'How do I get to Carnegie Hall?' The bystander answered, 'Practise, practise, practise.'

It's pretty basic: the more you practise, the better you sound. If you're really serious about learning how to play the piano, then you will make time each week to practise. At a minimum, you should practise for 90 minutes a week in three 30-minute practice sessions. And don't be restricted by your practice schedule – if you get the urge to play the piano, don't hold back; go ahead and play it. For the best use of your practice time, practise at a time of day or night that is free of any interruptions. This uninterrupted time will allow you to concentrate on what you are trying to achieve.

When assisting children, be sure to make it an enjoyable and positive experience. When they get frustrated or feel discouraged, give them some encouraging words. If they're having difficulty with an exercise, play it for them and explain it to them as you're playing it.

If your child is taking piano lessons, he or she is going to need your assistance; naturally, younger ones need the most help. Children should practise at least three times a week and, depending on their ability to keep their attention on practising, each session should be 20 to 30 minutes long. Children who have a high level of interest in the piano should practise five to seven days a week. For children 10 years old and over, it's best for them to practise on their own.

Keeping Your Concentration

The best way to keep your concentration is to minimize interruptions and distractions. Turn off the television, radio, all telephones (including your mobile phone) and pager. If you have a family and your piano is located in a separate room, lock the door. Mental distractions can also be very counterproductive when practising. As part of your discipline, clear your mind of any extraneous thoughts before you start practising; this will allow you to keep your concentration and, as a result, make more progress.

You shouldn't try to play something in a different way to the one your teacher has told you. Once you've learned something the wrong way, it's very difficult to unlearn that wrong way and make it right.

After you've taken piano lessons for two to three months and you feel fairly confident about your playing, record yourself playing your favourite piece of music. Listening to your playing is a very telling experience. When you're actually playing the piano, you're focused on playing the music to the best of your ability, and when you listen to the playback of a recording, you'll hear things you didn't hear when you were playing. You can learn a lot about your playing by listening to a tape, as it allows you to judge yourself, hear any imperfections and make adjustments in your playing.

When you are having difficulty with a certain passage, do your best to work it out using the instructions given to you by your teacher. Make several attempts to get it right. If you're still having difficulty with it, move on to another section or to an entirely different piece of music. At your next piano lesson, your teacher should show you how to work out the section you're having difficulty with.

Once you start your practice session, don't stop – it's very difficult to start and stop and try to start again, and this counterproductive bad habit should be avoided.

There are no shortcuts in getting to the Carnegie Hall or learning how to play the piano. Learning how to play comes with time, desire, discipline, dedication, instruction – and a lot of practising.

Physical Position

To avoid back pain, you have to sit at the piano with a straight spine – do not lean forward or slouch while playing the piano. In the interests of comfort, sit on a cushion. If you purchase a used piano, make sure to get a matching piano bench – if possible, a padded one. New pianos usually come with a matching piano bench, some of which are padded. The best padded piano benches are adjustable., and you can adjust the height according to your size and finger placement on the keyboard. In terms of height, you want to be sitting high enough so your fingers and forearms are slightly higher than the keyboard, making it easy to press down on the keys. If you don't have an adjustable bench, use cushions or pillows to get the height you need.

Don't put your fingers too far forward towards the back of the keys – instead, place them closer to the edge, or the front, of the keys, as this will give you a quicker and better response in pressing and releasing the piano keys.

tips

If the piano bench is not padded and you're going to be playing for an extended period of time, make sure to put a cushion or pillow on the bench. This will make a big difference in terms of comfort.

Good Habits

1. Always sit in an upright position.
2. Make sure you're sitting at the proper height.
3. Sit on a cushion or padded bench.
4. Minimize all interruptions.
5. Find a quiet place to practise.
6. Clear your mind before you start practising.
7. Create a routine.
8. When you get stuck in a passage, move on and come back to it later.
9. Learn to play the right way, as instructed by your teacher.

Bad Habits

1. Stopping and starting while practising; not getting into a steady momentum.
2. Repeating difficult passages, making no progress.
3. Learning something the wrong way.
4. Trying to make shortcuts. (There aren't any shortcuts.)
5. Allowing yourself to be interrupted while practising.
6. Letting anyone discourage you from wanting to play the piano.

CHAPTER 12

Recording the Piano or Keyboard

I f you want to record your practice sessions yourself, a very basic recording set-up should suffice; but as you improve, you may also want to upgrade the recorded quality of your piano, and that's where this chapter comes in. It may seem like jumping the gun to examine recording at this stage, but after this, the rest of the book is about playing.

Recording Studios

If you want to get the best possible quality recording of your keyboard playing, then look into professional digital recording studios. These studios come complete with producers, sound engineers, acoustic pianos, synthesizers, samplers and effects units. Most of them also have analog recording equipment for those who prefer an analog sound.

Because of their superior quality, equipment and services, they are expensive. If you're lucky and really talented, some studios might be willing to work out some type of barter arrangement: for example, they provide you with an engineer/producer during off hours, usually between midnight and 6:00 AM. You don't have to pay their hourly rate; you only pay for tape costs and tape dubs. In exchange, the studio owners own the copyright to the material you're recording if it's original, or they take a percentage of any future sales of your recording.

This type of barter arrangement is more likely to happen with a new studio with new equipment – they want to test out the studio on you. For instance, they may need to experiment with microphone placement when recording the grand piano, or they may have a new recording console board and effects units that they need to become familiar with.

Hourly recording studio rates range from as little as £15 an hour for a 'home studio' to £100 and up an hour for a fully staffed professional studio. In most cases, studios are willing to work out a package rate versus hourly rates, which definitely saves you money.

Home Recording Studios

If a professional recording studio doesn't suit you, you always have the option of creating a home recording studio. The first thing you have to do is find the best room or space to set up your home studio. Ideally, this will be in a separate room, basement or garage.

In any room – especially the garage – you're probably going to need to install insulation. Sound insulation minimizes room noise, absorbs the sound and also helps prevent the neighbours from complaining about the 'noise' issuing from the room.

If you're going to record using an electric piano, digital piano or synthesizer, this noise factor can be greatly diminished by using headphones while playing and recording, and even during playback.

It's best not to record an acoustic piano in a basement or garage because it could suffer from extreme changes in temperature and humidity. Your acoustic piano should be in your living room, family room or spare room.

You should set up a home studio in an uncluttered space. There will be quite a few cables, cords, extension leads, microphone leads and so forth that can very quickly get tangled up. Some people tape down the leads and cables, which prevents a tangled mess. Of course, once they're taped down, you don't have the flexibility to move them. The length of your leads and cables is important because it limits the distance between the recording deck, amplifier and keyboard – it's always better to have more than enough cable length than to be stuck with cables that are too short.

Recording Equipment

If you choose to set up your own home recording studio, you want to make sure that you have all the equipment you will need. Of course, if you choose to go with a professional recording studio, this equipment will be provided for you. Even so, it is a good idea to become familiar with the equipment used. Here's a quick checklist to get you started.

Recording Equipment Checklist
- ❏ Keyboard (acoustic, electric piano, digital piano or synthesizer)
- ❏ Recording deck
- ❏ Tapes
- ❏ Amplifier
- ❏ Speakers
- ❏ Microphones
- ❏ Effects unit (optional)
- ❏ Sampler (optional)
- ❏ Mix-down unit
- ❏ Power strips, extension leads, connecting cables etc.

Magnetic Tape Recorders: Audiocassette Decks

Audiocassette decks, which are analog instruments, use audiocassette tapes to record and store the data. It's always best to use the highest quality tape for recording purposes, such as metal bias, type IV or high bias, type II tapes. The number of recording tracks on audiocassette decks generally ranges from four to eight tracks. To minimize tape hiss, these decks are usually made with a noise-reduction system. Most come with variable tape speeds, zero return and pitch control functions. DAT, or digital audio tape, is more efficient at noise reduction, but the tapes and decks are much more expensive.

Variable tape speed allows you to record in slow, normal or fast mode. Recording using the fast speed setting gives the best quality sound; use this speed when you are well rehearsed and ready to record a finished piece of music. The normal and slow speeds are good for recording your practice sessions or for experimenting with microphone placements and recording techniques. The normal speed (and even more so, the slow speed) has more tape hiss than the fast speed setting. However, when using the normal or slow speeds, you can get more material on one tape because the tape turns slower than it does with the fast speed setting.

The zero return function is very helpful when you want to rerecord, overdub or simply find the beginning of a piece of music. Before you start recording, set the counter numbers to zero and put the zero return setting in play. Press the record key and start recording. If you want to go back to the beginning of the piece, press the rewind key. The tape will stop at zero, right at the beginning of the piece.

The pitch control device can raise or lower the collective pitch of music recorded on tape. When you raise the pitch, you are also increasing the speed and tempo of the music; when you lower the pitch, you are also slowing the speed and tempo of the music. You can be creative with this device – for instance, if you're recording a musical passage that is difficult to play at normal speed, set the pitch as low as possible and record it playing at a slower tempo. Once you have recorded it, increase the pitch to normal and it will sound faster (and higher) than what you recorded. If you want the recorded passage to sound even faster (and higher), increase the pitch to a higher setting.

If you're going to be recording your voice and want to sound higher or younger, record your voice with the pitch set normal and increase the pitch when listening to the playback.

Each track has EQ (equalization) settings and pan settings. Panning is used to place the sound within the stereo spectrum. With panning, you can place a track to the far right, centre (down the middle) or far left; all the variables in between right, left and centre are also available.

Magnetic Tape Recorders: Reel-to-Reel Tape Recorders

Every now and then, you might come across a reel-to-reel tape recorder; these machines were very popular in the 1950s, 1960s and 1970s. Reel-to-reel recorders use magnetic tape to record the sound. The size of the tape is usually 6mm (1/4in) in width, although professional recording studios have reel-to-reel recorders that use 12mm (1/2in), 25mm (1in) and 50mm (2in) tapes and are still in use today – quite a few people are convinced that these analog machines sound warmer than digital decks.

As with audiocassette decks, when using any size of magnetic tape, you're going to encounter tape noise. That's why noise-reduction systems, such as Dolby, were built. In addition to tape noise, over an extended period of time magnetic tapes can dry up and crack, losing some data and quality.

Because digital technology is so popular and offers so many functions not available with tape decks, 6mm (¹/₄in) reel-to-reel tape recorders have become fairly obscure, so as a result, it's difficult to purchase new blank reel-to-reel magnetic tapes.

Digital Recording Decks

If you're going to record using a digital recording deck, you don't have to be concerned with audiotapes; digital decks record and store the data using internal computer chips, also called a hard drive. As is true with digital sound instruments, the sound that digital decks record and play back is bright and crisp, and has an edge.

One of the big differences between audiotape decks and digital decks is tape noise. Since digital decks don't use tapes, there is no tape noise whatsoever. The number of recording tracks on digital recording decks designed for home studios range from eight to 24 tracks. Professional studios may have digital decks with as many as 48 tracks, and there a few instances where even more are used.

Thanks to digital technology, when recording using digital decks you have options that are not available with audiotape decks – for instance, you have the ability to copy and paste sections of music instead of having to play everything in real time, as you have to do with audiotape decks. When using the editing mode on digital decks, you can subsequently add harmony, counterpoint, bass or rhythm parts to a previously recorded piece of music.

Some digital decks come preloaded with hundreds of different rhythm patterns, incorporating a wide variety of musical styles, drum-kit combinations and percussion instruments.

Many digital decks have built-in sound effects, which can be assigned to each track. The effects can be edited and stored in the user-effect memory banks. Each track also has its own individual EQ settings: you can add treble to brighten up one track, while adding bass to deepen another. If you want to keep strict time while recording a piece of music, you can activate a built-in metronome and adjust the tempo accordingly.

Digital decks also have a punch-in/punch-out function that makes it easy to rerecord or add music to specific sections. You can set the exact record in-point and out-point with a trigger record function, which keeps the music up to the in-point and after the out-point completely intact and protected.

The internal hard disk of digital recorders can hold up to a specific amount of data; the bigger the size of the disk, the more data it can store. When the disk has reached its maximum storage capacity, the data can be downloaded to a DAT (digital audio tape) recorder or an external hard disk drive.

Amplifiers

Because recording decks don't have any speakers, all recording decks need to be connected to an external amplifier with speakers. Most decks come with a built-in amplifier, which works well while listening with headphones, but an external amplifier has much more wattage and sends the sound through external speakers. The amplifiers in home stereo systems are more than adequate – simply connect your recording deck to the amplifier using the tape or auxiliary inputs, and set your amplifier to the appropriate setting. Your recording deck will send its sounds to the amplifier and to the attached stereo speakers.

Another option is to use an amplifier made for guitars, keyboards or sound systems. However, the sound probably won't be as clean as the sound you get when using the amplifier in a receiver, and if the speakers are contained in one single cabinet, you won't hear the sounds in stereo.

Microphones

When recording an acoustic piano, you need microphones. It's best to get two quality microphones and two adjustable microphone stands. There are basically two different types of microphones: directional and omnidirectional. Directional microphones are sharper in recording tighter, focused sounds, while omnidirectional microphones record more room noise, sound fuller, and have more ambience. Both types of microphones work well; the specific type of sound you're striving for will determine which type you ultimately use.

What are directional and omnidirectional microphones?
Directional microphones receive sound signals from a narrow, semi-closed radius. Omnidirectional microphones receive sounds from a wider, more open radius.

Microphone prices start at the bottom end from around £20–25 and go up to hundreds of pounds – the more money you spend on a microphone, the better the quality. Generally speaking, you can get a good quality microphone for about £35, which should be more than adequate for recording your piano.

One microphone should be placed above the treble section and the other placed above the bass section of the piano. This will allow you to record the full range of sound the piano has to offer. Make sure you have long enough leads to reach the distance from the microphones to the inputs on your recording deck.

Effects Units

If you're recording using an audiocassette deck, it is unlikely to have built-in effects. This means that you'll need to connect it to an effects unit that contains numerous types of effects, including various kinds of reverb, echo, delay, chorus, gated effects and so forth. Effects units are digital and MIDI-compatible.

The recorded tracks on the cassette deck are sent to the effects unit, processed with a specific effect and sent back to the deck. Each track on the cassette deck can be processed with an effect. The amount or level of the effect can be adjusted on the cassette deck.

Digital recording decks are made with built-in effects, and the type and quality of effects are similar to those of external effects units. The built-in effects on digital decks are more than adequate, so you probably won't need an external effects unit.

Samplers

Samplers are separate sound units, similar to effects units, with one big difference: they record sampled sounds. A sampler allows you to take any external sound, such as a musical instrument, a slamming door or running water, and record and store it in memory.

The recorded sample sound is looped, making it continuous. Using the sampler as a controller, the sampled sound is sent through MIDI to a digital keyboard. When the keyboard is programmed to play the sampled sound, the entire keyboard will produce the sampled sound. So with the sound of running water, for instance, you can play high-pitched, fast-running water sounds or low-pitched, slow-running water sounds.

Sampling is really an extraordinary technical accomplishment: the possibilities of this technical capability are endless and are limited only by your imagination. And for analog fans, any analog sound can be sampled and then played on digital synthesizers. The sampling of sounds is possible because of digital technology and the use of MIDI.

tips

A good example of sampled keyboard sounds are the soundtracks to Ericka Beckman's films *Out of Hand*, *You the Better*, *Cinderella* and *Hiatus*. These soundtracks, which were composed by the author, use sampled sounds from striking metal pipes, chirping birds, water sprinklers and running water. The sampled sounds were manipulated through sound and effect processors.

At the low end of the price spectrum, you can purchase a portable battery-operated sampler for around £110. This type of sampler is very practical for sampling (recording) outside noises such as the sound of traffic, trains or low-flying jet engines. Jumping up in price to around £550, Yamaha and Roland make samplers that can record the sampled sound for a longer period of time, and come with many built-in special effects. For those of you who want to have a digital keyboard with a built-in sampler, you can get an Ensoniq, Kurzweil, Korg or Yamaha. These keyboard samplers have the best editing features and come equipped with sequencing, cutting and copying features.

Mix-Down Deck

This important piece of equipment is used during the final stage of the recording process. A mix-down deck can be an audiocassette deck/player, DAT recorder or CD burner, and must have a record function. Connect your recording deck to the mix-down deck using the appropriate outputs, inputs and leads. When you connect the mix-down deck to your amplifier, you can hear the incoming signal through the speakers, or, if the deck has a headphone option, you can listen with headphones.

Preparing to Record

One of the most important things to do when you purchase your recording equipment is to read the instruction manuals carefully and thoroughly. Take your time and set the equipment up properly. Explore all the different options and functions the equipment has to offer. Don't rush into the recording process without reading the manuals. If you do, you'll end up wasting time and failing to utilize the full capacity of the equipment.

If you're recording an acoustic piano, make sure it's in tune. It should be tuned to A-440, which is the universal tuning for all musical instruments; this is especially important if you're going to be recording both an acoustic piano and electric keyboards. The acoustic piano has to be tuned to A-440 so it will match and be in tune with the electric keyboard instruments.

Check the pedals on your acoustic piano and make sure they don't squeak. If they do, apply a small amount of oil and work it into the pedal mechanism. This will prevent the microphones from picking up any unwanted squeaking sounds when you use the pedals.

Also check your piano for any buzzes or vibrations before recording. It can happen that something drops into the casing and rests on the soundboard or strings, such as a pencil or paperclip. These little objects can cause buzzing and vibrating noises.

Make sure that the nuts and bolts inside or underneath the piano bench are tight – doing so will prevent the bench from making squeaking sounds as you play.

> Make sure to have a few pieces of music well rehearsed before you start the recording process. If possible, memorize them so you won't have to read the sheet music. Instead, your eyes can watch the record levels on the deck and make sure that the levels don't get too high and distort the incoming sound.

Recording an Acoustic Piano

Set up two microphones: one above the treble section and the other above the bass section of the piano. If you place the microphones close to the strings, you'll capture a direct, relatively dry sound from the strings and soundboard. When the microphones are in this position, you'll get a strong signal. You might also pick up some hammer and action sounds; the way to prevent this is to tip the microphones away from the hammers and action. If you place the microphones 100–150mm (4–6in) away from the strings, the sound will be softer, less dry and contain some room noise or ambience. The only disadvantage to having the microphones in this position is that you'll have to increase the record level to get a strong signal, and in doing so, you'll be picking up more room noise. There will also be noticeable differences in sound, depending on your choice of microphones: directional or omnidirectional.

Another variable affecting the sound of recording the piano is the position of the lid. If the lid is only slightly open, just enough to get the microphones in position, the sound will be somewhat compact and tight. If the lid is raised to its high position, the sound will be a great deal more open and fuller.

The only way to find a sound that you like is to experiment with different microphones, and microphone and lid positions. After you find the sound you like, set the record levels to as high as possible without getting too great a signal and distorting the incoming sound. Assign track one to one microphone and track two to the other. If you want to get a full-spread stereo sound, set the pan dial on track one to the left and the pan dial on track two to the right. Experiment with the varying degrees of the pan settings, from extreme left and right to moving the pan towards the centre – for example, you can place the pan setting halfway between far left and centre.

In the process of finding the best possible sound, you only need to play a few chords at your normal dynamic level of playing. Once you are satisfied with the sound and settings, play the softest and loudest passages from the piece you're going to record. Make sure that you're getting enough record level during the soft section and not too much level during the loud section. It's best to set the record level to an overall one, getting enough signal for the soft sections and not too much signal for the loud sections. Here again, you have to experiment with the record levels before you record an entire piece of music.

Recording a Non-acoustic Piano

The big difference between recording with electric pianos, digital pianos or synthesizers and recording an acoustic piano is that you don't have to use any microphones. Simply connect a patch lead from the output of your keyboard directly into the input on your recording deck and assign it to a designated track; going direct and not using microphones gives you a cleaner sound with less noise. The majority of these keyboards have two output jacks, which can be assigned to two different tracks on the recording deck, giving you a stereo recording.

Electric pianos don't offer much in terms of built-in effects; however, digital pianos do have some built-in effects. Synthesizers come equipped with electric piano and digital piano sounds, and some also have a variety of effects already built-in.

Recording Techniques

If you're recording an acoustic piano and using a four-track audiocassette deck, use the two-microphone set-up that was covered in the microphone section of this chapter. Set the pan dials to left and right to get a good stereo sound. Turning the pan dials slightly in either direction will give you varying degrees of stereo, from extreme left and extreme right to the sound of the tracks bleeding or overlapping each other. If you only have one microphone, you can still create a stereo sound by sending the incoming record signal to two different tracks. With track one, set the pan to the left. With track two, set the pan to the right. When using only one microphone, you'll be recording an overall sound of the piano as opposed to a treble-section and bass-section recording when using two microphones.

> tips
>
> If you want to simulate the sound of a bass track and treble track when using only one microphone, try increasing the bass equalization on track one, and increasing the treble on track two. This technique can give your piano a simulated stereo sound.

When recording using an electric piano, digital keyboard or synthesizer, plug directly into the recording deck. Send the incoming signal to two different tracks and experiment with different pan settings and EQ settings. As you will notice with your keyboard, some of the sounds are already processed with effects and may not need any changes. However, you might want to experiment with modifying the equalization.

You have the option to add additional sounds to your keyboard tracks by utilizing any unrecorded tracks on your recording deck – for instance, you can add a string line, string section, bass or percussion track to accompany your keyboard tracks. This process is called multitracking or overdubbing. If you plan to multitrack and want the additional track or tracks to start at the very beginning of the piece of music, you're going to have to record, using a microphone, a count-in so you know when to start playing the overdubs. For instance, if the piece of music is in 4/4 time, count off saying, *one, two, three.* Leave a space for *four* because it's close to the beginning of the recorded music and nobody wants to hear it! By doing a count-in, you set the tempo and know where the downbeat to the first measure is. A count-in can also be made by using a built-in metronome or beats from a drum machine.

If you are an ambitious, creative-type musical arranger and want to multitrack using more than the tracks available, you can mix two tracks down to one open track – for example, you can take the two piano tracks on tracks one and two and mix them down to track three. This will give you three open tracks for overdubbing.

Mixing two tracks down to one requires a lot of recording experience and experimentation with your equipment.

There are some disadvantages if you choose to use this mixing option when using an audiotape deck: you will lose the stereo sound of the two separate piano tracks, lose some sound quality and increase tape noise. Mixing two tracks down to one can also be done using a digital deck. Actually, this sounds much better because there is no increased tape noise; it's a process of finding the best balance and mix of both tracks before you mix them down to one track.

The Mix

Now comes the final stage in the recording process. Once you are completely satisfied with the sound and settings of your recorded piano or keyboard tracks, you can mix down the two tracks to an audiocassette, DAT tape, minidisk or CD. If mixing down to a tape, to ensure the best quality of sound, clean the tape heads on the mix-down deck by applying some methylated spirits or lighter fuel to a cotton bud and rubbing it gently over the tape heads before letting it dry – this will remove any dirt built up from repeated use. Be sure to use the highest quality tape as your mix-down tape, as it will be your master from which you can make copies (as will be the mix-down CD, minidisk or DAT tape).

When you're satisfied with the pan and EQ settings, assign different effects from the effects unit to the recorded tracks and listen to how the sound of the piano varies with each effect. Also experiment with the level of the effect – too much effect can wash out the definition and clarity of the recorded piano sound.

Play back the source tape on your recording deck, and adjust the incoming record levels on the mix-down deck. To get a strong sound level without distorting the sound, set the level to as high as possible without going into the red for any extended period of time. (Occasional peaks into the red zone are acceptable.) Rewind the tape to the beginning of the recorded piece of music. Start the mix-down tape first, to allow for preroll and so as not to miss or clip the very beginning of the music on your source tape. About four seconds later, start the source tape on your recording deck. At the end of the music, stop both decks. Rewind the mix-down tape and listen to its playback. If the sound level and quality sounds good, you have a master mix tape.

Pros and Cons of Digital Decks

The biggest advantage in recording with digital decks is that it's easier and quicker to record, edit and mix down music tracks. This is possible because the technology has advanced functions that are not available when using analog decks.

Another big advantage with digital decks is the superior sound quality. Because digital decks record and store data by using a microchip, the use of magnetic audiotapes is completely eliminated, and, as a result, there is no tape hiss or tape noise to contend with.

If you find the digital sound too bright or not warm enough, try adjusting the EQ by lowering the treble and increasing the bass or midrange.

Digital decks can be used with analog decks – you can very easily transfer pre-existing recordings from reel-to-reel tapes, audiocassettes or any other sound source to a digital recording deck. Simply record them onto assigned tracks on your digital recorder. Once you have done this, the music is safely stored on the hard drive and can be treated with all the options and functions available on the digital deck.

There are a few disadvantages to digital decks. There is a limit to how much data can be stored on the microchip's hard drive. Be sure to find out how much memory is available on the digital deck before you make your purchase; generally speaking, the larger the memory capacity, the higher the price. When the hard drive has reached its full capacity, you will not be able to make any additional recordings. In order to do so, you will have to delete some of the data on the hard drive or download some or all of the data onto an external digital disk or hard drive, which will free up the memory and allow you to make new recordings.

In terms of sound quality and recording functions, the advantages of digital recording decks far outweigh any disadvantages.

CHAPTER 13

Learning to
Play the Piano

Now it's time for you to take a seat at the piano and learn how to play. In this chapter, you're going to learn about basic music theory as it applies to the keyboard; and in doing so, you will learn to play several easy exercises.

Musical Terms and Definitions

Music is a universal language – anyone can listen to music. However, the making and playing of music requires more than listening; it requires knowledge. If you want to play the piano, you're going to have to study, take lessons and practise.

Before you dive into the exercises, you should know some of the basic terms used in music and their definitions.

Bar – A bar, sometimes called a measure, contains a number of beats, as designated by the time signature – for instance, when the time signature is 4/4, there are four beats per bar.

Bar lines – Bar lines are placed between bars. In 4/4 time, a bar line is placed after the fourth beat of each bar.

Bass line – The bass line, played by the left hand, accompanies the melody. Bass lines usually play the root of the chord and can also include the fifth and third of the chord and passing notes.

Beat – A beat is a measurement of time – for example, in a 4/4 time signature, there are four beats in a bar of music. The beats in music help you keep even time.

Chords – Basic chords are comprised of three notes: the root, the third and the fifth. Three-note chords are called triads.

Clefs – There are three clefs in music: treble, alto and bass clefs. (A fourth, the tenor clef, is almost unused.) In piano music, the treble and bass clefs are used. The treble clef is also called the G clef; the bass clef is also called the F clef. Clefs sit at the far left end of a stave and determine the letter names of the notes.

Harmony – Usually comprised of chords, harmony supports the melody. In piano music, the harmony is generally played with the left hand.

Key signature – The key signature tells you what key a piece of music is written in. There are two kinds of key signatures: sharp (♯) and flat (♭). The key signature is written on the stave to the immediate right of the clef.

Ledger lines – These are short horizontal lines found above and below the five lines of the staves. Ledger lines accommodate notes that are above G at the top of the treble-clef stave and below D at the bottom of the same stave – for instance, the middle C on your keyboard is written on one ledger line below the upper stave.

Melody – Melody is the dominant musical line, which is usually played by the right hand on the piano and is most often written in the treble clef.

Notes – Musical notes are used to determine the duration and value of the note being played. Notes and their values are: semibreves, minims, crotchets, quavers, semiquavers and demisemiquavers. (The breve, twice as long as a semibreve, is now obsolete.).

Pitch – Pitch is determined by where the note is played on the piano and its corresponding written note on manuscript paper.

Rests – Rests represent silence in music. When you see a rest, stop playing for the duration and value of what the rest is equal to. There are semibreve rests, minim rests, crotchet rests, quaver rests, semiquaver rests and demisemiquaver rests. Rests are of equal value to notes – for instance, a crotchet rest is equal in value to a crotchet note, which represents one beat.

Rhythm – Rhythm occurs when playing a series of notes.

Stave – Staves are made up of horizontal lines and spaces. When using a treble clef, the lines on a staff from bottom to top are: E, G, B, D, and F. To help remember these letter names to the corresponding lines, think of this saying: 'Every Good Boy Deserves Favour'. The letter names of the spaces on the staff between the lines are: F, A, C and E. When you put the letter names of the lines and spaces together, you get E, F, G, A, B, C, D, E and F, which correspond directly with letter names of the piano keys.

Stems – Stems are attached to notes. There are crotchet stems, quaver stems, semiquaver stems, and demisemiquaver stems.

Tempo – The tempo is the rate of speed at which you play music.

Time signature – The time signature tells you how many beats there are per bar.

Now you know the terminology, you are ready to begin your first lesson. The following series of exercises are written for the beginner level – the aspiring pianist. As the lessons and exercises progress, they reach a more intermediate level.

Learning the Names of the Notes

FIGURE 13-1:
Abbreviated
keyboard

1. 2. 3. 4. 5. - the fingers of your
right hand

Note that this illustration does not show the 88 keys found on most acoustic pianos – a full keyboard has an additional 24 keys above the far right C key and another 15 keys below the far left C key; the additional keys follow the same white key/black key configuration. The highest note on an acoustic piano is C; the lowest note is A. As you can see in FIGURE 13-1, the notes of the piano's white keys are C, D, E, F, G, A and B. The notes of the black keys are C sharp, D sharp, F sharp, G sharp and A sharp.

The black keys are located between the white keys and are grouped in sets of two and three: C sharp and D sharp make up a group of two black keys, while F sharp, G sharp and A sharp make up a group of three. This two- and three-group black note sequence is consistent up and down the keyboard. The black keys are called sharp keys because they're slightly higher (sharper) than the white keys that precede them – for instance, the black key C sharp is slightly higher in sound and pitch than the white key C. When playing in flat key signatures, the black keys are also called flat keys. This is further explained in Chapter 16.

The note called middle C is located approximately in the middle of the keyboard. To be exact, it's a little left of the middle – slightly left of the manufacturer's brand name on the fall. If you count up from the lowest note on a keyboard instrument that has 88 keys, middle C will be the 40th note up from the bottom.

Applying Your Fingers to the Keys

Looking at your right hand, let's assign numbers to each of your fingers. Your thumb is 1, index finger is 2, middle finger is 3, fourth finger (ring finger) is 4 and your smallest finger is 5. Now let's assign corresponding numbers to the keys, starting with middle C. C is 1 (your thumb), D is 2 (your index finger), E is 3 (your middle finger), F is 4 (your fourth finger) and G is 5 (your smallest finger). See FIGURE 13-1.

Two-Finger Exercise

This first series of exercises will use only your first two fingers: your thumb (1) and your index finger (2).

Place your thumb on middle C, press down on the key and release it. Repeat this action a number of times. Place your index finger on the D key and do the same. Play D a number of times. Using your thumb to play middle C and your index finger to play D, alternate playing both notes in the following sequence: C, D, C, D, C. Try to play the two notes evenly with the same measured time for each note. Keep playing this simple two-finger exercise until it feels comfortable and sounds smooth.

Three-Finger Exercise

Now let's add your third (middle) finger to the exercise. Place your third finger over the E key (key 3) and press and release it a few times. With your thumb positioned above middle C, your second finger above D and your third finger above E, play the following sequence of notes: C, E, D, E; C, E, D, E; C, E, D, E, C. Another way of thinking and playing this exercise is to use the corresponding number of your fingering sequence: 1, 3, 2, 3; 1, 3, 2, 3; 1, 3, 2, 3, 1 (1 represents your thumb, 3 represents your middle finger, 2 represents your index finger, 3 represents your middle finger).

The written music for this three-finger exercise is shown overleaf.

EXERCISE 13-1

It's important to note that the middle C on your keyboard corresponds to the written crotchet C, located on one ledger line below the stave. This note is the first written note in EXERCISE 13-1.

Now play EXERCISE 13-1 reading the music. Your fingers and hand stay in the same position, so you don't have to look down at them. Instead, keep your eyes on the music. Keep repeating this exercise until it feels good and sounds smooth and even.

FIGURE 13-2:

Abbreviated keyboard

Using the same three fingers (the thumb, index finger and middle finger), place your thumb above the D key, index finger above the E key and your middle finger above the F key (see FIGURE 13-2). Play the following sequence of notes: D, F, E, F; D, F, E, F; D, F, E, F, D. The corresponding numbers of your fingering sequence is exactly the same as EXERCISE 13-1: 1, 3, 2, 3; 1, 3, 2, 3; 1, 3, 2, 3, 1 (1 represents your thumb, 3 represents your middle finger, 2 represents your index finger, 3 represents your middle finger).

The written music looks like this:

EXERCISE 13-2

Congratulations! You have just played the first in a series of sequential exercises. The fingering configuration – 1, 3, 2, 3; 1, 3, 2, 3; 1, 3, 2, 3, 1 – can be played on any group of three piano keys. For example, in EXERCISE 13-1, you played this configuration starting with your thumb on the C key, and in EXERCISE 13-2, you played the same configuration starting with your thumb on the D key.

Noting the Symbols

Before we continue with the exercises, let's take a close look at all the symbols used in EXERCISE 13-2.

First, we see a treble clef sitting on the far left of the stave. The treble clef is also called the G clef because the curl wraps around and stops at the G line on the stave. This clef tells you that the letter names of the lines and spaces on the stave are: E, F, G, A, B, C, D, E and F.

Next, we see the first note D, which is a crotchet and whose value is one beat in the bar. The crotchet is shaped like a filled-in circle with a stem attached to it. The following F, E, and F are also crotchets. So we have four crotchets (D, F, E, F) in the first bar.

Immediately following the fourth crotchet in the first bar is a bar line. The bar line separates the bars on the stave and keeps the four crotchets together in one bar. The next bar (bar 2) is an exact repetition of bar 1: same notes, same keys, same fingering and same number of beats in the bar. The same is true in measure 3 – a direct repetition of measures 1 and 2. Again, note the bar lines separating each bar.

In bar 4 we see only one crotchet followed by a crotchet rest (the curved zigzag line) and a minim rest (the small rectangular block that sits on the middle line of the stave). A crotchet rest equals one beat, and a minim rest equals two beats. The combined value of one crotchet, one crotchet rest, and one minim rest gives us four beats in bar 4. The first beat has sound, which is the crotchet D. The second beat is silent, represented by the crotchet rest. And the third and fourth beats are silent, represented by the minim rest.

The symbol we see at the very end of the stave is called a double bar line. The double bar line means this is the end of the piece.

In reviewing the above material, answer the following questions.

1. How many bars are there in EXERCISE 13-2?

   ♪ ....

2. How many notes are there in bar 3 in EXERCISE 13-2?

   ♪ ....

3. How many notes are there in bar 4 in EXERCISE 13-2?

   ♪ ....

4. What kinds of notes are in EXERCISE 13-2?

   ♪ ....

5. How many beats are there per bar in EXERCISE 13-2?

   ♪ ....

6. What separates the bars?

   ♪ ....

7. What is the name of the clef?

   ♪ ....

8. What do the numbers above the notes represent?

   ♪ ....

9. What is the name of the zigzag line in bar 4, and how many beats is it equal to?

   ♪ ....

10. What is the name of the small rectangular block in bar 4, and how many beats is it equal to?

    ♪ ....

11. What is the final symbol at the very end of the stave called, and what does it mean?

    ♪ ....

(Answers can be found in the Appendix.)

Moving Up the Keyboard

Let's continue with the exercises using the same sequence starting on different notes.

As you can see below, in EXERCISE 13-3 the fingering is exactly the same as EXERCISES 13-1 AND 13-2 – the only differences are the pitches and letter names of the notes. You're simply moving your first three fingers up the keyboard and playing the same sequence. Play EXERCISE 13-3 starting with your thumb playing the E key, followed by your middle finger playing the G key and your index finger playing the F key.

EXERCISE 13-3

Remember: as you play the exercises, try to play the crotchets evenly, since they all have the same equal value.

If you get lost during the course of playing these exercises, refer to FIGURE 13-2. This illustration shows you where the letter names of the notes on the stave are relative to the piano keys – for instance, the first note in EXERCISE 13-4 is F, which is four notes above middle C on your piano.

Play EXERCISE 13-4 starting with your thumb playing the F key, followed by your middle finger playing the A key, etc.

EXERCISE 13-4

Now try EXERCISE 13-5.

EXERCISE 13-5

There's something new in EXERCISE 13-5: immediately following the treble clef are two fours, one on top of the other. This is a time signature. The top number four tells you there are four beats per bar, and the bottom number four represents the crotchet, telling you the crotchet gets the beat. EXERCISES 13-1, 13-2, 13-3 and 13-4 are also in 4/4 time.

This time start the sequence on the A key.

EXERCISE 13-6

Something new has been added to EXERCISE 13-6. The word *moderato* in the upper left-hand corner indicates the rate of speed at which the exercise should be played. *Moderato* is an Italian word that means 'moderately' – not too fast and not too slow. This is the tempo (rate of speed) at which the music is to be played.

The first note in EXERCISE 13-7 is B.

EXERCISE 13-7

There is a change in the position and direction of the crotchet stems in EXERCISES 13-5, 13-6, 13-7. In the previous exercises, all the crotchet stems are placed on the right side of the notes and go up. When notes are on the middle line of the stave (B) and higher, note stems are placed on the left side of the note and go down.

Directly below the 4/4 time signature is the symbol *mf*. This symbol stands for the Italian term *mezzo forte*, which in English means 'medium loud'. EXERCISE 13-7 should be played at a moderate tempo and played medium loud.

EXERCISE 13-8 introduces another musical symbol called the repeat sign. It is located immediately to the right of the 4/4 time signature and again at the end of bar 4. As you can see, a repeat sign is a double bar line with two small circles in the A and C spaces of the stave. There is also written text telling you to repeat three times at the end of bar 4. – this tells you that after you have played the exercise once, you are to repeat the entire exercise twice. In doing so, you will have played the exercise a total of three times.

Be sure to give the crotchet and the minim rest in bar 4 their full values totalling three beats of silence – one beat for the crotchet rest, two beats for the minim rest. It might help to count *one, two, three, four* for each beat per bar. For instance in bars 1, 2 and 3, as you're playing the crotchets C, E, D, E, say *one, two, three, four*. When you get to bar 4, count *one* for the C note, *two* for the crotchet rest, and *three, four* for the minim rest.

Play EXERCISE 13-8 starting with the C key.

EXERCISE 13-8

Introducing Octaves

There is a direct correlation between EXERCISE 13-1 and EXERCISE 13-8: Both exercises have the same letter names for the notes – C, E, D, E; C, E, D, E; C, E, D, E; C. The difference is the position of the notes on the stave and corresponding piano keys. The notes in EXERCISE 13-8 are an octave higher than those in EXERCISE 13-1. *Octave* is a musical term referring to a pitch that is eight notes above a note that has the same letter name.

Place your thumb on middle C (the first note in EXERCISE 13-1, written on one ledger line below the stave) and count the keys moving up the keyboard until you reach the C (the first note in EXERCISE 13-8, written in the third space of the stave). The high C is exactly eight white keys higher than middle C, thus an octave higher.

Using these two Cs as a model, do the same with the second note E in EXERCISE 13-1 and the second note E in EXERCISE 13-8. You will discover that there is the same number of white keys from the E on the first line of the stave in EXERCISE 13-1 to the higher E in the fourth space on the stave in EXERCISE 13-8. Now do the same comparison with the third note D in both EXERCISES 13-1 and 13-8, and you will discover the same thing: there are eight white keys from the low D to the high D.

Playing a Simple Melody

Now that you have played through EXERCISES 13-1 to 13-8, it's time to play your first piece of music. This little tune is comprised of sections from EXERCISES 13-1, 13-2 and 13-3. As you can see opposite, the fingering of the right hand is not indicated beyond bar 4. This is because the fingering pattern is already established and keeps repeating throughout the piece (1, 3, 2, 3, 1).

As the time signature indicates, there are four beats per bar. Be sure to give all the bars their full four beats, including the bars that have rests.

Let's take a closer look at EXERCISE 13-9. This piece is written using a two-bar pattern. The two-bar pattern is a series of four crotchets in the first bar followed by one crotchet, one crotchet rest and a minim rest in the second measure. This is a rhythmic pattern – it creates a specific rhythm that is repeated throughout the piece. The rhythm of the pattern is the same; however, the pitches change. In bars 1 and 2, the pitches are C, E, D, E, C. In bars 3 and 4, the pitches rise to D, F, E, F, D. In bars 5 and 6, the pitches rise to E, G, F, G, E. Bars 7 and 8 are exactly the same as bars 3 and 4. And bars 9 and 10 are exactly the same as bars 1 and 2.

This structural analysis identifies the patterns in the piece, which should make it easier to play the music.

EXERCISE 13-9

NICE and EASY

To review this material, answer the following questions.

12. What do you call the first thing you see to the immediate right of the treble clef in EXERCISE 13-5?

13. What does this symbol mean?

14. In EXERCISE 13-6, what does the word *moderato* command?

15. What is the English translation of the Italian word *moderato*?

16. In EXERCISE 13-7, what does the symbol *mf* mean?

17. Why are the stems on the crotchets in EXERCISES 13-7 and 13-8 going down?

18. In EXERCISE 13-8, what is to the immediate right of the time signature and also at the very end of bar 4?

19. What does this symbol mean?

20. When you see this symbol, how many times should you play the music?

    ♪ ....

21. What is the correlation between EXERCISE 13-1 and EXERCISE 13-8?

    ♪ ....

22. What type of pattern is used in EXERCISE 13-9?

    ♪ ....

23. What other pattern is consistent throughout the piece?

    ♪ ....

24. How many bars are there in EXERCISE 13-9?

    ♪ ....

25. How many bar lines are there in EXERCISE 13-9?

    ♪ ....

26. How many beats are there in bars 2, 4, 6, 8 and 10?

    ♪ ....

27. In those bars, how many beats are silent?

    ♪ ....

(Answers can be found in the Appendix.)

Minims and Semibreves

Before we continue on with the exercises, let's take a look at notes and their relative values. You are already familiar with crotchets, having played them in the previous exercises. As you know, a crotchet equals one beat. You also know that four crotchets equal four beats. For example, in EXERCISE 13-9 the time signature is 4/4, telling you that there are four crotchet beats per bar. Bars 1, 3, 5, 7 and 9 have four crotchets in each of them.

You are also familiar with the crotchet rest, which equals one beat of silence, and the minim rest, which equals two beats of silence. A minim looks like a white crotchet and equals two beats of sound. The sound of a minim is sustained, or held, for two beats. For example, in EXERCISE 13-10, the first note is a minim and represents the first and second beats in the bar. This is followed by a crotchet for the third beat and another crotchet for the fourth beat. When playing a minim, you hold the sound through the second beat.

Semibreves look like minims without stems. They are held for a full four beats. Semibreve rests look like upside-down minim rests and receive four counts of silence. You can find a semibreve in the next chapter, EXERCISE 14-1. Semibreve rests first appear in EXERCISE 15-9.

Adding the Fourth and Fifth Fingers

Now let's add fingers 4 and 5 to the exercises. Place your fifth finger above the G key (five keys above middle C), your fourth finger above the F key, your third finger above the E key and your second finger above the D key.

Play EXERCISE 13-10 starting with your fourth finger on the F key.

EXERCISE 13-10

A new symbol has been added in EXERCISE 13-10: the dynamic marking *mp*. This symbol means *mezzo piano*, which translated from Italian to English means 'medium soft'.

At this point, you might be wondering why musical terms and symbols are in Italian. This started with the Italian operatic composers Puccini, Rossini and Verdi, who wrote dynamic and tempo markings in Italian for the singers and musicians who performed their operas. Other countries in Europe adopted the Italian symbols, which eventually became the universal standard.

Make sure to follow the repeat sign in EXERCISE 13-10; at the end of bar 8, go directly back to the beginning of the piece (bar 1) and play the exercise again. Don't stop the even flow of beats when going from the end of bar 8 back to bar 1.

For the next exercise, place your fifth finger above the G key, your fourth finger above the F key, your third finger above the E key, your second finger above the D key and your thumb above the C key (middle C). This exercise is designed to strengthen your fourth and fifth fingers, which are normally the weakest fingers in the right hand. (Reminder: don't forget to follow the repeat sign.)

Play EXERCISE 13-11 starting with your thumb on middle C.

Play EXERCISE 13-11 frequently; in doing so, you will strengthen your fourth and fifth fingers.

The following are a few things to keep in mind when playing the exercises in this chapter.

1. Start playing the exercises slowly. Once you have played the exercise correctly, then increase your tempo (speed) to *moderato*.
2. If you get confused with your fingering, refer to FIGURES 13-1 and 13-2 as required.
3. Your hand and fingers should never be flat when playing the keyboard. Make sure to keep your right hand arched and your fingers curved when playing these exercises.
4. Play the crotchets evenly, giving them the same equal value (one beat).
5. Give the crotchet and minim rests their full values.
6. Enjoy playing the exercises – you should feel good about learning how to play the piano.

Adding Your Left Hand

Think of the left hand as providing the musical foundation that supports what the right hand is playing. This chapter introduces you to the bass line in a piece of music and shows how to use your left hand to play it. Then you are going to put both hands together to play a short piece of music.

Playing a Bass Line

For the most part, the left hand plays the bass line in a piece of music, which provides harmony to the melody played with the right hand. In more advanced piano compositions, the left hand plays both bass lines and chords; this is the case with most of the piano sonatas mentioned in Chapter 4. However, we're going to leave the more advanced stuff for now and concentrate on using the left hand to play just a bass line.

FIGURE 14-1:
Abbreviated
keyboard

5. 4. 3. 2. 1. - the fingers of your left hand

Let's assign numbers to the fingers in your left hand. Your thumb is 1, your index finger is 2, your middle finger is 3, your fourth finger is 4 and your fifth finger is 5. Referring to FIGURE 14-1, place the five fingers of your left hand above the following keys: thumb above middle C, index finger above the B key, middle finger above the A key, fourth finger above the G key and fifth finger above the F key.

When playing with your left hand, the corresponding notes are written on a stave using the bass clef. Refer to FIGURE 14-2: the bass clef has two dots immediately to the right of what is a curved, half heart-shaped semicircle.

FIGURE 14-2:
Bass clef

Starting with the top line and going down to the bottom line, the letter names of the lines of the bass stave are: A, F, D, B and G. The letter names of the spaces from the top space to the bottom space are: G, E, C and A. The F line is between the two dots of the bass clef.

Middle C plays a very important role in tying together the bass clef and the treble clef. As you can see in FIGURE 14-3, one ledger line above the bass clef is middle C, which is the same middle C located one ledger line below the treble clef.

FIGURE 14-3

In FIGURE 14-3, the time signature is 2/4. This time signature tells you two things: the top number tells you how many beats there are per bar (two) and the bottom number tells you the crotchet gets the beat.

As indicated in FIGURE 14-3, play the notes C, B, A, G and F with the corresponding fingers of your left hand.

In the next exercise, the fingering of the left hand starts on middle C in bar 1. In bar 3, the sequence begins with the thumb on B. In bar 5, the sequence begins with the thumb on A. And in bar 7, the sequence begins with the thumb on G.

The very last note in this exercise is C, which is one octave below middle C.

EXERCISE 14-1

The first note in EXERCISE 14-2 is C, located one octave below middle C. Place your fifth finger above the C key, fourth above the D key, third above the E key, second above the F key and your thumb above the G key. Keeping your fingers in this position, play EXERCISE 14-2.

EXERCISE 14-2

A few new symbols have been added to EXERCISE 14-2. The word *allegro* indicates the tempo; it means 'fast'. The *f* dynamic marking, which represents *forte*, means 'loud'.

Start the exercise slowly. Once you have worked out the notes and rhythm, increase your speed and play the exercise loudly.

FIGURE 14-4:
Abbreviated keyboard

*   = use first note in Fig 14-3
** = one octave below middle C

The first note in EXERCISE 14-3 is A, located two keys below the last note C in EXERCISE 14-2 (please see FIGURE 14-4). Starting with your fifth finger on the A key, play EXERCISE 14-3.

EXERCISE 14-3

There's a new tempo marking in EXERCISE 14-3, *adagio,* which means to play the exercise slowly. Did you follow the repeat sign and play the exercise twice through?

Before we continue with more exercises – and eventually play a piano piece using both your right and left hands – please answer the following questions.

1. What are the letter names of the lines on a stave from top to bottom when using a bass clef?

    ♪ ....

2. What are the letter names of the spaces from top to bottom?

    ♪ ....

3. Where is middle C located when using the bass clef?

    ♪ ....

4. What does *allegro* mean?

    ♪ ....

5. What does *f* mean?

    ♪ ....

6. What does *adagio* mean?

    ♪ ....

(Answers can be found in the Appendix.)

Playing Octaves with the Left Hand

By now, you are familiar with the term octave, which is a derivative of the Latin word *octavo*, meaning 'eight'. For example, the low note C in EXERCISE 14-2 is an octave below middle C.

In order to play an octave, you have to open up and stretch your left hand. The low note is played with your fifth finger, and the high note (located an octave above) is played with your thumb.

Place your fifth finger on the low C key and your thumb on middle C and play EXERCISE 14-4.

EXERCISE 14-4

Play EXERCISE 14-4 often so you can get accustomed to stretching the fingers on your left hand and getting the feel of playing octaves.

Learning Quavers

In the next exercise, you're going to play quavers, which are a subdivision of crotchets – two quavers equal one crotchet. As you can see in bars 2, 4, 7 and 9 in EXERCISE 14-5, there are two quavers for the third and fourth beats of each bar. In bar 2, the third beat is comprised of the two quavers E and D, and the quavers C and B make up the fourth beat. Your target is to play the quavers evenly within the third and fourth beats of the bar.

As you can see from the fingering in EXERCISE 14-5, your thumb will be playing more than one key; it will play the A, G, F and E keys. You will discover that the thumb on your left hand needs to be be very active when playing bass lines.

EXERCISE 14-5

In EXERCISE 14-6 you're going to play a series of quavers in every bar except the last bar, which has a semibreve. With the steady flow of quavers, this exercise is designed to help you play quavers evenly.

Start playing this exercise slowly. When you have worked out the positioning of notes on the keyboard and the corresponding fingering, increase your speed to the designated *allegro* tempo.

EXERCISE 14-6

Practising Techniques When Playing With Both Hands

By now, you should have a good feel for playing bass lines using the left hand. Are you ready to put both the left and right hands together?

Before you start playing a piano piece written for both hands, keep the following practice techniques in mind:

1. Start with only playing the right-hand part, and keep playing that part until you have perfected it and, if possible, have memorized it.
2. Once you have achieved that, move on to the left hand. Now play only the left-hand part and keep playing it until you have perfected it.
3. Try your best to play either the right- or left-hand part automatically, without having to think about what you're playing; try to play the part instinctively. This will make it a lot easier when putting both hands together and playing both parts simultaneously.
4. Don't try to play the whole piece at once. Instead, take it one bar at a time. Once you have perfected bar 1, add the second bar. Before going on to the third bar, repeat the first two until they flow together without any hesitation or pauses. Keep adding bars one at a time, until you have played them all.
5. Take your time; don't rush into the exercise.
6. Start playing it slowly. Once you are comfortable with the parts, increase the tempo.
7. If you choose to use pedals, keep in mind that when using the loud pedal, a common practice is to press it down at the beginning of each measure and release it at the end of each measure. This pedal technique will prevent the blurring of chords, harmonies and melodies from bar to bar. For practising purposes, you might want to use the soft pedal; and if you have one on your piano, experiment with the sustain pedal. The use of pedals is determined by your subjective ear and aesthetic taste.

With all of the above tips in mind, play EXERCISE 14-7.

EXERCISE 14-7

Let's take a closer look at EXERCISE 14-7. As you can see, this is the first exercise to use two staves – one for the right hand (treble clef) and one for the left hand (bass clef). A bracket ties the two staves together.

In measures 1 and 2, the right hand plays semibreves while the left hand plays crotchets. As you can plainly see, the semibreve equals four crotchets. Similarly, the four crotchets equal the semibreve. In the third bar, the minim E, played by the right hand, equals the two crotchets C and B, played by the left hand. The same note values occur with the second minim F, played by the right hand, and the two crotchets A and B, played by the left hand.

As indicated by the time signature, EXERCISE 14-7 is in 4/4 time. The first beat in bar 1 has two notes: the semibreve in the right hand and the

crotchet in the left hand. Both of these notes are to be played at exactly the same time. In the first beat of the second bar, the F note in the right hand and the F note in the left hand are to be played at exactly the same time. (Incidentally, the distance between the F note in the left hand and the F note in the right hand is an octave.)

In the first beat of the third bar, the E note in the right hand and middle C in the left hand are to be played at the same time. In the third beat of this same bar, the F note in the right hand and the A note in the left hand are to be played at the same time.

Finally, in the first beat of the last bar, the exercise is concluded with the right hand playing the semibreve E and the left hand playing the semibreve middle C.

When playing the piano using both hands and reading the corresponding music, a vertical and horizontal sound experience occurs simultaneously. The vertical sound occurs when two notes are played at the same time. For instance in EXERCISE 14-7, bar 1, the right hand plays the E while the left hand plays the middle C below it. Looking at the written music, you see the vertical relationship of the E above the middle C. Once this vertical sound occurs, the horizontal sound takes place with the descending bass notes of the left hand. Your eyes are reading the music both vertically and horizontally at the same time.

The Thumb Goes Under the Fingers

There are eight white keys from middle C down to the C key an octave lower. When playing descending bass lines with your left hand that span an octave, you can run out of fingers. For instance, after playing the A with your third finger in FIGURE 14-8, how do you play five more notes? By putting your thumb under your third finger. If F is your lowest note and middle C is your highest note, then you don't have to alter the fingering. However, if you have to play all eight notes from middle C down to the C located an octave lower, then your thumb is going to go under your middle finger.

EXERCISE 14-8

As the fingering indicates, after playing the third crotchet in the first bar with your third finger, the next note is to be played with the first finger of your left hand. The way to do this is to move your thumb under your third finger immediately after playing the A note. In doing so, you will be repositioning the fingers of your left hand to be able to play all the notes down to the low C without running out of fingers.

Play EXERCISE 14-8 slowly, and keep repeating it until you are comfortable with this new fingering technique. In playing the repeat, you will be leaping an octave from the last note C (played with your fifth finger) up to the first note middle C (played with your thumb).

Leaping Over the Thumb

When playing ascending bass notes with the left hand, you have to leap your finger over the thumb to avoid running out of fingers. As indicated in EXERCISE 14-9, in the third bar, after playing the G note with your thumb, move your middle finger over your thumb to play the A note. The last two ascending notes are played with your second finger playing the B note and your thumb playing middle C.

EXERCISE 14-9 will help you to learn to play both descending and ascending bass notes, moving the thumb under your fingers on the way down and moving your middle finger over the thumb on the way up.

Play EXERCISE 14-9 slowly, and keep repeating it until you get comfortable with the descending and ascending fingering.

EXERCISE 14-9

Putting It All Together

EXERCISE 14-10 is a piece I wrote that incorporates a lot of the material covered in this chapter. Before you play this piece, take a close look at all of the elements that make up the piece. Note the rhythm of the right hand, which comprises a two-bar sequence made up of two quavers followed by two crotchets, two more quavers and a semibreve in the second bar. The left hand plays a series of minims, with fingering that includes the thumb going under the middle finger in measure 5. The tempo is *moderato* (moderate) and the dynamic level is *mp* (medium soft).

It's very important to look at all of the elements in a piece of music before you play it.

This allows you to get mentally prepared and to anticipate what you have to do in order to perform it properly and play what's written.

Refresh your memory and look over the tips listed earlier in this chapter about practising techniques to use when playing a piano piece with both hands.

When you are mentally prepared and quite ready, play EXERCISE 14-10 and enjoy this simple little tune.

EXERCISE 14-10

LAZY DAY

In reviewing the material covered in this chapter, please answer the following questions.

7. What is an octave?

    ♪ ....

8. What fingers on the left hand play an octave?

    ♪ ....

9. How many quavers equal one crotchet?

    ♪ ....

10. In EXERCISE 14-5, what bars have quavers?

    ♪ ....

11. What beats in those bars have quavers?

    ♪ ....

12. What should you do before practising a two-hand piano exercise or piece?

    ♪ ....

13. What does a bracket do?

    ♪ ....

14. What do your eyes do when reading both right- and left-hand parts?

    ♪ ....

15. When does the thumb on the left hand go under the fingers?

    ♪ ....

16. Why does the thumb go under the fingers?

    ♪ ....

17. When does the middle finger on the left hand leap over the thumb?

    ♪ ....

18. What is the two-bar sequence comprised of in EXERCISE 14-10?

    ♪ ....

(Answers can be found in the Appendix.)

CHAPTER 15

Learning Sharp Key Signatures

Y ou've done a great job so far! Now it's time to take things a bit further. In this chapter you are introduced to the circle of fifths, learn scale degrees and, of course, learn sharp key signatures.

C Major

All the exercises and piano pieces you have played thus far have one thing in common: they are all in the key of C major or A minor. Why is that? Because the key of C major and its relative minor, A minor, have no sharps or flats – you play only the white keys. In this key, the sharps and flats are located on the black keys on the keyboard.

The key of A minor is C major's relative minor because it uses the same key signature, which has no sharps or flats. Notes that have no sharps or flats are also called naturals. So all the notes in the C major scale and the A minor scale are natural.

Key signatures tell you what the notes are in a specific scale and what the corresponding keys are on the keyboard. Having played the exercises in Chapter 14, you are already familiar with the key of C major. The consecutive sequence of eight notes from middle C up an octave to the C on the third space of the treble stave is called a scale. Let's take a look at the C major scale.

EXERCISE 15-1

As you can see, the notes in the C major scale are C, D, E, F, G, A, B and C. Scales go up, scales go down, and scales in a specific key are the same in all octaves.

The notes in scales are numbered from one to eight.

1. C is the tonic; also called the root.
2. D is the supertonic.
3. E is the mediant.
4. F is the subdominant.

5. G is the dominant.
6. A is the submediant.
7. B is the leading note or subtonic.
8. C is the octave.

All these scale degrees have an intervallic relationship with the root C. An interval is the distance between any two pitches or notes. For instance, the intervallic distance between C and D is a second, between C and E is a third, between C and F is a fourth and so on.

Practise the C major scale in EXERCISE 15-1 with your right hand. Notice that the thumb goes under the middle finger on the third beat in bar 1, and the middle finger goes over the thumb on the fourth beat in bar 3. Repeat this exercise several times.

In the next exercise you're going to play the C major scale with your left hand. Notice that the middle finger goes over the thumb on the first beat in bar 2, and that the thumb goes under the middle finger on the second beat in bar 3. Repeat EXERCISE 15-2 several times.

EXERCISE 15-2

In EXERCISE 15-3 you're going to play the C major scale covering two octaves, from middle C to the C two ledger lines above the treble stave. As indicated in the fingering, when you see 1 after 3 and 4, the thumb goes under the middle finger going up the scale. And going down the scale, when you see 3 and 4 after 1, the middle finger goes over the thumb.

EXERCISE 15-3

Moving on to the left hand, play the C scale covering two octaves in the bass. Before you do, notice that in the fingering on the way up the scale, the middle finger goes over the thumb in bar 2, the fourth finger goes over the thumb in bar 3, and the middle finger goes over the thumb in bar 4. On the way down the scale, the thumb goes under the middle finger in bar 5 and under the fourth finger and third finger in bar 6. The first note is two octaves below middle C.

EXERCISE 15-4

Next you are going to play the C major scale at the distance of two octaves. Note that EXERCISE 15-5 is a combination of EXERCISES 15-3 and 15-4.

EXERCISE 15-5

As you can see in the next exercise, the fingering for the left hand and the right hand is exactly the same as the fingering in EXERCISE 15-5. In EXERCISE 15-6 play the A minor scale at a distance of two octaves between both hands.

EXERCISE 15-6

The Circle of Fifths

Music theory is very logical. All the notes in music are in alphabetical order from A to G. The treble and bass staves are joined by the common note middle C. Notes from high ledger lines above the treble stave to ledger lines below the bass stave follow the alphabetical order.

The sequence of key signatures with sharps follows a circle of fifths. For example, the first sharp key signature, using one sharp, is the key of G, which happens to be five notes, or a fifth, above C.

Below is a visual representation of the circle of fifths. It is easy to see, for example, that the major key of E has a relative minor of C sharp. Both keys contain four sharps.

Major Key	Relative Minor Key	Number of Sharps & Flats	Sharps or Flats
C	A	none	all naturals
G	E	1 sharp	F
D	B	2 sharps	F, C
A	F sharp	3 sharps	F, C, G
E	C sharp	4 sharps	F, C, G, D
B	G sharp	5 sharps	F, C, G, D, A
F sharp	D sharp	6 sharps	F, C, G, D, A, E
C sharp	A sharp	7 sharps	F, C, G, D, A, E, B
F	D	1 flat	B
B flat	G	2 flats	B, E
E flat	C	3 flats	B, E, A
A flat	F	4 flats	B, E, A, D
D flat	B flat	5 flats	B, E, A, D, G
G flat	E flat	6 flats	B, E, A, D, G, C
C flat	A flat	7 flats	B, E, A, D, G, C, F

You may ask yourself the question, 'Why does the key of G have an F sharp?' It's because it follows the same scale degrees and intervallic relationships of all major keys. Using the C major scale as an example, the distance between C and the seventh scale degree B is a semitone.

Looking at your keyboard, you can see that the B key is next to the C key. In the key of C, there are two semitones: between B and C, and between E and F. The relationships among the other notes in the key of C are tones. For example, going from C to D is a tone; there is a black key between the two notes. It's also a tone from D to E, F to G, G to A, and A to B. As you can see on your keyboard, there are black keys between each of these tones.

All major key signatures have exactly the same tone/semitone pattern, which is:

· A tone from the root to the second scale degree.
· A tone from the second to third scale degree.
· A semitone from the third to fourth scale degree.
· A tone from the fourth to fifth scale degree.
· A tone from the fifth to sixth scale degree.
· A tone from the sixth to seventh scale degree.
· A semitone from the seventh scale degree to the octave.

To summarize, there are two semitones and five tones in all major key signatures. The semitones are from the third to fourth scale degrees and from the seventh scale degree to the octave.

G Major

Using this parallel tone/semitone relationship, the seventh scale degree in the key of G has to be a semitone away from the octave G. That's why the F is sharp. So when playing the G major scale, you're going to play the black key between the F and G keys, which is called F sharp. In EXERCISE 15-7, a sharp sign (♯) is on the F line in the treble clef, telling you to play the black key F sharp. Be sure to play all of the F notes F sharp, even though there isn't a sharp sign on the F space in the staff. With that in mind, play EXERCISE 15-7 with your right hand.

EXERCISE 15-7

In keeping with the parallel relative logic of music theory, just as C major's relative minor is A minor, G major's relative minor is E minor. The relative parallel connection is that the relative minors are built on the sixth scale degree of the major key. In the key of C major, the sixth scale degree is A, and in the key of G major, the sixth scale degree is E.

G is the root, the tonic.

A is the second, the supertonic.

B is the third, the mediant.

C is the fourth, the subdominant.

D is the fifth, the dominant.

E is the sixth, the submediant.

F is the seventh, the leading note.

G is the eighth, the octave.

Both G major and E minor use the same key signature, which has one sharp – F sharp. In the key of E minor, the scale degrees are:

E is the root, the tonic.

F sharp is the second, the supertonic.

G is the third, the mediant.

A is the fourth, the subdominant.

B is the fifth, the dominant.

C is the sixth, the submediant.

D is the seventh, the subtonic.

E is the eighth, the octave.

It's important to note that all natural minor scales have a different tone/semitone pattern from major scales. In minor scales, the pattern is:

· A tone from the root to the second scale degree.
· A semitone from the second to the third scale degree.
· A tone from the third to the fourth scale degree.
· A tone from the fourth to the fifth scale degree.
· A semitone from the fifth to the sixth scale degree.
· A tone from the sixth to the seventh scale degree.
· A tone from the seventh to the eighth scale degree.

In natural minor key signatures, the semitones are from the second to third scale degree and from the fifth to sixth scale degree.

When playing EXERCISE 15-8, please note that the F sharp is the second note in the E minor scale and is played with the second finger on your right hand and the fourth finger on your left hand.

EXERCISE 15-8

Music in major keys tends to be bright and cheerful. On the other hand, music in minor keys can sound introspective, moody and even sad. EXERCISE 15-9, written in E minor, should create an introspective mood. Before you start playing it, there's a lot of new information that you need to grasp.

First of all, note the 3/4 time signature. That tells you there are three beats per bar and the crotchet gets the beat. This time signature creates a different feel from the customary 4/4 time signature. Time signatures that are in 2/4 and 4/4 create an even feel – the numbers are even – whereas a 3/4 is uneven because of the odd number of beats.

In EXERCISE 15-9 you can see a series of three crotchets per bar in the left hand, except for bar 16 and 24, which have dotted minims. The series of three crotchets will help you keep a steady 3/4 time. In order to get comfortable with the 3/4 time signature, look at the crotchets and count one, two, three. The first beat of each bar is a little more pronounced than the second and third beats. The first beat is called the downbeat; the second and third beats are called upbeats. Downbeats are generally stronger than upbeats.

Look at the notes in the right hand in bars 1, 3, 4, 5, 7, 8, 9, 11, 12, 13, 14, 17, 19, 20, 21 and 24, and you'll see dotted minims. The dot represents half the value of a minim, which is equal to one crotchet. Therefore, a dotted minim equals three crotchets – the minim equals two crotchets, and the dot equals one crotchet. These three beats satisfy the 3/4 time signature, which tells you that there are three beats per bar.

In bars 3, 4, 7, 8, 11, 12, 13, 14, 19 and 20, the dotted minims are tied to each other. This means you hold the dotted E in bar 3 through to the end of bar 4. The collective value of the two dotted minims tied together equals six beats, tying together the three beats in bar 3 with the three beats in bar 4. When you play the E in bar 3, keep that key depressed through to the end of bar 4 – by doing so, the sound will continue through both bars. The same is true in bars 7 and 8, 11 and 12, 13 and 14, and 19 and 20. Please observe the whole rests in the right hand in bars 15 and 16.

Also look at the fingering of both hands before playing the piece (the left-hand fingering is the same throughout). Notice the tempo marking *andante*, the metronome marking crotchet = 108, and the dynamic marking *mp*. *Andante* means 'moderately slow'. If you have a metronome, set it to crotchet = 108, and you will hear the rate of the pulse of the crotchet. The metronome marking makes the tempo marking much more specific.

In the left hand, the third note in bars 1, 5, 17, 21 and 23 is on two ledger lines above the bass stave, which is one octave above the first note in these bars. This ledger line is two tones above middle C. It is also exactly the same pitch as the tied dotted minims in bars 3 and 4, 7 and 8, and 19 and 20.

Because EXERCISE 15-9 is in E minor, the key signature has an F sharp in both the treble and bass clefs. In noting the key signature, be sure to play the F sharps. Even though there is only one sharp symbol on the top line of the treble clef and one sharp symbol on the second from the top line of the bass clef, *all* Fs have to be played sharp. The first and third notes played by the right hand in the second bar are F sharps.

Once you have studied and are mentally prepared, play EXERCISE 15-9 starting with only the left-hand part. Then add the right hand, one bar at a time.

LATE AT NIGHT

Andante ♩ = 108

D Major

As we go through the circle of fifths, we'll be adding one sharp at a time for each new key signature.

The next key signature in the circle of fifths is D major, a fifth above G. The key of D major has two sharps: F sharp (carried over from G major) and C sharp. As with all major key signatures, there has to be a semitone from the seventh scale degree to the octave and a semitone from the third to the fourth scale degree. Therefore the C is raised to a C sharp, and the F is raised to an F sharp.

If the relative minor of C major is A minor, and the relative minor of G major is E minor, what is the relative minor of D major? Knowing that the relative minor is built on the sixth scale degree of every major scale, B minor is D major's relative minor. B minor and D major use the same key signature, which has two sharps: F sharp and C sharp.

In the next exercise, you're going to see a different fingering pattern for the left hand when playing the B minor scale. As indicated, you start with your fourth finger instead of the customary fifth finger when playing C major and G major scales and A minor and E minor scales. Make sure to catch the over-the-thumb action going up the scale and the under-the-thumb action on the way down.

With that in mind, play EXERCISE 15-10 with the left hand, starting with the low B, located below the second ledger line below the bass clef.

EXERCISE 15-10

Move on to EXERCISE 15-11 and put your hands together to play the B minor scale up and down two octaves. Make sure to catch the under-the-thumb action in the right hand going up the scale and the over-the-thumb action going down the scale.

EXERCISE 15-11

In EXERCISE 15-12, play the D major scale with both hands.

EXERCISE 15-12

Now that you are familiar with the D major and B minor scales, let's take a close look at the next exercise. This piece is designed to strengthen all the fingers in your right hand. It is composed utilizing a sequence of a crotchet followed by six quavers. As the metronome marking indicates (crotchet = 92), EXERCISE 15-13 is slower than EXERCISE 15-9. Given its title, the piece is to be played lightly and, as the dynamic marking indicates, medium soft.

Make your preparations and enjoy this light little piece.

EXERCISE 15-13

QUITE LIGHTLY

We have covered quite a bit of ground so far in this chapter. Before we move on, please answer the following questions.

1. How many sharps does C major have?

   ♪ ....

2. What is C major's relative minor?

   ♪ ....

3. On what scale degree is a major key's relative minor built on?

   ♪ ....

4. What is a note called that has no sharps or flats?

   ♪ ....

5. The first scale degree in the key of C is called the tonic. What else is it called?

   ♪ ....

6. What key signatures have one sharp?

   ♪ ....

7. What is the distance between the seventh and eighth scale degrees in a major key?

   ♪ ....

8. What is the distance between the second and third scale degrees in a major key?

   ♪ ....

9. What is the distance between the second and third scale degrees in a minor key?

   ♪ ....

10. In EXERCISE 15-9, what is the first beat called?

    ♪ ....

11. What does a dotted minim equal?

    ♪ ....

12. What happens when notes are tied together?

    ♪ ....

13. What does *andante* mean?

    ♪ ....

14. What is 'crotchet = 108'?

    ♪ ....

15. What does it tell you?

    ♪ ....

16. In the key of E minor, are all the Fs played sharp?

    ♪ ....

17. What should you do before starting a two-handed piano piece?

    ♪ ....

18. What key signatures have two sharps?

    ♪ ....

19. When playing the B minor scale with the left hand, which finger plays the first note B?

    ♪ ....

(Answers can be found in the Appendix.)

A Major

So far we have covered C major (A minor), G major (E minor) and D major (B minor). A fifth above D is A, so the next key in the circle of fifths is A major and its relative minor, F sharp minor.

There are three sharps in the key of A major and F sharp minor: F sharp, C sharp and G sharp. In the next exercise, you will be playing the A major scale with both hands. Start playing with only the right hand, then move on to only the left hand, and eventually put both hands together.

EXERCISE 15-14

In the next exercise, please notice the different fingering for both hands when playing the F sharp minor scale.

EXERCISE 15-15

E Major

The next sharp key is E major and its relative minor, C sharp minor. E major and C sharp minor have four sharps in the key signature: F sharp, C sharp, G sharp and D sharp. Play EXERCISE 15-16 starting with the right hand and eventually adding the left hand.

EXERCISE 15-16

In the next exercise, please notice the different fingering in both hands when playing the C sharp minor scale. In the same way as with F sharp minor, the fingering is different because the scale starts on a black key.

EXERCISE 15-17

B Major

Continuing with the circle of fifths, the next sharp key is B major and its relative minor, G sharp minor. The new sharp added to this key signature is A sharp, the seventh scale degree in B major. The five sharps in B major and G sharp minor are: F sharp, C sharp, G sharp, D sharp and A sharp.

By now you have probably noticed the pattern in the addition of sharps: the new sharp is always a fifth above the previous sharp. For example, in the key of E major, the fourth sharp is D. B major uses the same four sharps in E major plus the new sharp A. A sharp is a fifth above D sharp.

Before playing the B major scale, notice that the fingering in the left hand starts with the fourth finger. And watch out for those A sharps!

EXERCISE 15-18

The fingering for playing the G sharp minor scale is the same as the fingering for the C sharp minor scale – the right hand starts with the second finger, and the left hand starts with the third finger. The following exercise shows the G sharp minor scale in action.

EXERCISE 15-19

F Sharp Major

In the next key signature, you're going to discover a sharp that isn't on a black key. In the F sharp major scale, the seventh scale degree (which you know has to be raised a semitone) is E sharp. As you also know, E natural is the white key on the piano, two tones above C.

When raising E a semitone and making it E sharp, it happens to be the same pitch as F, which is one white key above E.

With that in mind, play the F sharp major scale in EXERCISE 15-20.

EXERCISE 15-20

Here's the D sharp minor scale, which uses the same key signature as F sharp major. Note the different fingering in both hands, and watch out for those E sharps!

EXERCISE 15-21

Let's review the key signatures. The sequence of key signatures in the circle of fifths starting with C major (and their relative minors) is:

Major Key Signature	Relative Minor
C major	A minor
G major	E minor
D major	B minor
A major	F sharp minor
E major	C sharp minor
B major	G sharp minor
F sharp major	D sharp minor

As you can see, the relative minors also follow the circle of fifths: E minor is a fifth above A minor; B minor is a fifth above E minor, and so on.

The major sharp key signatures and their relative minors have:

No sharps – C major, A minor
One sharp (F sharp) – G major, E minor
Two sharps (F sharp, C sharp) – D major, B minor
Three sharps (F sharp, C sharp, G sharp) – A major, F sharp minor
Four sharps (F sharp, C sharp, G sharp, D sharp) – E major, C sharp minor
Five sharps (F sharp, C sharp, G sharp, D sharp, A sharp) – B major, G sharp minor
Six sharps (F sharp, C sharp, G sharp, D sharp, A sharp, E sharp) – F sharp major, D sharp minor

Continuing the Circle of Fifths

In this chapter, we have covered the most common sharp key signatures used in piano music – and music in general. However, sharp key signatures do continue beyond F sharp major. Continuing the circle of fifths, the remaining major sharp key signatures and their relative minors are:

C sharp major, A sharp minor
G sharp major, E sharp minor
D sharp major, B sharp minor

Even though you probably won't play piano pieces written in these key signatures, you should be aware of them.

CHAPTER 16

Learning Flat Key Signatures

Now that you know the sharp key signatures, it makes sense to move on to the flat key signatures. Take a deep breath, relax, and get ready to tackle the circle of fourths.

The Circle of Fourths

As we have seen, sharp key signatures follow a circle of fifths, and sharps raise any given pitch up a semitone. Flats, on the other hand, lower a pitch down a semitone, and flat key signatures follow a circle of fourths. Refer to the chart on page 160 to remind yourself of this system.

The first flat key is F major. Going up four notes is B; however, in keeping with the tone/semitone scale degree pattern of major scales, the B is flat in F major. There has to be a semitone between the third and fourth scale degrees. F to G and G to A are tones; A to B flat is a semitone. The B flat is the black key located between A and B on your keyboard. In keeping with the tone/semitone pattern of minor key scales, there has to be a semitone from the fifth scale degree to the sixth scale degree. So in the key of D minor (which is F major's relative minor), the fifth scale degree is A, and a semitone above that is the sixth scale degree, B flat.

As you recall, sharps are located on the seventh scale degree in major key signatures and on the second scale degree in their relative minor key signatures. For example, in the key of G major, the seventh scale degree is F sharp; in E minor, F sharp is the second scale degree. Unlike sharps, flats are located on the fourth scale degree in major key signatures and on the sixth scale degree in minor key signatures.

The major flat key signatures and their relative minors are:

Major Flat Key Signature	Relative Minor
F major	D minor
B flat major	G minor
E flat major	C minor
A flat major	F minor
D flat major	B flat minor
G flat major	E flat minor

F Major

Play EXERCISE 16-1 and pay special attention to the B flat.

EXERCISE 16-1

By now, you're quite familiar with the way major scales sound, and you've become accustomed to scale degrees and the pattern of tones and semitones. With that in mind, try a little experiment and play the F major scale with B natural (the white key), not B flat (the black key). Your ears should tell you that the B natural doesn't sound right because it's not in the key signature.

In the next exercise, play the D minor scale, which uses the same key signature as F major.

EXERCISE 16-2

B Flat Major

Moving up a fourth is the key signature of B flat major and its relative minor, G minor. Notice that the fingering in the right hand starts with the second finger. The fingering in the left hand starts with the third finger.

As always, start playing with only the right hand. Then play with only the left hand. When you have both parts worked out, play the B flat major scale with both hands.

EXERCISE 16-3

EXERCISE 16-4 is a piano piece I wrote called 'Octavia'. (When you look at the left-hand part, you'll understand just why I called it that.) Let's take a close look at this exercise before you start playing it.

First of all, the key signature, which has the two flats B flat and E flat, tells you the piece is in the key of B flat major. The time signature tells you the piece is in 4/4 time. The tempo is *moderato*, with a metronome marking of crotchet = 108. The dynamic marking *mp* tells you to play the music medium soft. But then there's a new sign, which looks like a stretched-out part of a triangle. This is a crescendo sign, which means to play the music gradually louder by increasing the volume of sound. This pertains to the first four quavers: D, E flat, F and G. In the next measure, the *mf* dynamic marking tells you to play medium loud. So there is a gradual increase from medium soft to medium loud from the first quaver D in bar 1 to the crotchet A in bar 2.

EXERCISE 16-4 starts out differently to the other pieces you have played so far. It starts off with rests – a semibreve rest in the left hand and a minim rest in the right hand. What you have to do is count off and feel the first two beats, which are silent, and then play the quavers representing the third and fourth

beats for the right hand. The four quavers in the first bar are called grace or pick-up notes, which lead the way up to the downbeat (crotchet A) in bar 2.

Compositionally, EXERCISE 16-4 uses a two-bar sequence, or motif, which is comprised of a minim rest followed by four quavers followed by a crotchet, two quavers and a minim. This two-bar sequence is repeated throughout the piece until bar 13, when the sequence is broken with two crotchets (instead of four quavers) followed by a tied semibreve.

Another dynamic sign appears in bar 15 that is just the opposite of the crescendo sign in bar 1. This is a diminuendo sign, which tells you to play the music softer. Because the right hand is holding the sound of the tied semibreve, the diminuendo sign applies to the notes played in the left hand. In terms of volume, EXERCISE 16-4 starts off medium soft, becomes medium loud and ends medium soft.

Note the fingering in the right hand in bars 9, 11 and 12. The thumb goes under the second finger to play the middle C in measures 9 and 11; and in bar 12, the second finger goes over the thumb to play the minim B flat.

Starting slowly with the right hand only, play EXERCISE 16-4.

OCTAVIA

In the next exercise, which is in the key of G minor, take a close look at the fingering in the right hand before playing it. As you will discover in the first bar, it feels natural to simply move the fifth finger of the right hand down a semitone from B flat to A. In the third bar, the first note is played by the second finger by going over the thumb on the last note played in the preceding bar. In the third bar, the fifth finger moves down a semitone from E flat to D. When playing this exercise, please observe the repeat sign.

EXERCISE 16-5

E Flat Major

The next flat key signature in the circle of fourths is E flat major and its relative minor, C minor. As you can see, E flat major and C minor have three flats: B flat, E flat and A flat. In comparison to the evolution of sharp key signatures and their corresponding sharps, the addition of flats in flat key signatures follows the evolving circle of fourths. In other words, the first flat key signature, F major, has one flat: B flat. The second flat key signature, B flat major, has two flats: B flat and E flat. And the third flat key signature, E flat major, has three flats.

In the next exercise, note that the fingering in the right hand starts with the second finger,

and the fingering in the left hand starts with the third finger. When going up the E flat major scale, the thumb in the right hand will go under the fingers twice in each octave, and the third and fourth fingers go over the thumb on the way down. The fingering in the left hand starts with the third finger. On the way up the scale, the fourth and third fingers go over the thumb twice in each octave. On the way down the scale, the thumb goes under the fingers twice per octave.

With all this in mind, now play the E flat major scale in EXERCISE 16-6, starting with the right hand.

EXERCISE 16-6

In **EXERCISE 16-7**, try your hand at E flat's relative minor, C minor. Make sure you play the B flats, E flats and A flats!

EXERCISE 16-7

As you discover each key signature, compare how they sound. The biggest difference in sound is between major and minor keys. But in addition to that, each major key has its own distinct sound. For instance, play the C major scale, then play the B flat major scale. Even though they're both major scales, they sound very different. The difference in sound is attributed largely to the two flats in the B flat scale: the B flat and the E flat. Most people consider that C major sounds brighter than B flat major.

With minor scales, the difference in sound can be even more striking. For example, play the A minor scale. Then play the C minor scale. You may well hear quite a difference in sound between these two different minor scales. Here again, the difference is because of the three flats in the key of C minor. In the key of A minor, the B, E and A are natural, and in C minor, the B, E and A are flat – that's what creates the striking difference in sound between these two minor keys.

Now take a look at EXERCISE 16-8. The key signature tells you the song is in C minor. The time signature is in 4/4 time. The tempo is *andante* with a metronome marking of crotchet = 96, and *mf* tells you to play the song medium loud.

In the first bar, the first three beats are silent (as indicated by the minim rest and crotchet rest), and the fourth beat has two quavers (E flat and F), which are grace notes leading up to the first crotchet in the second bar. In the sixth bar, notice that the last quaver (E flat) is played with the first finger as it goes over the thumb.

For those of you who are vocally inclined, you might want to sing along with the melody played by the right hand.

DON'T YOU EVER LET ME DOWN

Before we continue with the remaining flat key signatures, see if you can answer the following questions.

1. Flat key signatures follow what kind of circle?

   ♪ ....

2. What do flats do?

   ♪ ....

3. In major flat key signatures, what scale degree gets the flat?

   ♪ ....

4. In minor flat key signatures, what scale degree gets the flat?

   ♪ ....

5. What is the first major flat key and its relative minor?

   ♪ ....

6. Where is the B flat key located on the keyboard?

   ♪ ....

7. How did 'Octavia' get its name?

   ♪ ....

8. What should you do when you see a crescendo sign?

   ♪ ....

9. What does diminuendo mean?

   ♪ ....

10. What are the first four quavers called in the first bar of EXERCISE 16-4?

    ♪ ....

11. In EXERCISE 16-4, what type of sequence is used in the melody played by the right hand?

    ♪ ....

12. How many flats does the key of C minor have?

    ♪ ....

(Answers can be found in the Appendix.)

A Flat Major

The next flat key is A flat major and its relative minor, F minor. The new flat in this key is D flat, which is the fourth scale degree in A flat major and the sixth scale degree in F minor. As you can see in the fingering of both the right and left hands, a lot of under- and over-the-thumb action takes place while playing the A flat major scale in two octaves.

With that in mind, please play the A flat major scale starting with your second finger in the right hand and your third finger in the left hand.

EXERCISE 16-9

You'll see that the fingering in EXERCISE 16-10 is quite different from the fingering of the A flat major scale in EXERCISE 16-9. With that in mind, play the F minor scale in EXERCISE 16-10.

Overleaf is a challenging piece I wrote for you to get your right hand accustomed to moving from E flat down a fifth to A flat. In order to achieve this, your third finger goes over the thumb, and your thumb goes under your third finger and leaps down to A flat. As indicated in the fingering of the right hand in bars 8 and 16, the last quaver is played with your third finger, while your thumb quickly goes under your fingers and plays the A flat.

The tempo of EXERCISE 16-11 is *allegro* with a metronome marking of crotchet = 126. Start playing EXERCISE 16-11 slowly and gradually speed up to the *allegro* tempo. But before you do, make sure to note that EXERCISE 16-11 is written in the key of A flat, which has four flats. So concentrate on playing all the Bs, Es, As and Ds flat.

As you can see, this piece starts off with the right hand, while the left hand rests for the first eight bars. Even though the left hand isn't playing at the beginning, have it ready in position, resting lightly above A flat and E flat for the left hand in bar 9.

Do yourself a favour and play only the right hand for the entire piece several times before adding the left hand. Be careful with the last four quarters in bar 20; they're one note higher than the sequence of quavers in bars 4 and 12. The fingering for the left hand is the same throughout the piece, alternating between the fifth finger and the thumb.

As you play the descending quavers in bars 8 and 16 and the following crotchet in bars 9 and 17, you might be able to hear the title 'Leaping Down a Fifth'.

LEAPING DOWN A FIFTH

D Flat Major

A fourth above A flat gives us the next key signature, D flat major, and its relative minor, B flat minor. D flat major has five flats: B flat, E flat, A flat, D flat and the new flat, G flat. With five flats in the key signature, you'll be playing five black keys and only two white keys on the keyboard. As a result, the fingering in the right hand starts with the second finger, and the fingering in the left hand starts with the third finger. At the top of the two-octave scale, the thumb on the right hand goes under the fingers to play the C, and the second finger goes over the thumb to play the high D flat. Similarly, the thumb on the left hand plays the high C, and the second finger goes over the thumb to play the high D.

EXERCISE 16-12

The next exercise is the B flat minor scale, which starts with the second finger on both hands.

Enharmonic Equivalents

Before we move on to G flat major, we need to discuss enharmonic equivalents. What's one of these when it's at home, then? Let me explain. For example, the pitch G flat, which is located on the black key (one semitone lower than the white key G), is the same pitch as F sharp (a semitone higher than F). G flat and F sharp are enharmonic equivalents; they are the same pitch – the same black key – but have different letter names.

In addition to individual notes having enharmonic equivalents, there are enharmonic equivalent scales. For example, when you play the D flat major scale, you're also playing the C sharp major scale. The pitches, the keys and even the fingering are the same, but all the letter names are different.

Looking at the letter names in both keys we have:

D flat major	equals	C sharp major
D flat	=	C sharp
E flat	=	D sharp
F	=	E sharp
G flat	=	F sharp
A flat	=	G sharp
B flat	=	A sharp
C	=	B sharp

So every note in the C sharp major scale is an enharmonic equivalent of the notes in the D flat major scale. Furthermore, the entire C sharp major scale is the enharmonic equivalent of the D flat major scale. Instead of having to play seven sharps in C sharp major, simply play five flats in D flat major. Looking back to Chapter 15, you can see that C sharp major was not included in the sharp key signatures list.

The same is true with the relative minors. When you're playing the B flat minor scale, you're also playing the A sharp minor scale because B flat and A sharp are enharmonic equivalents.

G Flat Major

Just as D flat major is the enharmonic equivalent of C sharp major, G flat major is the enharmonic equivalent of F sharp major. It is more than likely that if someone is going to write a piece of music in G flat major, it will be written in the enharmonic equivalent key, F sharp major.

Here are the note-for-note enharmonic equivalents in both keys:

G flat major	equals	F sharp major
G flat	=	F sharp
A flat	=	G sharp
B flat	=	A sharp
C flat	=	B
D flat	=	C sharp
E flat	=	D sharp
F	=	E sharp

Now go back to Chapter 15 and play the F sharp major scale in EXERCISE 15-20. When playing the F sharp major scale, say the enharmonic equivalent letter names in G flat major (G flat, A flat, B flat, C flat, D flat, E flat and F). To all intents and purposes, you will have played the G flat major scale.

Do the same with the enharmonic equivalent relative minors, E flat minor and D sharp minor. Play D sharp minor in Chapter 15, EXERCISE 15-21, and say the letter names for the corresponding scale degrees (E flat, F, G flat, A flat, B flat, C flat, and D flat). In doing so, you will have played the E flat minor scale.

Here are the note-for-note enharmonic equivalents in both relative minor keys:

E flat minor	equals	D sharp minor
E flat	=	D sharp
F	=	E sharp
G flat	=	F sharp
A flat	=	G sharp
B flat	=	A sharp
C flat	=	B
D flat	=	C sharp

Here are some more questions to finish off this chapter.

13. What is the fourth flat in the key of A flat major?

   ♪ ....

14. How many flats does F minor have?

   ♪ ....

15. What does *allegro* mean?

   ♪ ....

16. In EXERCISE 16-11, where does the leaping fifth occur?

   ♪ ....

17. What does the left hand do in the first eight bars of EXERCISE 16-11?

   ♪ ....

18. What should you do before adding the left-hand part to EXERCISE 16-11?

   ♪ ....

19. How many flats does B flat minor have?

   ♪ ....

20. What is the harmonic relationship between the notes G flat and F sharp?

   ♪ ....

21. Are the notes E sharp and F natural enharmonic equivalents?

   ♪ ....

22. What is B flat minor's enharmonic equivalent scale?

   ♪ ....

23. What is F sharp major's enharmonic equivalent scale?

   ♪ ....

24. What is D sharp minor's enharmonic equivalent scale?

   ♪ ....

25. What is the note A flat's enharmonic equivalent?

   ♪ ....

26. What is the note B's enharmonic equivalent?

   ♪ ....

(Answers can be found in the Appendix.)

CHAPTER 17

Learning
Chords

Y ou've learned so much already, but
do you feel ready to perform in front
of an audience? Probably not.
Something is missing. You sound good,
but you could sound better. This chapter
will help you take things a step further by
introducing chords.

What Is Harmony?

Let's start this chapter with a few definitions of harmony in the general sense: an agreement in feeling or opinion; accord; a pleasing combination of elements in a whole.

And now here's a definition of harmony in terms of music: the study of the structure, progression and relation of chords; simultaneous combination of notes in a chord; the structure of a work or passage as considered from the point of view of its chordal characteristics and relationships; a combination of sounds considered pleasing to the ear. Got all that?

As you have discovered in the previous chapters, melody is commonly (but by no means always) played with the right hand on the piano or keyboard. Melodies are comprised of a specific series of singular notes, from simple tunes to more challenging melodic lines.

What's fascinating about music is the many different ways of arranging harmony juxtaposed to melody. For instance, in piano and keyboard music, the right hand can play a simple melody, while the left hand can play consonant, harmonically pleasing chords or dissonant, unresolved chords.

For our purposes, let's focus primarily on harmony that constitutes 'a combination of sounds considered pleasing to the ear'.

Major Chords

As you already know, an interval is the measured distance between any two pitches. (For instance, in the key of D major, from the root D up to B is an interval of a sixth.) Chords are comprised of intervals. A D major chord is the combination of two intervals: a major third from the root (D) up to the third scale degree (F sharp), and a minor third from F sharp up to the fifth scale degree (A). A major third contains two whole tones: D to E and E to F sharp. A minor third contains one semitone, F sharp to G, and one tone, G to A. So a D major chord contains the three notes D, F sharp and A. Three-note chords are also called triads.

All major chords follow the same two-interval formula: a major third followed by a minor third. Choose any pitch and make it the root of a major chord, count up two tones and you have the third of the chord, count up a semitone and tone above the third and you have the fifth. For example, with A flat as the root, the third is C and the fifth is E flat.

Here's a table showing the construction of major triads (chords) starting with various roots:

TABLE 17-1

Root	Third	Fifth
C	E	G
C sharp	E sharp	G sharp
D	F sharp	A
E flat	G	B flat
E	G sharp	B
F sharp*	A sharp*	C sharp*
G flat*	B flat*	D flat*
A	C sharp	E
B	D sharp	F sharp

* enharmonic equivalents

Now let's apply these major chords to the keyboard. Starting with C major and using your right hand, place your thumb on middle C, your second finger on E and your fifth finger on G. Strike the keys all at the same time. This right-hand finger configuration is the same for all major chords, and is the same in any octave. For example, when you play the C major chord an octave higher, use the same fingering. Please see FIGURE 17-1.

FIGURE 17-1:
Root position
major chords

Do the same with the rest of the major chords listed in the table (C sharp, D, E flat, E, F sharp, G flat, A and B major chords). Make sure you are aware of the specified sharps and flats per each chord. Also, when playing the C sharp major chord, note the white key E sharp. Please refer below to **FIGURE 17-2**.

FIGURE 17-2:
Root position
major chords

Minor Chords

The intervallic structure of all minor chords is comprised of two intervals: a minor third followed by a major third. For example, the D minor chord has a minor third from the root, D, up to the third, F. This minor third interval is comprised of a tone from D to E and a semitone from E to F. The D minor chord has a major third from the third of the chord, F, up to the fifth, A. This major third interval is comprised of two tones, from F to G and G to A.

Opposite is a table showing the construction of minor triads (chords), starting with various root notes.

TABLE 17-2

Root	Third	Fifth
C	E flat	G
C sharp	E	G sharp
D	F	A
E flat	G flat	B flat
E	G	B
F	A flat	C
F sharp	A	C sharp
G	B flat	D
A	C	E
B flat	D flat	F

Please note that all of the minor chords above have the same intervallic structure: a minor third followed by a major third.

The right-hand fingering of these minor chords is the same as the fingering used when playing major chords: thumb on the root, second finger on the third and fifth finger on the fifth. With that in mind, play the chords as shown in FIGURE 17-3.

FIGURE 17-3:

Root position major chords

Chords in a Major Key

When you played the C major scale, you played the scale degrees from the root note C up one or two octaves. A piece of music written in the key of

C major can use all or some of the chords within the key. Chords in the key of C major are built on each scale degree.

Here's a table of the chords in the key of C major and their intervallic structures and chord qualities.

TABLE 17-3

Scale Degree	Chord Number	Root	Third	Fifth	Quality
1st	I	C	E	G	major
2nd	ii	D	F	A	minor
3rd	iii	E	G	B	minor
4th	IV	F	A	C	major
5th	V	G	B	D	major
6th	vi	A	C	E	minor
7th	vii	B	D	F	diminished

Note that each chord has a number, and that all the chords have their own root, third and fifth. The major chords in the key of C are the I, IV and V chords. They are major because they are comprised of two intervals: a major third and a minor third. For instance, the IV chord F has a major third from the root F to A and a minor third from A to C. To refresh your memory, the interval of a major third is comprised of two tones, and the interval of a minor third is comprised of one tone and a semitone.

The minor chords in the key of C are the ii, iii and vi chords. To make it easier to differentiate between the major and minor chords in a given key, the major chord numbers are in uppercase roman numerals, and the minor chords are in lowercase roman numerals. The D minor, E minor and A minor chords are minor because they are made up of a minor third and a major third. Using the ii chord D minor, for example, there's a tone from D to E and a semitone from E to F (which makes up the interval of a minor third), and from F to G and G to A are two tones (which makes up the interval of a major third).

Diminished Chords

Chords built on the seventh scale degree are called diminished chords, which are a semitone smaller than minor chords. The intervallic structure of all diminished chords is made up of two minor intervals. For instance, the B diminished chord has a minor second from B to D (a semitone from B to C and a tone from C to D) and another minor second from D to F natural (a tone from D to E and a semitone from E to F).

The chords in the key of C major are:

C major
D minor
E minor
F major
G major
A minor
B diminished

EXERCISE 17-1 overleaf utilizes some of the chords in the key of C played by the right hand.

There are 12 chords in this exercise. The rhythmic pattern is the same throughout – two crotchet chords followed by a minim chord per bar. As you can see, the chords are comprised of three-note triads, and the notes are stacked up together, making the chord. The sequence of chords is called a chord progression.

Look at TABLE 17-4 carefully before playing EXERCISE 17-1.

Augmented Chords

Augmented notes are raised a semitone above the standard position in chords or scales. An augmented chord contains a root, a major third and an augmented fifth. It's almost an ordinary major chord, but the fifth is one semitone higher.

Play a C major chord: C, E and G. Now raise the G a semitone to G sharp. C, E and G sharp is an augmented chord.

TABLE 17-4

Chord	Notes in the Chord	Chord Quality	Fingering
1st	C–E–G	I (major)	thumb-C, 2nd-E, 5th-G
2nd	B–D–G*	V (major)	thumb-B, 2nd-D, 5th-G
3rd	A–C–E	vi (minor)	thumb-A, 2nd-C, 5th-E
4th	A–C–E	vi (minor)	thumb-A, 2nd-C, 5th-E
5th	B–D–F	vii (diminished)	thumb-B, 2nd-D, 5th-F
6th	C–E–G	I (major)	thumb-C, 2nd-E, 5th-G
7th	C–F–A**	IV (major)	thumb-C, 2nd-F, 5th-A
8th	D–G–B**	V (major)	thumb-D, 2nd-G, 5th-B
9th	E–A–C**	vi (minor)	thumb-E, 2nd-A, 5th-C
10th	E–A–C**	vi (minor)	thumb-E, 2nd-A, 5th-C
11th	D–G–B**	V (major)	thumb-D, 2nd-G, 5th-B
12th	E–G–C*	I (major)	thumb-E, 2nd-G, 5th-C

* first inversion

** second inversion

As the fingering indicates above, the right hand uses the same finger configuration for all of the chords in this exercise (thumb, second finger and fifth finger).

EXERCISE 17-1

Let's add a left-hand bass line to the same chord progression for EXERCISE 17-2.

EXERCISE 17-2

Root Position and First- and Second-Inversion Chords

The first, third, fourth, fifth and sixth chords in EXERCISE 17-2 are in root position, meaning that the first note in each chord is the root of the chord, followed by the third and fifth. However, the second chord and the chords in bars 3 and 4 are not in root position. The second chord in the first bar is in a first-inversion position, meaning that the first note in the chord is not the root, but the third, followed by the fifth and the root. Indicated by one asterisk in Table 17-4, the first note in the G major chord is B, the third, followed by the fifth, D, and the root, G.

Chords seven to eleven are in a position called second inversion, meaning that the first note of the chord is the fifth, followed by the root and the third. Looking at Table 17-4, the second-inversion chords have two asterisks by their letter names. For example, in bar 3, the first note in the F major chord is C, which is the fifth of the chord. Similar to the second chord in the first bar, the last chord in the exercise is also in a first-inversion position (the first note of the chord is the third, followed by the fifth and the root).

Chords in a Minor Key

When you played minor scales in Chapters 15 and 16, you played natural minor scales – notes that observe the key signature. For example, when you played the E minor scale, you were aware of the F sharp key signature and played the series of notes E, F sharp, G, A, B, C, D and the octave E. That's the E natural minor scale.

When building chords on the scale degrees of E natural minor we get the following chords:

TABLE 17-5

Scale Degree	Chord Number	Root	Third	Fifth	Quality
1st	i	E	G	B	minor
2nd	ii	F sharp	A	C	diminished
3rd	III	G	B	D	major
4th	iv	A	C	E	minor
5th	v	B	D	F sharp	minor
6th	VI	C	E	G	major
7th	VII	D	F sharp	A	major

As you can see by doing a comparison with the chords built on major scale degrees, the quality of chords is different in a natural minor key.

Chords built on major scale degrees have the following qualities:

- Major chords: I, IV, V
- Minor chords: ii, iii, vi
- Diminished chords: vii

Chords built on natural minor scale degrees have the following qualities:

- Major chords: III, VI, VII
- Minor chords: i, iv, v
- Diminished chords: ii

Harmonic minor scales are different from natural harmonic scales because of one scale degree: the seventh scale degree is sharp in a harmonic minor scale. As you already know, the seventh scale degree in a natural minor scale is not sharp, it's natural. Using E minor as an example, the seventh scale degree is D natural in E natural minor, and D sharp in E harmonic minor. When applying the sharp seventh scale degree to chords in E harmonic minor, the III chord (G) becomes augmented, the V chord (B) becomes major, and the vii chord (D) becomes diminished because of the D sharp.

When building chords on the scale degrees of E harmonic minor, we get the following chords:

TABLE 17-6

Scale Degree	Chord Number	Root	Third	Fifth	Quality
1st	i	E	G	B	minor
2nd	ii	F sharp	A	C	diminished
3rd	III	G	B	D sharp	augmented
4th	iv	A	C	E	minor
5th	V	B	D sharp	F sharp	major
6th	VI	C	E	G	major
7th	vii	D sharp	F sharp	A	diminished

Here's a comparison of chord qualities between natural minor scale degrees and harmonic minor scale degrees:

	Natural Minor	**Harmonic Minor**
Major chords:	III, VI, VII	V, VI
Minor chords:	i, iv, v	i, iv
Diminished chords:	ii	ii, vii
Augmented chords:		III

The most striking difference between these two different minor scales is the quality of the fifth scale degree. As you remember from Chapter 15, the fifth scale degree is called the dominant. The dominant/tonic relationship is harmonically very strong because the dominant chord, built on the fifth scale degree, wants to resolve to the tonic, the root. This is referred to as tension/resolution in harmonic terms. Using E harmonic minor as an example, the tension is caused by the D sharp, which is the third in the V chord B major (see Table 17-6). Harmonically, the D sharp wants to resolve to the tonic E. In the E natural minor scale, the fifth scale degree is B minor, with D natural as the third in the B minor chord. The harmonic tension is less between B minor and E minor because of the D natural.

The next two exercises illustrate these harmonic differences.

In EXERCISE 17-3, you will be playing chords in E natural minor, noting the D natural in the root position VII chord (first minim chord in the second bar) and the root position v chord (first minim chord in the fourth bar). Similarly, the left hand plays a D natural (second crochet in the fourth bar).

Before playing the exercise, take a close look at the following table.

TABLE 17-7

Chord	Notes in the Chord	Chord Quality/ Position	Fingering		
1st	E–G–B	i-minor/root	thumb-E,	2nd-G,	5th-B
2nd	E–A–C**	iv-minor/2nd	thumb-E,	2nd-A,	5th-C
3rd	D–F#–A	VII-major/root	thumb-D,	2nd-F#,	5th-A
4th	E–G–B	i-minor/root	thumb-E,	2nd-G,	5th-B
5th	B–E–G**	i-minor/2nd	thumb-B,	2nd-E,	5th-G
6th	A–C–E	iv-minor/root	thumb-A,	2nd-C,	5th-E
7th	B–D–F#	v-minor/root	thumb-B,	2nd-D,	4th-F#
8th	B–E–G**	i-minor/2nd	thumb-B,	2nd-E,	5th-G

** second-inversion chords

As you can see, EXERCISE 17-3 has a repeat sign. As also indicated, play this exercise the first time with only the right hand. If you need to, keep repeating only the right-hand part. Once you have the right-hand part worked out, play only the left-hand part. Then play the piece as written: once with the right hand only, the second time with both hands. Make sure to use the numbered fingering for the left hand.

EXERCISE 17-3

EXERCISE 17-4 utilizes chords built on the E harmonic minor scale degrees, acknowledging the D sharp. As you can see, the sharp sign is written on the stave just before the D, telling you to play the D up a semitone. Unlike the F sharp, the sharp sign is written before each D note because D sharp is not in the key signature of E minor. Be prepared to play the D sharp in the first-inversion V chord (first minim chord in bar 2) and the second-inversion V chord (first minim chord in bar 4). Similarly, make sure to play the D sharps in the left hand (second crotchet in the second and fourth bar).

Before playing EXERCISE 17-4, take a close look at the table overleaf.

TABLE 17-8

Chord	Notes in the Chord	Chord Quality/ Position	Fingering
1st	E–G–B	i-minor/root	thumb-E, 2nd-G, 5th-B
2nd	E–A–C**	iv-minor/2nd	thumb-E, 2nd-A, 5th-C
3rd	D#–F#–B*	V-major/1st	thumb-D#2nd-F#,5th-B
4th	E–G–B	i-minor/root	thumb-E, 2nd-G, 5th-B
5th	D–G–B**	III-major/2nd	thumb-D, 2nd-G, 5th-B
6th	E–A–C**	iv-minor/2nd	thumb-E, 2nd-A, 5th-C
7th	F#–B–D#**	V-major/2nd	thumb-F#,2nd-B, 4th-D#
8th	G–B–E*	i-minor/1st	thumb-G, 2nd-B, 5th-E

* first-inversion chords

** second-inversion chords

As you can see, the exercise below also has a repeat sign. As indicated, play this exercise the first time with only the right hand. If you need to, keep repeating only the right-hand part. Once you have it worked out, then play only the left-hand part. When you have both parts worked out independently, then play the piece as written: once with the right hand only, the second time with both hands. Use the numbered fingering for the left hand.

EXERCISE 17-4

EXERCISE 17-4 utilizes both first- and second-inversion chords. Inverted chords serve two purposes: they make the fingering easier in the chord progression, and the voices of one chord flow to the next chord by tones or semitones. For instance, in the second measure, the first minim chord (the V chord B major) in second-inversion position has the notes D sharp, F sharp and B. To get to the next chord (the root position E minor), the thumb and second finger simply move up a semitone from D sharp to E and F sharp to G. What's even easier is the B played by the fifth finger – it plays the top note B in the B major chord and plays the top note B in the E minor chord (B being the common tone in both chords).

Another example is the first-inversion B major chord in the fourth measure with the notes F sharp, B and D sharp. To get to the first-inversion E minor chord, you simply move your thumb a semitone from F sharp to G, and your fourth finger a semitone from D sharp to E. The second finger stays put and plays the B in the B major chord and then plays the same B in the E minor chord. Here again, B is the common tone in both chords.

Playing chords only in root position is difficult and requires a lot of moving up and down the keyboard. Unlike inverted chords, when playing only root position chords in a chord progression, the changing notes from chord to chord don't flow smoothly.

A Harmonic Relationship

Let's take a look at EXERCISE 17-3 and see what the harmonic relationship is between the chords in the right hand and the bass line in the left hand. In the first measure, the bass plays the crotchet E, located an octave below the root-position chord E minor in the right hand. It then jumps down an octave to play the second crotchet E. Both of these notes are playing the root of the chord (E) in two different octaves. It then goes back up and plays the minim E, while the right hand plays the second-inversion A minor chord. This minim E sounds good because E is a note in the A minor chord. Instead of playing the root (A), it's playing the fifth (E) in the A minor chord.

In the second bar, the left hand plays exactly the same as it did in the first bar. However, the chords in the right hand are different. The right hand plays a minim D major chord over the two crotchets E in the left hand. This creates harmonic tension because there are no common tones between the D major chord and the bass note E. But the tension is quickly resolved in the third beat of the same bar when the right hand plays the root-position E minor chord, and the left hand plays E. The D major chord over the E in the bass is sometimes referred to as a pedal tone; the pitch remains the same in the left hand while the right hand plays different chords.

In bar 3, the bass again plays an E, supporting the E minor chord in the right hand, and then plays a passing crotchet G before playing the minim A. The passing note G works well harmonically for two reasons: G is the third in the E minor chord, and in terms of scales, leads directly to the A.

In bar 4, the left hand plays the crotchets B and D, which are the root and third in the B minor chord played by the right hand, and lands on the root E with the E minor chord played by the right hand.

To summarize, in EXERCISE 17-3 the left hand plays the root of the chords, with the exception of the first two beats in the second bar. And it plays two passing notes, both of which are notes in the chords played by the right hand.

In EXERCISE 17-4 the left hand plays the root of the chords and passing notes, which are also notes in the chords played by the right hand. As you can see, the left-hand bass line plays roots, fifths and thirds of the chords played by the right hand, while the right hand plays chords in all three positions (root, first inversion or second inversion).

The Use of Chords in the Right Hand

So far, the exercises in this chapter have dealt with playing chords with the right hand, while the left hand plays bass lines. Playing chords in the right hand is used primarily for accompaniment purposes – when accompanying a singer or solo instrumentalist. This is because the melody is being sung by the singer or played by the instrumentalist. In this scenario, the piano provides the chordal, harmonic and rhythmic support for the melody.

Now let's put the chords in the left hand and melody in the right hand.

The Use of Chords in the Left Hand

A pianist can play melody, harmony and bass on the piano. The right hand can play the melody and/or chords, and the left hand can play the bass line or chords, and can also play melody.

When the piano is not in the accompaniment role, but rather in the solo role, the left hand usually plays a combination of bass lines and chords, while the right hand usually plays the melody and chords. This is the case with piano sonatas, piano concertos and instrumental piano pieces.

In the next two exercises you will play chords in the left hand and melody in the right.

In EXERCISE 17-5 the left hand plays chords supporting the melody in the right hand. Take a close look at the following table before playing EXERCISE 17-5.

TABLE 17-9

Chord	Notes in the Chord	Chord Quality/ Position	Fingering
1st	D–F#–A	I-major/root	5th-D, 2nd-F#, thumb-A
2nd	D–G–B**	IV-major/2nd	5th-D, 2nd-G, thumb-B
3rd	D–F#–A	I-major/root	5th-D, 2nd-F#, thumb-A
4th	C#–E–A*	V-major/1st	4th-C#, 3rd-E, thumb-A
5th	D–F#–B*	vi-minor/1st	5th-D, 2nd-F#, thumb-B
6th	D–G–B**	IV-major/2nd	5th-D, 2nd-G, thumb-B
7th	D–G–B**	IV-major/2nd	5th-D, 2nd-G, thumb-B
8th	C#–E–A*	V-major/1st	4th-C#, 3rd-E, thumb-A
9th	D–F#–A	I-major/root	5th-D, 2nd-F#, thumb-A

* first-inversion chords

** second-inversion chords

Note that EXERCISE 17-5 is in 3/4 time, the tempo is *andante* (slowly), and as the two-sharp key signature indicates, it's in the key of D major (F sharp and C sharp). Make sure to play all Fs and Cs sharp in both the right- and left-hand parts. As Table 17-9 indicates, most of the chords are inverted, making the harmony smooth and the fingering easy. As always, play the right- and left-hand parts separately before playing them together.

If it helps, write the left-hand chord fingering in the left-hand part.

EXERCISE 17-6 is written in D harmonic minor. That's why there's a sharp sign before the C in the first-inversion V chord in the second bar. A natural sign appears before the C in the second-inversion IV chord in the third bar, cancelling out the previous C sharp. However, the C sharp returns again in the fourth bar. Look closely at Table 17-10 before playing the exercise.

EXERCISE 17-5

QUIET SUNDAY

TABLE 17-10

Chord	Notes in the Chord	Chord Quality/ Position	Fingering
1st	D–F–A	i-minor/root	5th-D, 2nd-F, thumb-A
2nd	D–G–B♭**	iv-minor/2nd	5th-D, 2nd-G, thumb-B♭
3rd	D–F–A	i-minor/root	5th-D, 2nd-F, thumb-A
4th	C#–E–A*	V-major/1st	4th-C#, 3rd-E, thumb-A
5th	D–F–B♭*	VI-major/1st	4th-D, 2nd-F#, thumb-B♭
6th	C–F–A**	III-major/2nd	5th-C, 2nd-F, thumb-A
7th	C#–E–A*	V-major/1st	4th-C#, 2nd-E, thumb-A
8th	D–F–A	i-minor/root	5th-D, 2nd-F, thumb-A

* first-inversion chords

** second-inversion chords

EXERCISE 17-6 is in 4/4 time, and the tempo is *andante* (metronome marking: crotchet = 80). This makes the tempo in this exercise slower than the tempo in EXERCISE 17-5. In the same way as EXERCISE 17-5, most of the chords in EXERCISE 17-6 are inverted.

In the third bar, there's a crescendo sign from *mp* to *f* followed by a diminuendo sign in the fourth bar, bringing the volume back down to *mp*. Note the repeat sign. This time, start with only playing the left hand. Add the right hand once you have your left-hand chords in place.

EXERCISE 17-6

CHANGING Cs

You have covered a lot of new material in this chapter. And now for the questions...

1. Why am I answering these questions?

2. What is harmony?

3. What's another word for a three-note chord?

4. How many intervals are there in a major chord?

5. What type of intervals are they?

6. What note is a fifth above A flat?

7. What note is a major third above C sharp?

8. What is the relationship between an F sharp major chord and a G flat major chord?

9. What is E sharp's enharmonic equivalent?

10. What types of intervals comprise minor chords?

11. What note is a minor third above F?

12. What note is a fifth above F sharp?

13. What is the third chord in the key of C major?

14. What is the seventh chord in the key of C major?

15. What is a root-position chord?

16. What is a first-inversion chord?

17. What is a second-inversion chord?

18. What is the sequence of letter note names of a first-inversion A major chord?

19. What is the sequence of letter note names of a second-inversion E minor chord?

20. What is the fifth chord in the key of E natural minor?

21. What is the seventh chord in the key of E natural minor?

22. What chord is diminished in the key of E natural minor?

23. What chords are diminished in the key of E harmonic natural minor?

24. Why is the fifth chord in E harmonic minor a major chord?

25. Why are chords inverted?

(Answers can be found in the Appendix.)

CHAPTER 18

Listening and
Basic Music Theory

By now, you're familiar with reading piano music. But you may not realize that your eyes are taking in information both vertically and horizontally – the vertical reading of singular notes and chords, and the horizontal reading of melodies and the flow of notes (voices) within chord progressions. This chapter will show you how it all fits together.

Listen to the Music

There's a big difference between hearing and listening. You hear a lot of sounds all day long. People might ask you, 'Did you hear that?' Your response could be, 'I'm not sure.' But when someone has something important to say to you, they might preface it by saying, 'Listen very carefully to this.'

Listening is an acquired skill. It requires full attention, being focused and not being distracted. And listening to music is very important. Not just hearing music as background music, but focused listening. And with repeated listening to the same piece of music, you will hear things you didn't hear the first or second time.

Listening is so important that some music schools have a required class for students called ear training, which is designed to develop their listening skills. Through the process of taking ear training classes, the student can more easily recognize and identify intervallic relationships, chord qualities and chord progressions, and the harmonic relationship between melody and harmony.

When you're playing a piece of music on your keyboard, give it your full listening attention. Listen to the melody; listen to the harmony and bass line. Listen to the parts individually, and listen to them collectively. Good musicians are very good listeners.

Analyze the Piece of Music

Before playing any piece of music, it's always best to analyze all the different parts: the key signature, tempo/metronome marking, time signature, the right-hand part, the melody, the left-hand part, the harmony, the fingering, the rhythm and dynamic markings. The vast majority of piano pieces don't have the right- and left-hand fingering written in the part, so you have to go through the piece and determine which fingers to use for each hand.

This preparation helps with your ability to play a piece of music as written and to anticipate what's coming. It's always good practice for your eyes to be slightly ahead of your fingers – for instance, when you're playing the first bar, your eyes should be looking at bars 2 and 3.

Piano pieces can be written in a specific style or left open for your own stylistic adaptation. Musical styles cover a wide range, including baroque, classical, romantic, impressionistic, ragtime, stride, abstract, jazz, bebop, boogie-woogie, rhythm and blues, country, gospel, rock and roll, show tunes (West End musicals), pop, soul, disco, funk, reggae and New Age. If it's specified, try to play the piece in the style it's written in.

While reading and playing music, you're mentally registering what you're seeing. At the same time, you're also hearing what you're reading (seeing) and playing. These multisensory events are taking place all at once. Playing music is a multisensory experience utilizing the visual, audio, physical and mental facilities. It's interesting to note that some pianists have very strong reading skills, can read any style and multiple parts simultaneously, but have difficulty playing without the written music in front of them. On the other hand, some pianists possess strong listening skills; they can hear a piece of music and replicate it without the written music. But when they try to read the same piece of music, they find it difficult, and the attempt to read impairs their playing ability. Some pianists 'play by ear', while others play by reading – then there are those very fortunate pianists who are gifted with having both very sharp eye and ear skills.

Repetition is a very effective methodology that helps when learning a piece of music. When playing the same piece of music repeatedly, it becomes more committed to your memory. As a result of repeated practising, some pianists can memorize lengthy pieces of music.

Four-Note Chords

Both the right hand and left hand can play four-note chords. They are based on the span of an octave, usually from the root of the chord up eight notes to its octave, along with the third and fifth of the chord in between. Four-note chords also include the first and second inversions of the root-position chords.

Using some of the three-note chords (triads) from Chapter 17, let's make them four-note chords. Following Table 18-1 below, you can see the octave has been added for each of the chords.

TABLE 18-1

Chord	Root	Third	Fifth	Octave
C major	C	E	G	C
D major	D	F sharp	A	D
E flat major	E flat	G	B flat	E flat
F major	F	A	C	F
G major	G	B	D	G
A major	A	C sharp	E	A
B major	B	D sharp	F sharp	B

The following table shows the same chords in the first-inversion position.

TABLE 18-2

Chord	Third	Fifth	Root	Third
C major	E	G	C	E
D major	F sharp	A	D	F sharp
E flat major	G	B flat	E flat	G
F major	A	C	F	A
G major	B	D	G	B
A major	C sharp	E	A	C sharp
B major	D sharp	F sharp	B	D sharp

Note that with four-note first-inversion chords, the octave occurs from the low third to the high third, eight notes above.

Here are the same chords in the second-inversion position.

TABLE 18-3

Chord	Fifth	Root	Third	Fifth
C major	G	C	E	G
D major	A	D	F sharp	A
E flat major	B flat	E flat	G	B flat
F major	C	F	A	C
G major	D	G	B	D
A major	E	A	C sharp	E
B major	F sharp	B	D sharp	F sharp

Notice that with four-note second-inversion chords, the octave occurs from the low fifth to the high fifth, eight notes above.

Right Hand

When playing four-note chords with the right hand, the fingering of the notes that make up the chord is consistently the same for each chord:

Root: thumb
Third: second finger
Fifth: third finger
Octave: fifth finger

The same fingering applies to first- and second-inversion chords played by the right hand. While the fingering is the same, the sequence of the notes in the chord change as follows:

First-Inversion Chords, Right Hand
Third: thumb
Fifth: second finger
Root: third finger
Third: fifth finger

Second-Inversion Chords, Right Hand
Fifth: thumb
Root: second finger
Third: third finger
Fifth: fifth finger

As you can see, when playing four-note first-inversion chords with the right hand, there's an octave from the third played by the thumb to the third played by the fifth finger, eight notes above. When playing four-note second-inversion chords, an octave occurs from the fifth of the chord to the fifth, eight notes above.

Left Hand

When playing four-note chords with the left hand, the fingering of the notes that make up the chord is also consistently the same for each chord:

Root: fifth finger
Third: third finger
Fifth: second finger
Octave: thumb

The same fingering applies to first- and second-inversion chords played by the left hand. While the fingering is the same, the sequence of the notes in the chord changes as follows:

First-Inversion Chords, Left Hand
Third: fifth finger
Fifth: third finger
Root: second finger
Third: thumb

Second-Inversion Chords, Left Hand
Third: fifth finger
Fifth: third finger
Third: second finger
Fifth: thumb

Here again, when playing four-note first-inversion chords with the left hand, there's an octave from the third played by the fifth finger to the third played by the thumb, eight notes above. When playing four-note second-inversion chords, an octave occurs from the fifth of the chord to the fifth, eight notes above.

Four-Note Chord Exercises

In EXERCISE 18-1, you play four-note chords with your right hand. Use the same fingering for each chord: root – thumb; third – second finger; fifth – third finger; octave – fifth finger.

In EXERCISE 18-1, all of the chords are major chords: C major, D major and E flat major. As a group, these chords don't belong to one specific key signature. Therefore, no key signature is written on the stave. Generally speaking, when there isn't a sharp or flat key signature, this means the music is in the key of C major or A minor. However, this is not the case here because we are using major chords from more than one key signature, and we're even mixing sharp (the D major chord) and flat (the E flat major chord) major chords together. Make sure to play the F sharp in the D major chord, and the E flat and B flat in the E flat major chord.

In EXERCISE 18-2, a rhythmic bass line is added to the same chord progression. This bass line, played by the left-hand thumb, stays on the C note, an octave below middle C. As you can see, there is a curved line called a tie, which ties together the first crotchet with the first quaver in the second beat of bars 1, 2, 3 and 4. The tie means the first quaver is heard but not played because it is tied to the crotchet. But you do play the second quaver, which is the subdivision of the second beat in the bar.

To get a feel for the tied rhythm played by the left hand, count out loud the following:

ONE	two	**AND**	**THREE**	four
(Crotchet	quaver	**quaver**	**minim**	**)**

The above numbers in bold and the corresponding note values represent the beats and notes to play with the left hand in EXERCISE 18-2. When counting out loud, put an emphasis on *one, and* and *three*. As you recall, two quavers equal one crotchet. A subdivision is simply dividing a single crotchet into two quavers.

Harmonically, the moving right-hand chords over the repeated C in the bass create tension in bars 2, 3, and 4, and then resolve in the fifth bar, with the left hand playing the root of the C major chord, doubled down an octave. The harmonic tension in measures 2, 3 and 4 is created because the bass note C is not a note within the triadic structure of the D and E flat chords. As a reminder, the triadic structure of a chord is comprised of the root, third and fifth.

As indicated, the right-hand chords have their letter names written above each chord.

EXERCISE 18-2

Another name for a tied rhythm is a dotted rhythm. The value of a dotted note is equal to the note's value plus half its value. For example, a dotted crotchet equals one crotchet beat plus a half beat, or in other words, a beat and a half. As you can see in EXERCISE 18-2, the crotchet tied to the quaver equals a beat and a half. So another way of writing the exact same rhythm is to use a dotted crotchet followed by a single quaver, instead of a crotchet tied to an quaver. Refer to EXERCISE 18-3.

EXERCISE 18-3

The rhythm of the bass line in EXERCISE 18-3 is exactly the same as the rhythm of the bass line in EXERCISE 18-2. However, as you can see, there is a difference between these two exercises: in EXERCISE 18-3, the pitches are different in the second, third and fourth bars.

Now let's move on to playing four-note chords with the left hand.

In EXERCISE 18-4, the left hand plays the following four-note chords: C major, D major and E major (not E flat major). Make sure you are aware of the sharps in the D major and E major chords. The left-hand fingering of all of the chords in this exercise is: root – fifth finger; third – third finger; fifth – second finger; octave – thumb. Also notice that the last chord (E major) played in bar 7 is tied to the same chord in bar 8. Play the E major chord in bar 7, keep it held down, and let it sustain through to the end of bar 8.

EXERCISE 18-4

As you can see in the next exercise, a dotted, or tied, rhythm is played by the right hand. The rhythm is written in two different ways: a crotchet tied to a quaver (bars 1 and 4) and a dotted crotchet (bars 2, 3, 5, and 6). The rhythm in bars 1 to 6 is exactly the same, and sounds the same, even though the rhythm is written in two different ways.

This dotted rhythm is the same rhythm that the left hand played in EXERCISES 18-2 and 18-3, with one exception: the rhythm is different in the seventh bar. The rhythm of the third and fourth beats in the seventh bar is also a tied (dotted) rhythm (the fourth beat is tied to the preceding crotchet; the *and* of the fourth beat, the second quaver, is played). It's exactly the same rhythm as the first two beats in the measure.

Let's look at the harmonic relationship between the right-hand melody and left-hand chords in EXERCISE 18-5. The repeated E note played by the right hand is harmonically consonant (resolved) with the chords played by the left hand in bars 1, 3, 5, 7 and 8. This is because the note E is also the third in the C major chord and the root and octave in the E major chord. Because both the C major and E major chords have the note E in their triadic structure, E is referred to as the common tone between the two chords. In bars 2, 4 and 6, the E note in the right hand creates some tension against the D chord because the E note is not a pitch that makes up the D major triad.

EXERCISE 18-5

Breaking It Down

EXERCISE 18-6 is comprised of a simple melody in the right hand and moving four-note chords in the left hand. It's the moving harmony of the chords juxtaposed to the simple melody that makes this exercise interesting.

The following table identifies the quality, position and fingering of the chords used in EXERCISE 18-6.

TABLE 18-4

Measure	Notes in the Chord	Quality/Position	Fingering
1	E♭–G–B♭–E♭	I-major/root	5th-E♭, 3rd-G, 2nd-B♭, thumb-E♭
2	E♭–G–B♭–D	I-major 7th/root	5th-E♭, 3rd-G, 2nd-B♭, thumb-D
3	C–E♭–G–C	vi-minor/root	5th-C, 3rd-E♭, 2nd-G, thumb-C
4	C–E♭–A♭–C*	IV-major/1st	5th-C, 3rd-E♭, 2nd-A♭, thumb-C
5	C–F–A♭–C**	ii-minor/2nd	5th-C, 3rd-F, 2nd-A♭, thumb-C
6	D♭–F–A♭–D♭^	VII-major/root	5th-D♭, 3rd-F, 2nd-A♭, thumb-D♭
7	D–F–B♭–D*	V-major/1st	5th-D, 3rd-F, 2nd-B♭, thumb-D
8	E♭–G–B♭–E♭	I-major/root	5th-E♭, 3rd-G, 2nd-B♭, thumb-E♭

* first-inversion chords

** second-inversion chords

^ lowered seventh chord

Two new chords are introduced in EXERCISE 18-6. In the second bar, the chord is E flat major seventh. It's called a major seventh chord because the distance between the root E flat and D is an interval of a major seventh. This interval is added on to the E flat major triad. In the sixth bar, the chord is D flat major. This is an altered chord because in the key of E flat major, the seventh scale degree is D natural, not D flat. Even though D flat is not in the key of E flat major, this chord works well because the D flat is a passing tone from C to D. In addition, F minor and D flat major have two common tones: F and A flat. We will discuss altered chords more extensively in Chapter 19.

While all the notes of the chords provide harmony for the melody, take a look at the top note in each chord. The top notes of the chords measure by measure are: E flat, D, C, C, C, D flat, D natural and E flat. This top harmonic voice moves smoothly in a tonal motion while the other notes (voices) in the chord move beneath it. This top note is also strong harmonically because it is doubled an octave lower throughout the chord progression, with the exception of the second bar. When notes are doubled and played in octaves, their sounds dominate the other notes in the chord.

Play only the left-hand chords several times before adding the right-hand melody. In doing so, you will discover common tones among the chords and smooth harmonic changes by playing inversions. As indicated, EXERCISE 18-6 is in the key of E flat major. Make sure to play all the flats as indicated in the key signature.

EXERCISE 18-6

SAFE and SOUND?

Pulling It All Together

EXERCISE 18-7 is in 6/8 time. That means that there are six quavers, or the equivalent thereof, per bar. When counting the quavers, count 1-2-3, 2-2-3 for each bar, with an accent on the first quaver in each group of three. This gives the 6/8 time signature a two-beat feel with three quaver subdivisions per beat. When playing this piece with a two-beat feel, the tempo is *largo*, which is slow. Keep in mind that there are two sets of three even quavers per beat.

Because EXERCISE 18-7 is in the key of D harmonic minor, the seventh scale degree is C sharp. As indicated in bars 4 and 8, the C sharp makes the V chord A major. The dotted crotchet chords equal three quavers (two quavers in a crotchet plus the dot equals half the value of a crotchet, which is a quaver). The dotted minim chords equal two dotted crotchets or six quavers. The left hand plays four-note chords throughout the piece except for the very last D minor chord, which is a three-note chord. This occurs because the right hand plays the top note D. The fingering of the chords in the left hand is the same throughout: fifth finger, third finger, second finger and thumb, except for the last chord, played with the fifth finger, third finger and second finger. The G minor chord in bars 2, 3, 6 and 7 are second inversions, starting with the fifth of the chord D, followed by G, B flat and D. The A chords in bars 4 and 8 are first inversions, starting with the third of the chord C sharp, followed by E, A and C sharp.

Play only the left-hand chords several times. Take time, practise the chords, listen to the four voices that make up the chord and how the voices change from chord to chord. You'll hear the common tone (D) between D minor and G minor, and how the first-inversion A chord makes a smooth harmonic progression to D minor.

Once you have the chords worked out comfortably with your left hand, play only the melody with your right hand. Notice how bars 5, 6 and 7 are exactly the same as bars 1, 2 and 3.

Note the D minor key signature and play all the Bs flat.

UNDERGROUND

To help you absorb the material that has been covered in this chapter, answer the following questions.

1. What should you do before playing any piece of music?

2. When reading music, where should your eyes be?

3. What is listening?

4. What are four-note chords based on?

5. What is the sequence of notes in a four-note, first-inversion, E flat major chord?

6. What is the sequence of notes in a four-note, first-inversion, E minor chord?

7. What is the sequence of notes in a four-note, second-inversion, B major chord?

8. What is the sequence of notes in a four-note, second-inversion, D minor chord?

   ♪ ....

9. Compared to four-note root-position chords, how does the fingering change when playing their first inversion with the right hand?

   ♪ ....

10. Where does the octave occur when playing four-note second-inversion chords?

    ♪ ....

11. Why is there no key signature in EXERCISE 18-1?

    ♪ ....

12. What happens when notes are tied together?

    ♪ ....

13. In EXERCISE 18-2, do you play the quavers that are tied to the crotchet?

    ♪ ....

14. Why is there harmonic tension between the D major and E flat major chords and the C in the bass in EXERCISE 18-2?

    ♪ ....

15. What's another way of writing a tied rhythm?

    ♪ ....

16. How many quavers are there in a dotted crotchet?

    ♪ ....

17. In EXERCISE 18-5, is the rhythm the same in bars 1 and 2?

    ♪ ....

18. What is a common tone?

    ♪ ....

19. C major and E major chords have a common tone. What is it?

    ♪ ....

20. What are the common tones between C minor and A flat major chords?

    ♪ ....

21. What are the common tones between F minor and D flat major chords?

    ♪ ....

22. What are the common tones between D flat major and B flat major chords?

    ♪ ....

23. How many quavers are there in a dotted minim?

    ♪ ....

24. Why does a 6/8 time signature feel like two beats per measure?

    ♪ ....

25. Why does the left hand only play a three-note chord at the end of EXERCISE 18-7?

    ♪ ....

(Answers can be found in the Appendix.)

CHAPTER 19

Advanced Chord Structures

At this point, you are familiar with most major and minor chords in root position and first and second inversions. In this chapter, we add notes to the basic chord structure, which will allow you more freedom to express yourself through music.

Major Sevenths

Major seventh chords are consonant. They are built on major key scale degrees; in major key scales, the seventh scale degree is a semitone below the octave.

As you know, chords are comprised of thirds: a major third and a minor third equal a major triad; a minor third and a major third equal a minor triad. Going up another third from the fifth of a chord gives us the seventh. For example, the notes in a C major chord are C (root), E (third) and G (fifth). A major third above G is B. When you stack up the thirds in a C major seventh chord, you have: C, E, G, B (C to E is a major third, E to G is a minor third, and G to B is a major third). So the formula for all major seventh chords is a sequence of a major third, minor third and major third.

The following table shows you the notes and consecutive thirds in major seventh chords.

TABLE 19-1

Chord	Root	Third	Fifth	Seventh
D major 7th	D	F sharp	A	C sharp
F major 7th	F	A	C	E
G major 7th	G	B	D	F sharp
A major 7th	A	C sharp	E	G sharp
B major 7th	B	D sharp	F sharp	A sharp

In keeping with the major seventh formula, note that the interval from the root to the third with all of the chords is a major third, from the third to the fifth is a minor third, and from the fifth to the seventh is a major third.

When playing the D major, G major, A major and B major seventh chords in Table 19-1 with the right hand, the fingering is:

Root: thumb
Third: second finger
Fifth: third finger
Seventh: fourth finger

The fingering is slightly different for the F major seventh chord:

Root: thumb
Third: second finger
Fifth: third finger
Seventh: fifth finger

The difference in the fingering is because of the following: when the seventh in a major seventh chord is located on a black key, the fourth finger plays the seventh because it is longer than the fifth finger and can easily reach the black key. However, when the seventh in a major seventh chord is located on a white key, the fifth finger is a better choice. (For those of you who have small hands, you might not be able to reach the seventh on a black key with your fourth finger, in which case, try using your fifth finger.)

In EXERCISE 19-1, play the major seventh chords in Table 19-1 with your right hand.

EXERCISE 19-1

Major seventh
chords

When playing the chords with your left hand, the fingering is:

Root: fifth finger
Third: third finger
Fifth: second finger
Seventh: thumb

This left-hand fingering applies to all major seventh chords, black and white keys alike. When playing sevenths that are on black keys, you're going to have to play deeper into the keys, moving your hand towards the fall. In doing so, it will be easier for your relatively short thumb to reach the black keys.

In EXERCISE 19-2, play the major seventh chords in Table 19-1 with your left hand.

EXERCISE 19-2:

Major seventh
chords

In EXERCISE 19-3 you're going to build major seventh chords following the major third, minor third, major third formula. Build up from the roots starting with middle C. (Reminder: the major seventh is a semitone below the octave.)

EXERCISE 19-3

Constructing Major Seventh Chords

	Root	Third	Fifth	Seventh
C				
E flat				
F sharp				
A				
B flat				

Now that you have constructed the chords, play them with your right hand in EXERCISE 19-4.

EXERCISE 19-4:
Major seventh
chords

Minor Seventh Chords

The following minor seventh chords are built on natural minor scale degrees. The seventh scale degree in natural minor scales is a tone below the octave.

The stacking up of thirds for natural minor seventh chords follows this formula: minor third, major third and minor third.

The following table shows you the notes and consecutive thirds in natural minor seventh chords.

TABLE 19-2

Chord	Root	Third	Fifth	Seventh
C minor 7th	C	E flat	G	B flat
D minor 7th	D	F	A	C
E minor 7th	E	G	B	D
F minor 7th	F	A flat	C	E flat
G minor 7th	G	B flat	D	F
A minor 7th	A	C	E	G
B minor 7th	B	D	F sharp	A

Please note that all of the chords in Table 19-2 follow the natural minor seventh formula – from the root to the third is a minor third, from the third to the fifth is a major third, and from the fifth to the seventh is a minor third.

When playing minor seventh chords with the right hand, the fingering is the same as playing major seventh chords. As indicated by one asterisk in Table 19-2, the sevenths that are on black keys are played using the fourth finger – all the other sevenths, which are on white keys, are played using the fifth finger.

In EXERCISE 19-5, play the chords in Table 19-2 with your right hand.

EXERCISE 19-5:

Minor seventh chords

When playing minor seventh chords with the left hand, the fingering is the same as playing major seventh chords.

In EXERCISE 19-6, play the minor seventh chords in Table 19-2 with your left hand.

EXERCISE 19-6:

Minor seventh chords

In EXERCISE 19-7, build natural minor seventh chords following the minor third, major third, minor third formula. Start with the root, E flat. (Reminder: the minor seventh is a tone below the octave.)

EXERCISE 19-7

Constructing Minor Seventh Chords

	Root	Third	Fifth	Seventh
E flat				
F sharp				
A				
B flat				

Now that you have constructed the chords, play them with your right hand in EXERCISE 19-8.

EXERCISE 19-8:

Minor seventh chords

Harmonic Minor Sevenths

Minor seventh chords with an interval of a major seventh from the root to the seventh are built on harmonic minor scale degrees. The seventh scale degree in harmonic minor scales is a semitone below the octave.

The stacking up of thirds for harmonic minor seventh chords follows this formula: minor third, major third and major third. Rather than calling them harmonic minor seventh chords, they are commonly referred to as minor chords with a raised seventh – raised because the seventh is a semitone higher than the natural minor seventh. For example, the notes in a G minor seventh chord are G, B flat, D and F. In a G minor with a raised seventh, the notes are: G, B flat, D and F sharp. The shorthand version chord symbol for harmonic minor chords is Gm+7. The '+' is shorthand for raised.

The difference between major seventh chords and minor chords with a raised seventh is only one pitch: the third of the chord. For example, the notes in a C major seventh chord are C, E, G and B. The notes in a C minor with a raised seventh are C, E flat, G and B. The simple change of a lowered semitone with the third of the chord makes a big difference in the way these two chords sound.

To illustrate this difference, alternate playing between C major seventh and C minor with a raised seventh, using middle C as the root of both chords.

Dominant Seventh Chords

The seventh chords we have covered so far are all built on the first scale degree – the root. Dominant seventh chords are built on the fifth scale degree – the dominant.

In the key of C major, the dominant seventh is G7. This chord is comprised of the G major triad plus a minor seventh interval from the root G up to F. The notes in the G7 chord are G, B, D and F.

Dominant seventh chords want to resolve to the root. When playing in a major key, C major for instance, the G7 also has a sense of resolution by going to the vi chord, A minor. The formula for all dominant seventh chords is a sequence of a major third, minor third and minor third.

Dominant seventh chords are also used in harmonic minor keys. For example, in the key of E harmonic minor, the V chord is B major. B major becomes B7 by adding the note A. The notes in the B7 chord are B, D sharp, F sharp and A.

In the next exercise, build dominant seventh chords following the major third, minor third, minor third formula. Start with the root E, two tones above middle C. (Reminder: the minor seventh is a whole step below the octave.)

EXERCISE 19-9

Constructing Dominant Seventh Chords

	Root	Third	Fifth	Seventh
E				
F				
G				
A				
B flat				
C				

When you have constructed the dominant seventh chords in EXERCISE 19-9, play them with your right hand in EXERCISE 19-10.

EXERCISE 19-10:

Dominant seventh chords

Seventh-Chord Inversions

Seventh chords can be inverted to first, second or third positions. With a first-inversion, E-dominant seventh chord, the notes are G sharp, B, D and E. In a second-inversion, C major seventh, the notes are G, B, C and E. The first note in a third-inversion chord is the seventh; for example, the notes in an F major seventh third-inversion chord are E, F, A and C.

The table below shows seventh chords in third-inversion positions.

TABLE 19-3

Chord	Seventh	Root	Third	Fifth
C minor 7th	B flat	C	E flat	G
D major 7th	C sharp	D	F sharp	A
E dominant 7th	D	E	G sharp	B
F minor 7th	E flat	F	A flat	C
G major 7th	F sharp	G	B	D
A minor +7th	G sharp	A	C	E
B major 7th	A sharp	B	D sharp	F sharp

Play the chords in Table 19-3 with your right hand in EXERCISE 19-11. The fingering is the same for all of the chords:

Seventh: thumb
Root: second finger
Third: third finger
Fifth: fifth finger

EXERCISE 19-11:
Third-inversion seventh chords

EXERCISE 19-12 uses a variety of seventh chords in the right hand over a rhythmic bass line. Table 19-4 identifies the chord qualities and their positions.

TABLE 19-4

Measure	Chord	Notes	Quality	Position
1	C major 7th*	E–G–B	I-major 7th	1st inversion
2	F major 7th	E–F–A–C	IV-major 7th	3rd inversion
3	E major**	E–G#–B	V-dominant	root position
4	A minor	E–A–C	iv-minor	2nd inversion
5	F major 7th*	E–A–C	IV-major	3rd inversion
6	E dominant 7th**	E–G#–B–D	V-dominant 7th	root position
7	A minor	E–A–C	iv-minor	2nd inversion
8	A minor	E–A–C–E	iv-minor	2nd inversion

* root in bass

** borrowed dominant

The table for EXERCISE 19-12 reveals new harmonic information. Up to now, you have been playing closed-position chords. In the next exercise you will be playing two open-position chords.

Looking at the very first chord (C major seventh), it looks as if the right hand is playing an E minor chord. But when you add the root of the chord, C, played by the bass, the E minor chord becomes a C major seventh chord. Similarly, in bar 5, the root of the F major seventh chord is played by the bass. The voicings of the C major seventh and F major seventh chords are good examples of open-position chords, where the notes that make up the chord are played in different octaves. All other chords in EXERCISE 19-12 are closed-position chords.

As indicated by two asterisks, the E major and E dominant seventh chords are borrowed dominants from the key of A minor. In the key of C major, the iii chord is minor. By making it major, it becomes the V chord in the key of A minor. In doing so, we move from the key of C major to A minor. EXERCISE 19-12 starts in the key of C major, but after two bars transposes to the key of A minor and stays in that key for the remainder of the piece.

In the left-hand part, note the dotted rhythm on the first two beats of every bar except for the last bar. The rhythm of the bass part in bar 1 is repeated in bars 3, 4, 6 and 7. A variation of this rhythm takes place on the fourth beat in bars 2 and 5.

There is a common tone among all of the chords in this exercise. One note is played in the same position throughout the chord progression – the note E, which is the first note in every chord played by the thumb in the right hand.

Play only the right-hand chords several times. Then play only the left-hand bass part several times. When you're ready, play with both hands together. You'll notice how significantly the sound of the harmony changes when you add the bass part to the chords in bars 1, 2 and 5.

EXERCISE 19-12

MOVING ON

Ninth Chords

An octave is eight notes above any given pitch. A tone above an octave is a ninth – for example, starting with the root G, eight notes above is the octave G, a tone above the octave G is A, which is the ninth.

Ninths can be added to all types of major chords and all minor chords. With that in mind, add the ninth to the following chords.

EXERCISE 19-13

Constructing Ninth Chords

Root/Chord	Third	Fifth	Ninth
C major	E	G	_____
D minor	F	A	_____
E flat major	G	B flat	_____
F minor	A flat	C	_____
F sharp major	A- sharp	C sharp	_____
G minor	B flat	D	_____
A major	C sharp	E	_____
B flat minor	D flat	F	_____

Ninths can also be added to all types of seventh chords. Add the ninth to the following seventh chords:

EXERCISE 19-14

Adding Ninths to Seventh Chords

Root/Chord	Third	Fifth	Seventh	Ninth
C sharp minor 7th	E	G sharp	B	_____
D major 7th	F sharp	A	C sharp	_____
E minor 7th	G	B	D sharp	_____
F dominant 7th	A	C	E flat	_____
G minor 7th	B flat	D	F	_____
A major 7th	C sharp	E	G sharp	_____
B dominant 7th	D sharp	F sharp	A	_____

There are also flat ninth chords, which are built on a dominant seventh chord. They are flat because the ninth is lowered a semitone. Using an F dominant seventh chord as an example, by adding a G flat it becomes a flat ninth chord. The notes in the chord are F, A, C, E flat and G flat. The abbreviated chord symbol for flat ninth chords is F7♭9. Flat ninth chords are very dissonant.

EXERCISE 19-15 has a variety of seventh and ninth chords in various positions with a bass line that leaps octaves every now and then.

Table 19-5 identifies the chord qualities, the notes in the chord and their positions.

TABLE 19-5

Bar	Chords	Notes	Position
1	A major 7, 9*	C#–E–G#–B	1st inversion
	A major	C#–E–A	1st inversion
	A major 7th*	C#–E–G#	1st inversion
	A major	C#–E–A	1st inversion
2	B minor 7th*	D–F#–A	1st inversion
	E dominant 7th	D–E–G	3rd inversion
3	A major 7, 9*	C#–E–G#–B	1st inversion
	A major	C#–E–A	1st inversion
	A major 7th*	C#–E–G#	1st inversion
	A major	C#–E–A	1st inversion
4	B minor 7th*	D–F#–A	1st inversion
	E dominant 7th	D–E–G	3rd inversion
5	F sharp minor	F#–A–C#	root
6	D major 7th*	F#–A–C#	1st inversion
7	B minor	D–F#–B	1st inversion
	B minor 7th*	D–F#–A	1st inversion
8	E dominant 7th	D–E–G#	3rd inversion
	E major	E–G#–B	root
9	A major 7, 9*	C#–E–G#–B	1st inversion
	A major	C#–E–A	1st inversion
	A- major 7th*	C#–E–G#	1st inversion
	A major	C#–E–A	1st inversion
10	B minor 7th*	D–F#–A	1st inversion
	E dominant 7th	D–E–G	3rd inversion
11	A major 7, 9*	C#–E–G#–B	1st inversion
	A major	C#–E–A	1st inversion
	A major 7th*	C#–E–G#	1st inversion
	A major	C#–E–A	1st inversion
12	B minor 7th*	D–F#–A	1st inversion
	E dominant 7th	D–E–G	3rd inversion
13	A- major 7th	E–G#–A–C#	2nd inversion

* root in bass

As you can see by looking at the key signature, EXERCISE 19-15 is in the key of A major; make sure to play all Fs, Cs and Gs sharp. The tempo of this piece is *adagio* (crotchet = 72).

In this piece, the right hand plays both chords and melody. The top note in the chords, along with the passing quavers, makes up the melody. Isolating the melody, the notes in the first two bars are: (bar 1) B, A, G sharp and A, and (bar 2) A, G sharp, F sharp, G sharp, A and B. This two-bar phrase melody, along with the chord progression and bass line, is repeated in bars 3 and 4, 9 and 10, and 11 and 12.

EXERCISE 19-15 has two parts. The first part is the two-bar phrase, repeated in bar 3 and 4. The second part is bars 5 to 8. This second part starts on A major's relative minor, F sharp minor, and works its way back to the first part, which is repeated in bars 9 to 12. In terms of form, this exercise follows an abbreviated A-B-A form – A: part one; B: part two; A: part one repeated.

When playing the A major ninth chords in bars 1, 3, 9 and 11, the root of the chord is in the bass. Similarly, in the B minor seventh chords in bars 2, 4, 10 and 12, the root is in the bass.

For the purpose of illustration, the rhythm of the bass part in bar 5 is the same as the rhythm in bar 6. The dotted minim in bar 5 equals three beats; the minim tied to the crotchet in bar 6 also equals three beats.

The thumb and the second finger of the right hand play the bottom two notes of the chords, while the third, fourth and fifth fingers play the chords' third and fourth notes. Additionally, as indicated in the right-hand part, the second, third, fourth and fifth fingers also play the melody's passing quavers.

Play only the right-hand chords several times before adding the left-hand part.

KEEP ON TRYING

Suspended Chords

Suspended chords include the second and fourth scale degrees in major and minor chords. The written shorthand for suspended chords is sus. They are called suspended chords because the suspended pitch (note) wants to resolve to either the root, third or fifth of the chord. For example, a C sus2 chord contains the second scale degree D, which can resolve to either C (the root) or E (the third). A C sus4 chord contains the fourth scale degree F, which can resolve to E (the third) or G (the fifth). The second (D) resolves by either going up a tone to E or down a tone to the root; the fourth (F) resolves by moving down a semitone to E or up a tone to G.

The following table includes a variety of suspended chords.

TABLE 19-6

Root/Chord	Sus2	Third	Sus4	Fifth
C minor sus2	D			G
D major sus4			G	A
E minor sus4			A	B
F major sus2	G			C
G major sus4			C	D
A minor sus4			D	E
B major sus2	C#			F#

As you can see in the table above, when playing sus2 or sus4 chords, the third of the chord is not included. Chord progressions that contain suspended chords generally move from a suspended chord to a resolved chord that includes the third.

Diminished Chords

Going back to Chapter 17, chords built on the seventh scale degree in major keys are diminished chords – to diminish means to make smaller.

Diminished chords are a semitone smaller than minor chords. For example, the two third intervals that make up a G minor chord are a minor third (from G to B flat) and a major third (from B flat to D). By lowering the major third a semitone and making it a minor third, we have two minor thirds that equal a diminished chord. The notes in a G diminished chord are G, B flat and D flat.

Adding to the two minor third triads that make up a diminished chord (by adding another minor third on top of the fifth), we get a diminished seventh chord. Using the G diminished triad, a minor third above the fifth is F flat.

Diminished chords are dissonant and want to be resolved. For example, a G diminished seventh chord can resolve to A flat major or its relative minor, F minor. Note by note, this is how the G diminished chord resolves to A flat:

G moves to A flat
B flat moves to A flat
D flat moves to C
F flat moves to E flat

Diminished chords are similar to dominant (V) seventh chords. For example, the dominant seventh chord in the key of A flat major is E flat (E flat, G, B flat, D flat). The first three notes in a G diminished chord are the same as the last three notes in the E flat dominant seventh chord: G, B flat, D flat. To further illustrate this similarity, play a G diminished chord with the right hand (G, B flat, D flat) and add an E flat with your left hand. By adding the E flat, the G diminished chord becomes an E flat dominant seventh (E flat, G, B flat, D flat). The shorthand for writing diminished chords is dim. (G dim.7).

Augmented Chords

You may recall that the III chord built on a harmonic minor scale is an augmented chord – to augment means to make larger. Augmented chords are a semitone larger than a major triad – the two third intervals that make up a D major chord are a major third (from D to F sharp) and a minor third (from F sharp to A). By raising the minor third a semitone and making it a major third, we have two major thirds that equal an augmented chord. The notes in a D augmented chord are D, F sharp and A sharp.

Augmented chords are also dissonant chords that want to be resolved. For example, the D augmented chord wants to resolve to G major. Note by note, this is how a D augmented chord resolves to G major:

D stays on D (common tone with both chords)
F sharp moves to G
A sharp moves to B

The shorthand for writing augmented chords is aug. (A aug.).

Arpeggio Chords (Broken Chords)

In contrast to the way you have been playing chords thus far, another way of playing chords is to arpeggiate, or break up, the notes that make up the chord and play each note individually. The Italian word *arpeggio* means 'harp-like'. Arpeggio chords can be played by either the right hand or the left hand.

The next exercise uses arpeggio chords in the left hand with a simple melody in the right hand. The following table identifies the chords and their qualities used in EXERCISE 19-16.

TABLE 19-7

Bar	Chords	Notes	Position
1	C major	C–E–G–C	root
	C major 7	C–E–G–B	root
2	F major	F–A–C–F	root
	F minor	C–F–A–C	2nd inversion
3	B dim. 7	A♭–B–A♭–C	2nd inversion
	G dominant 7	D–F–G–B	2nd inversion
4	C major	C–E–G–C	root

TABLE 19-7 (*continued*)

5	A minor	C–E–A–C	1st inversion
	A minor	C–E–A–C	1st inversion
6	D major	D–F#–A–D	root
	D 7	D–F#–A–C	root
7	D minor 7	D–F–A–C	root
	D minor 7	D–F–A–C	root
8	G 7 sus4	D–F–G–C	2nd inversion
	G 7	D–F–G–B	2nd inversion
9	F major	C–F–A–C	2nd inversion
10	F minor	C–F–A♭–C	2nd inversion
11	D minor 7	D–F–A–C	root
	G dominant 7	D–F–G–B	2nd inversion
12	C major	C–E–G–C	root
13	C major	C–E–G–C	root
	C major 7	C–E–G–B	root
14	F major	C–F–A–C	2nd inversion
	F minor	C–F–A♭–C	2nd inversion
15	B dim. 7	D–F–A♭–B	1st inversion
	G dominant 7	D–F–G–B	2nd inversion
16	C major	C–E–G–C	root

The broken chord pattern in EXERCISE 19-16 is made up of a series of quavers, with the exception of minims representing the third and fourth beats in bars 4, 8, 12 and 16. The quavers should be played evenly, so that they all have the same equal value. Each set of four quavers represents one chord – for example, the first set of four quavers in bar 1 (C, E, G, C) represents the C major chord. Similarly, the first set of quavers in bar 5 (C, E, A, C) represents the A minor chord in first-inversion position.

BACK ON TRACK

Notice that the right-hand melody part in bars 9 to 12 is exactly the same as the right-hand notes in bars 1 to 4. What's different is the harmony – the chords in the left hand in bars 9 to 12 play chords that are different than those played in bars 1 to 4. In bars 13 to 16, the melody is repeated once again.

Also notice that the fourth quavers in bars 9 and 10 are tied to minims. Simply play the fourth quaver and hold it down, giving it the full combined value equal to five quavers (the minim C equals four quavers plus the tied quaver C).

In bars 3 and 15 you can see how the first-inversion, B diminished seventh chord resolves to the G dominant seventh chord. Also note how the second-inversion, G 7 sus4 chord in bar 8 resolves to the second-inversion, G dominant seventh chord.

The left-hand fingering of the set of four ascending quavers is the same throughout the piece: 5, 3, 2, 1.

Play only the left-hand part several times, trying to play all the quavers evenly. When you have worked out the fingering and timing, add the right-hand melody part.

And now for the questions...

1. What is the formula for building major seventh chords?

2. How far is a major seventh from the octave?

3. What note is a major seventh above E flat?

4. What are the notes in a root-position, A flat major seventh chord?

5. How far is a minor seventh from the octave?

6. What note is a minor seventh above F sharp?

7. What are the notes in a root-position, F sharp minor seventh chord?

8. What are the notes in a root-position, A harmonic minor seventh chord?

9. What are the notes in a root-position, B flat minor seventh chord?

10. What are the notes in a root-position, E dominant seventh chord?

11. What are the notes in a second-inversion, C major seventh chord?

12. What are the notes in a first-inversion, B natural minor seventh chord?

   ♪ ....

13. What are the notes in a second-inversion, F sharp dominant seventh chord?

   ♪ ....

14. What are the notes in a third-inversion, C natural minor seventh chord?

   ♪ ....

15. What are the notes in a third-inversion, A major seventh chord?

   ♪ ....

16. What is an open-position chord?

   ♪ ....

17. What is a borrowed dominant chord?

   ♪ ....

18. What interval is a tone above an octave?

   ♪ ....

19. What are the notes in a root-position, E natural minor 7, 9 chord?

   ♪ ....

20. What are the names of the two suspended chords?

   ♪ ....

21. A suspended fourth resolves to what note in a triad?

   ♪ ....

22. A suspended second resolves to what note in a triad?

   ♪ ....

23. What's the difference between a minor chord and a diminished chord?

   ♪ ....

24. What are the notes in a B diminished seventh chord?

   ♪ ....

25. What's the difference between a major chord and an augmented chord?

   ♪ ....

26. What's another name for broken chords?

   ♪ ....

(Answers can be found in the Appendix.)

CHAPTER 20

Applying Music Theory to Playing the Piano

As you know, there's practice and there's theory. In practical terms, theory by itself doesn't really accomplish much. It is the application of the theory to the keyboard that makes it come to life and makes the practice of playing the piano easier to grasp.

Abbreviated Chord Symbols

Every chord has a symbol representing its quality. The following list is an example of chords, their quality and their corresponding symbol.

Chord/Quality	Symbol
C major	C*
D major seventh	Dmaj7
E dominant seventh	E7**
F minor	Fm
G minor seventh	Gm7
A flat major ninth	A♭9
A minor ninth	Am9
B suspended second	Bsus2
C suspended fourth	Csus4
D diminished	Ddim.
E flat diminished seventh	E♭dim.7
F augmented	Faug.
B flat minor, raised seventh	B♭min+7
C-dominant seventh, flat nine	C7♭9

*: A letter name without any abbreviations or numbers represents a major chord.
**: A letter name followed by a seven represents a dominant seventh chord.

Some piano music has the melody, harmony (chords) and bass line written out in fine detail. This is the case with classical pieces. With jazz, pop and rock piano music, sometimes the specific harmony is not written – instead, chord symbols are written above the melody. The sequence of chords is called a chord progression.

Playing a chord chart requires a lot of keyboard experience and the ability to construct chords based on chord symbols. The pianist has to know all the notes that belong in the chord and which position to play the chord: root, first inversion, second inversion or third inversion.

The first step in this process is to go through the entire chord progression and work out the fingering and positions of the chords with the left hand. Once that is accomplished, then you can add the melody with the right hand.

Take a look at EXERCISE 20-1, which has only a melody with chord symbols above it. The following table identifies the chord qualities and the notes for each chord in this exercise.

TABLE 20-1

Bar	Chords	Notes
1	D major 7th	D–F#–A–C#
2	A major 7th	A–C#–E–G#
3	B minor 7th	B–D–F#–A
4	A major 7th	A–C#–E–G#
5	B minor 7th	B–D–F#–A
6	F sharp minor	F#–A–C#
7	D major	D–F#–A
8	A major	A–C#–E

With your left hand, try to work out the fingering and position of the chords. As you know, first and second inversions make it easier to go from one chord to another, minimizing the repositioning of the hand and fingers. When playing a chord chart, the rhythm of the chords also has to be determined. In EXERCISE 20-1, simply play one dotted half note chord per bar, starting with the D major seventh in root position and building up from D, one tone above middle C.

As indicated in the key signature, EXERCISE 20-1 is in the key of A major and is in 3/4 time.

NIKKI

If you didn't find it easy to construct the chords in EXERCISE 20-1, the following table shows the positions of the chords in the progression.

TABLE 20-2

Bar	Chords	Notes	Position
1	D major 7th	D–F#–A–C#	root
2	A major 7th	C#–E–G#–A	1st inversion
3	B minor 7th	B–D–F#–A	root
4	A major 7th	A–C#–E–G#	root
5	B minor 7th	B–D–F#–A	root
6	F sharp minor	A–C#–F#	1st inversion
7	D major	A–D–F#	2nd inversion
8	A major	A–C#–E	root

Improvisation

Some chord charts have no written melody or harmony at all; the rhythm is indicated by slanted slash marks. This type of chord chart is used primarily by pianists who accompany singers or solo instrumentalists. The singer or instrumentalist sings or plays the melody while the pianist provides the chordal (harmonic) rhythmic accompaniment. In order to do this successfully, it helps to have years of keyboard experience and working with other musicians – soloists and singers alike. It also requires the ability to improvise or fill in. A keyboard player in a band typically plays solos; when playing from a chord chart that has no written notes to play, the pianist has to improvise; in other words, to make up solos on the spot.

Improvisation is a very special skill. Some pianists can acquire and develop this skill, while others have difficulty with improvising and prefer to play from much more detailed written music. Playing from chord charts is certainly for the advanced keyboard player who knows how to improvise.

The next exercise is an example of a chord chart with no written melody or harmony. Each slanted slash mark represents a crotchet. It's a fast-moving, bouncy, bright little piece. Go straight ahead and play with it; start slowly and work out the fingering and chords, and gradually work your way up to the given tempo (*allegro*). Play the chords with your right hand, and play the root of the chords with your left hand. There's an introduction in the first four bars, with changing chords every two beats. You can repeat it as often as you like.

EXERCISE 20-2

BOUNCING BACK

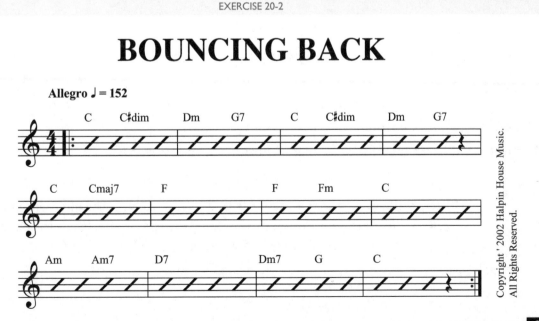

Chord Formulas

The following table identifies the formulas for constructing the chords we have covered in this book. The sequence of thirds starts from the root of the chord and builds up accordingly.

TABLE 20-3

Major Chord	*dominant 7*	*dominant 7, 9*	*major 7*	*major 7, 9*
		major third		minor third
	minor third	minor third	major third	major third
minor third	minor third	minor third	minor third	minor third
major third	major third	major third	major third	major third

Minor chord	*minor 7*	*minor 7, 9*	*minor +7*	*minor +7, 9*
		major third		minor third
	minor third	minor third	major third	major third
major third	major third	major third	major third	major third
minor third	minor third	minor third	minor third	minor third

diminished	*dim. 7*	*augmented*	*aug. 7*	*aug. 7, 9*
				minor third
	minor third		minor third	minor third
minor third	minor third	major third	major third	major third
minor third	minor third	major third	major third	major third

One of the most dissonant chords in the table above is the augmented 7, 9 chord. The tension is caused by the raised (augmented) fifth in the chord. The notes in a C aug. 7, 9 are C, E, G sharp, B and D.

Tied Rhythm

The next exercise has a tied rhythm in the melody over chords played with the left hand. As you already know, another way of writing this tied rhythm is a dotted rhythm – a dotted crotchet followed by a quaver. With a dotted rhythm, you don't see the second beat, whereas with the tied rhythm, you can see the second beat – even though you don't play it.

EXERCISE 20-3 begins with a two-bar introduction, which sets up the key of B flat major, the 4/4 time signature and the melody. As you can see in the second bar, the melody begins with the two crotchet grace notes C and D. In the fourth bar, there are accent marks above and below the chords and melody, so that you can play these notes and chords forcefully.

The following table contains the notes in the chords, quality, position of the chords and left-hand fingering for EXERCISE 20-3.

TABLE 20-4

Bar	Chords	Notes/Fingering	Position
1	B♭ major	B♭–D–F–B♭ 5 3 2 1	root
	E♭ major	B♭–E♭–G–B♭ 5 3 2 1	2nd inversion
2	B♭ major	B♭–D–F–B♭ 5 3 2 1	root
3	C minor 7th C minor 7th	C–E♭–G–B♭ C–E♭–G–B♭ 5 3 2 1	root root
4	F major F major	C–F–A C–F–A 52 1	2nd inversion 2nd inversion
5	B♭ major B♭ major	B♭–D–F B♭–D–F 3 2 1	root root
6	B diminished	B natural–D–F 3 2 1	root

TABLE 20-4 *(continued)*

7	C minor 7th	C–E♭–G–B♭	root
	C minor 7th	C–E♭–G–B♭	root
		5 3 2 1	
8	F major	C–F–A	2nd inversion
	F major	C–F–A	2nd inversion
		52 1	
9	B♭ major	B♭–D–F–B♭	root
		5 3 2 1	
	F major	C–F–A	2nd inversion
		52 1	
10	E♭ major	E♭–G–B♭	root
		3 2 1	
11	C minor 7th	C–E♭–G–B♭	root
	C minor 7th	C–E♭–G–B♭	root
		5 3 2 1	
12	F major	C–F–A	2nd inversion
	F major	C–F–A	2nd inversion
		52 1	
13	B♭ major	B♭–D–F–B♭	root
		5 3 2 1	
	E♭ major	B♭–E♭–G–B♭	2nd inversion
		5 3 2 1	
14	B♭ major	B♭–D–F–B♭	root
		5 3 2 1	

In terms of compositional form, there are two patterns in EXERCISE 20-3. The first pattern takes place in the first two bars: the tied rhythm in the melody followed by a minim over the I (B flat), IV (E flat), and I (B flat) chords. This is repeated with some variation in bars 9 and 10: the same rhythm with different pitches in the melody over the I (B flat), V (F), and IV (E flat) chords. The same pattern is repeated again in bars 13 and 14.

EXERCISE 20-3

POSITIVE

The same rhythm with different pitches appears in the melody over the I (B flat), IV (E flat) and I (B flat) chords.

The second pattern begins with the two crotchet grace notes C and D in the second bar, followed by the tied rhythm in the melody in bar 3, and concludes with the two accented crotchets F in bar 4. In this pattern, the left hand plays Cm7 and F chords. This pattern is repeated in bars 6, 7 and 8. It is repeated once again, with different pitches in the melody, in bars 10, 11 and 12.

The third beat in the right-hand part in bars 4, 8 and 12 is a crotchet rest. This rest lets the melody take a breath and sets up the grace notes in the fourth beat.

With that in mind, play EXERCISE 20-3, making sure to raise the B flat to B natural in the left-hand B diminished chord in bar 6. As always, play only the left hand several times. Then play only the right hand several times. The fingering for the right hand is written above the melody. Refer to Table 20-4 for the left-hand fingering. When you have worked out both parts individually, play the exercise with both hands.

Suspensions and Resolutions

EXERCISE 20-4 has a busy right-hand part, playing chords, broken chords with suspensions and the melody. The left-hand part simply plays steady crotchets and a few semibreves. This piece uses a harmonic structure of suspensions and resolutions throughout.

In EXERCISE 20-4 there are two suspensions in the melody. The top note in the first chord in bars 1, 2, 5, 6, 9, 10, 17, 18, 21 and 22 is a suspended fourth, and the second quaver in the third beat is a passing suspended second, which resolves to the root in the fourth beat. The melodic pattern emphasizes the quavers that play the fourth, third, second and root. For example, in the first bar, the quavers C, B, A and crotchet G make up the melody. The other quavers, D and G, are notes in the G major arpeggio or broken chord. This melodic pattern is repeated with different chords throughout the piece.

The following table identifies the right-hand chords played on the first beat in each bar of EXERCISE 20-4.

TABLE 20-5

Bar	Chord/Quality	Notes	Position
1	G sus4	D–G–C	2nd inversion
2	G sus4	D–G–C	2nd inversion
3	C maj7*	E–G–B	1st inversion
4	C maj7*	E–G–B	1st inversion
5	Am sus4	E–A–D	2nd inversion
6	Am sus4	E–A–D	2nd inversion
7	G	D–G–B	2nd inversion
8	D	D–F–A	root
9	Em sus4	B–E–A	2nd inversion
10	Em sus4	B–E–A	2nd inversion
11	Bm	B–D–F#	root
12	Bm	B–D–F#	root
13	Am 7, 9*	C–E–G–B	1st inversion
14	Am 7, 9*	C–E–G–B	1st inversion
15	D7sus	C–D–G	3rd inversion
16	D7	C–D–F#	3rd inversion
17	G sus4	D–G–C	2nd inversion
18	G sus4	D–G–C	2nd inversion
19	C maj7*	E–G–B	1st inversion
20	C maj7*	E–G–B	1st inversion
21	Am sus4	E–A–D	2nd inversion
22	Am sus4	E–A–D	2nd inversion
23	D sus	D–G–A	root
24	G	D–G–B	2nd inversion

* root in bass

The left hand plays the root of the chord in every bar except bar 7, where it plays the fifth (D) of the G major chord. As you can see in bars 1, 2, 3, 4, 5, 6, 9, 10, 17, 18, 19, 20, 21 and 22, the left hand plays the lower octave on the fourth crotchet beat.

The second bar is exactly the same as the first, the fourth bar is exactly the same as the third, and the sixth bar is exactly the same as the fifth. Bars 17 to 22 are an exact repetition of bars 1 to 6.

EXERCISE 20-4 has two different sections: section A (bars 1 to 8) and section B (bars 9 to 16). Section A is repeated in bars 17 to 24. This exercise follows an A-B-A form.

You'll discover that the fingering pattern in the right hand feels very natural and makes it easy to play the part. EXERCISE 20-4 is a light piano piece, thus the *mp* dynamic marking.

Staccato

EXERCISE 20-5 is in the key of C sharp minor. The tempo is a quick-paced *moderato* (crotchet = 120) in 4/4 time. As you can see, the left-hand part has small dots written above and below the introductory crotchets in bars 1 and 2, all the following chords (with the exception of bar 18) and the very last note in bar 26. When any note or chord is articulated with dots, it means to play the value of the note shorter – in other words, the dots above and below the crotchets and chords in the left-hand part do not get their full crotchet values; instead, the value is closer to that which equals a quaver. Staccato is the musical term that describes playing notes and chords shorter than their written values.

EXERCISE 20-5 is written in A-B-A form. After a two-bar introduction played by the left hand, the A section is stated in bars 3 to 10. As indicated by repeat signs, bars 3 to 10 are repeated. After playing the repeat, we move on to the B section, which is stated in bars 11 to 18. The A section returns in bars 18 to 26 (which is a repetition of bars 3 to 10), with the addition of the final crotchet played by the left hand in bar 26.

Chord symbols are written above the left-hand chords. By now, you should be able to work out the fingering for the left-hand chords. Start by using the following fingers from the bottom note of the chord and going

EXERCISE 20-4

TIME

up: fifth, third, second and thumb. Notice that the F minor chords in bars 4, 6, 7, 13, 17, 20, 22 and 23 are second inversions, and in that bar 9, the B chord is in second-inversion position. Make sure to play the A sharp in the second-inversion F sharp major chord in bars 12 and 16, and to take note of the natural sign before the A note in the second-inversion F sharp minor chords in bars 13 and 17, which cancels out the preceding A sharp in bars 12 and 16. Also notice the raised B sharp in the second-inversion G sharp 7 chord in the third and fourth beats in bar 14. In bar 18, the A major chord is in first-inversion position, followed by the first-inversion B chord. And in bar 25, the B chord is in second-inversion position.

The right-hand fingering is written in the part. Make sure to use the second-finger-over-the-thumb technique for the first and last quavers in bar 9. In contrast to the rhythm played by the right hand in section A, the rhythm of the right-hand part is a dotted rhythm in the B section: dotted crotchet followed by a quaver. As you know, the dotted crotchet equals the first beat and half of the second beat. To emphasize the ending of the musical phrase and resolution on the E major chord (C sharp minor's relative major), as indicated by accent marks in bars 10 and 26, play the staccato E chords and left-hand E notes with force.

Now that we have analyzed EXERCISE 20-5, start with working out the left-hand chords. Make sure to note where the staccato marks are, and to play them short. The right-hand melody should fall into place without any difficulty.

As indicated by the dynamic marking f, play this piece loudly.

FREEDOM MARCH

Syncopated Rhythm

EXERCISE 20-6 is in the key of D major and B minor, and is in 4/4 time. The tempo is *andante*, with a metronome marking of crotchet = 104. The exercise starts off with a four-bar chord introduction, followed by the A section in bars 5 to 8. The B section takes place in bars 9 to 16, followed by a repeat of the four-bar introduction. As indicated by the repeat signs, after playing the chords in bars 17 to 20, go back to bar 5 and play to the end (bar 20).

The right hand plays a syncopated rhythm and plays both chords and melody, while the left hand plays even crotchets and minims. What makes the right-hand part syncopated is the tied notes – for example, in bars 5 to 16, the second quaver in the second beat is tied to the third beat. In addition, in bars 9, 10, 11, 13, 14 and 15, the second quaver in the third beat is tied to the fourth beat. The syncopation occurs with the bass part playing the third and fourth beats and the right hand playing only the second quaver, the second part of the third and fourth beats.

The following table identifies the qualities and positions of the chords in EXERCISE 20-6.

TABLE 20-6

Bar	Chords	Notes	Position
1	G major	D–G–B	2nd inversion
	A major	E–A–C#	2nd inversion
2	B minor	F#–B–D	2nd inversion
3	G major	D–G–B	2nd inversion
	A major	E–A–C#	2nd inversion
4	D major	F#–A–D	1st inversion
5	D major	A–D–F#	2nd inversion
	A major	E–C#–A	arpeggio
6	G major	B–D–G	1st inversion
	D major	A–D–F#	2nd inversion
7	E minor	B–E–G	1st inversion
	B minor	F#–D–B	arpeggio

TABLE 20-6 *(continued)*

8	G major	B–D–G	1st inversion
	F# major	C#–F#–A#	2nd inversion
9	B minor	D–F#–B	1st inversion
	B minor sus 2*	C#–D (no 5th)	open
10	G maj 7*	D–F#–B	2nd inversion
	G maj 7, sus 4*	C#–D (no 3rd)	open
11	E minor 7	E–G–D	root
12	F# major sus 4	C#–F#–B	2nd inversion
	F# major*	A# (no 5th)	open
13	B minor	D–F#–B	1st inversion
	B minor sus 2*	C#–D (no 5th)	open
14	G maj 7*	D–F#–B	2nd inversion
	G maj 7, sus 4*	C#–D (no 3rd)	open
15	E minor 7	E–G–D	root
16	F# major sus 4	C#–F#–B	2nd inversion
	F# major*	A# (no 5th)	open
17	G major	D–G–B	2nd inversion
	A major	E–A–C#	2nd inversion
18	B minor	F#–B–D	2nd inversion
19	G major	D–G–B	2nd inversion
	A major	E–A–C#	2nd inversion
20	D major	F#–A–D	1st inversion

* root in bass

Before you play EXERCISE 20-6, take a close look at the melody and bass line – the top note of the right-hand chords is the melody. In bars 5 and 7, the right hand plays arpeggio chords in the third and fourth beats; in bars 6 and 8, there's a quick suspended second in the second quaver in the first beat. We modulate to B minor on the first beat in bar 9, using the borrowed dominant F sharp from B minor in the previous bar, so the A is raised a semitone to A sharp on the fourth beat in bar 8.

HOPEFUL

In bar 9, once the B minor chord is established in the first beat, the fifth of the chord (F sharp) is no longer played. This creates an open sound, with the bass playing the root in the lower octave. Another open sound with no third takes place in bar 10, and with no fifth in bar 12. Also in bar 9, the right hand plays a suspended second in the melody, which resolves up to D. This occurs while the bass, on the fourth beat, goes to the passing note A on its way down to G in bar 10.

The second G major seventh chord in bar 10 is also in the open position with the root in the bass. In that same measure, notice that the suspended fourth in the melody is C sharp, brought about by the C sharp in the D major key signature. Note too that the bass on the fourth beat goes to the passing note F sharp on its way down to E in bar 11. As you can see, the right hand is playing a repeated pattern in bar 10, with a pitch variation (the passing note C sharp in the melody) in bar 11, and a harmonic resolution and rhythm change in bar 12.

In bar 11, notice that the bass note on the fourth beat is E sharp, which is a passing note to the F sharp in bar 12. Bars 13 to 16 are exactly the same as bars 9 to 12.

By now, you should be able to work out the fingering for the left hand. The fingering for the top note melody in the right hand is as indicated in the part.

Use your newly acquired knowledge to answer the following questions.

1. What is the abbreviated chord symbol for a D dominant seventh chord?

2. What is the abbreviated chord symbol for an E minor seventh chord?

3. What is the abbreviated chord symbol for a C dominant seventh, flat 9 chord?

4. What are the notes in a first-inversion, A major seventh chord?

5. When reading a chord chart that has no written melody or chords, what does the pianist have to do?

6. What is the sequence of triads that make a dominant seventh chord?

7. What is the sequence of triads that make a major seventh, ninth chord?

8. What is the sequence of triads that make a minor raised seventh chord?

   ♪ ....

9. What is the sequence of triads that make a diminished seventh chord?

   ♪ ....

10. What is the sequence of triads that make an augmented seventh chord?

    ♪ ....

11. What is the sequence of triads that make an augmented seventh, ninth chord?

    ♪ ....

12. What are the notes in a C augmented 7, 9 chord?

    ♪ ....

13. What does the word *staccato* mean?

    ♪ ....

14. How does EXERCISE 20-6 begin?

    ♪ ....

15. What type of rhythm does the right hand play in EXERCISE 20-6?

    ♪ ....

16. What makes it syncopated?

    ♪ ....

17. What note is suspended in a B minor suspended second chord?

    ♪ ....

18. What note is suspended in an F sharp major suspended fourth chord?

    ♪ ....

19. The borrowed dominant F sharp major chord belongs to what key?

    ♪ ....

20. What causes the C sharp in the G major seventh, suspended fourth chord in measure 10?

    ♪ ....

    (*Answers can be found in the Appendix.*)

APPENDIX

Quiz Answers

Chapter 13

1. Four.
2. Four.
3. One.
4. Crotchets.
5. Four.
6. Bar lines.
7. Treble clef; also called a G clef.
8. The first three fingers of the right hand.
9. A crotchet rest; one beat.
10. A minim rest; two beats.
11. A double bar line; the end of the exercise or piece of music.
12. A time signature.
13. It means that there are four beats per measure, and the crotchet gets the beat (the crotchet rest gets the silent beat).
14. Tempo; the rate of speed at which the exercise is to be played.
15. Moderately (not too fast; not too slow).
16. *Mezzo forte*; medium loud.
17. Because the notes are on the B line of the stave and higher.
18. A repeat sign.
19. It means to repeat playing the music between the repeat signs.
20. Twice; however, in this exercise, because the written text says repeat three times, it is played three times.
21. Exercise 13-8 is an octave higher than Exercise 13-1.
22. A two-bar pattern.
23. The fingering.
24. Ten.
25. Ten.
26. Four.
27. Three.

Chapter 14

1. A, F, D, B, G.
2. G, E, C, A.
3. One ledger line above the stave.
4. Fast.
5. Loud.
6. Slow.
7. An octave is the distance of eight notes between two pitches.
8. The fifth finger and the thumb.
9. Two.
10. 2, 4, 7 and 9.
11. The third and fourth beats.
12. Review 'Practising Techniques When Playing with Both Hands'.

13. It ties the treble and bass staves together.
14. They read music vertically and horizontally at the same time.
15. When playing descending bass notes.
16. So you don't run out of fingers; so you can play all of the descending bass notes.
17. When playing ascending bass lines.
18. In the first bar, two quavers followed by two crotchets, two more quavers and a semibreve in the second bar.

Chapter 15

1. None.
2. A minor.
3. The sixth.
4. Natural.
5. The root.
6. G major and E minor.
7. A semitone.
8. A tone.
9. A semitone.
10. A downbeat.
11. Three crotchets.
12. They equal their combined value.
13. Moderately slow.
14. A metronome marking.

15. It tells you the rate of speed of the crotchet.
16. Yes.
17. Review 'Practising Techniques When Playing with Both Hands' (Chapter 14).
18. D major and B minor.
19. The fourth finger.

Chapter 16

1. A circle of fourths.
2. They lower a pitch down a semitone.
3. The fourth scale degree.
4. The sixth scale degree.
5. F major, D minor.
6. It's the black key between the white keys A and B.
7. Because of the octaves played by the left hand.
8. Gradually play louder.
9. Gradually play softer.
10. Grace notes.
11. A two-bar sequence.
12. Three.
13. D flat.
14. Four.
15. Fast.
16. From the E flat down to the A flat.
17. While resting, it is waiting and prepared to play the notes in bar 9.
18. Play only the right-hand part several times.
19. Five.
20. They are enharmonic equivalents.
21. Yes.
22. A sharp minor.

23. G flat major.
24. E flat minor.
25. G sharp.
26. C flat.

Chapter 17

1. To get a better understanding of how melody, harmony and bass lines work together to make piano music.
2. A combination of sounds considered pleasing to the ear.
3. A triad.
4. Two.
5. A major third followed by a minor third.
6. E flat.
7. E sharp.
8. They are enharmonic equivalents.
9. F.
10. A minor third followed by a major third.
11. A flat.
12. C sharp.
13. E minor.
14. B diminished.
15. A chord that starts with the root followed by the third and fifth.
16. A chord that starts with the third followed by the fifth and root.
17. A chord that starts with the fifth followed by the root and third.
18. C sharp, E, A.
19. B, E, G.
20. B minor.
21. D major.

22. The ii chord: F sharp diminished.
23. The ii and vii chords.
24. Because of the D sharp.
25. To make the fingering easier; to make the notes from one chord to another flow smoothly by moving a semitone or tone.

Chapter 18

1. Analyze all its parts.
2. Two or three measures ahead of your fingers.
3. An acquired skill.
4. The span of an octave.
5. G, B flat, E flat, G.
6. G, B, E, G.
7. F sharp, B, D sharp, F sharp.
8. A, D, F, A.
9. The fingering doesn't change; it's exactly the same as playing four-note root-position chords.
10. From the fifth to the fifth.
11. Because the chords don't belong to one specific key signature.
12. You play their combined value.
13. No.
14. Because C is not a note in the triadic structure of D major and E flat major chords.
15. Writing a dotted rhythm.
16. Three.
17. Yes.
18. When two or more chords have the same note in their triadic structure.
19. E.
20. C and E flat.

21. F and A flat.
22. There's only one: F.
23. Six.
24. Because the two beats include three quavers per beat.
25. Because the fourth note, D, is played by the right hand.

Chapter 19

EXERCISE 19-3

Root/Chord	Ninth
C major	D
D minor	E
E flat minor	F
F minor	G
F sharp minor	G sharp
G minor	A
A minor	B
B flat minor	C

EXERCISE 19-4

Root/Chord	Ninth
C sharp minor 7th	D sharp
D major 7th	E
E minor 7th	F
F dominant 7th	G
G minor 7th	A
A major 7th	B
B dominant 7th	C sharp

1. From the root of a chord, build a major third (root to third), minor third (third to fifth) and a major third (fifth to seventh).
2. A semitone.
3. D.
4. A flat, C, E flat, G.
5. A tone.
6. E.

7. F sharp, A, C sharp, E.
8. A, C, E, G sharp.
9. B flat, D flat, F, A flat.
10. E, G sharp, B, D.
11. G, B, C, E.
12. D, F sharp, A, B.
13. C sharp, E, F harp, A sharp.
14. B flat, C, E flat, G.
15. G sharp, A, C sharp, E.
16. When the notes of a chord are spread out in more than one octave.
17. It's a V chord that belongs to the new key; it's a pivotal chord that moves from one key to another.
18. A ninth.
19. E, G, B, D, F sharp.
20. Suspended fourth and suspended second.
21. The third.
22. The root or the third.
23. The fifth in a diminished chord is lowered by a semitone.
24. B, D, F, A flat.
25. The fifth in an augmented chord is raised a semitone.
26. Arpeggio chords.

Chapter 20

1. D7.
2. Em7.
3. C7♭9.
4. C sharp, E, G sharp, A.
5. Construct the chords, determine their position and improvise.
6. Major third, minor third, minor third.

7. Major third, minor third, major third, minor third.
8. Minor third, major third, major third.
9. Minor third, minor third, minor third.
10. Major third, major third, minor third.
11. Major third, major third, minor third, minor third.
12. C, E, G sharp, B, D.
13. To play the dotted notes shorter than their written values.
14. With a four-bar introduction.
15. A syncopated rhythm.
16. The tied notes over even crotchets in the bass.
17. C sharp.
18. B.
19. B minor.
20. The D major key signature.

Index

A

A flat major key, 188–190
A major key, 170–171
A minor key, 156–159, 185
accordion, 6, 8
acoustic piano. *See* piano
action
    in piano, 69–70
    in pianoforte, 3
adagio, 145
adults
    teachers for, 104–105
when to start lessons, 103
allegro, 144
altered chord, 227
amplifiers, 115
analog synthesizers, 81–82
andante, 164
arpeggio chords, 252–255
Ashby, Irving, 57
audiocassette decks, 112–113
augmented chords, 201–203,
    251–252

B

B flat major key, 180–183,185
B flat minor key, 191–192
B major key, 172–173

B minor key, 166–169
Babcock, Alpheus, 5
Bach, Johann Sebastian, 3, 17
backposts, 73
bar, defined, 127
bar lines
    use of, 131–132
defined, 126
Bartok, Bela, 18
bass line
    defined, 126
    learning to play, 142–147
beat, defined, 126
Beatles, 21–23, 24
bebop, 52
Bechstein pianos, 91
Beethoven, Ludwig van
    concertos of, 18
    sonatas of, 10, 14–15, 32
benches, piano, 107
big band music, 52
Blutner pianos, 91
Borge, Victor, 30–31
Brahms, Johannes
    concertos of, 17, 18
    Liszt and, 42
Brendel, Alfred, 31
bridge, of piano, 70–71
Brown, Ray, 57
Brubeck, Dave, 20

Brunner-Schwer, Hans Gerg, 57
Buchbinder, Rudolph, 28
Busch, Adolf, 49

C

C major key, 156–159, 185
    chords in, 199–203
C minor key, 183–187
C sharp minor key, 171–172
cabinet/casing, of piano, 66
celesta, 6
Charles, Ray, 53–54
children
    encouragement of, 105–106
    teachers for, 103
    when to start lessons,
        102–103, 104
Chopin, Fryderyk François
compositions of, 16, 17
    concertos of, 18
    life of, 36–37
chords, advanced, 233–256
    abbreviated symbols for,
        258–260
    arpeggio, 252–255
    augmented, 251–252
    improvisation with, 261
    sevenths, dominant, 240–241

sevenths, harmonic major, 239–240
sevenths, inversions, 241–244
sevenths, major, 234–237
sevenths, minor, 237–239
ninth, 245–249
staccato, 267, 270–271
suspended, 250
suspensions, resolutions, 266, 268, 269
syncopated rhythm with, 272–275
tied rhythm with, 263–266, 267
chords, defined, 126
chords, four-note, 219–231
exercises, 223–231
playing with left hand, 222
playing with right hand, 221–222
chords, three-note
augmented, 201–203
diminished, 201
major, 196–198, 199–200
minor chords, 198–199, 200, 204
root position, first and second inversion, 203
table of, 197
circle of fifths, 155–176
circle of fourths, 177–194
classical compositions, 9
concertos, 16–18
contrasted with romantic, 36
sonatas, 10–11, 15

classical pianists, 27–34
recordings of, 28–29
clavichord, 6
clefs
defined, 126
use of, 131
Clementi, Muzio, 13, 28, 29
Cliburn, Van, 37–38
composers
pianoforte and, 4
of sonatas, 11–16, 28
concertos, 16–18
console pianos, 64, 89
Corelli, Arcangelo, 17
crescendo sign, 181
Cristofori, Bartolomeo, 2–3
crotchet note, 131, 138
crotchet rest, 132, 138

D
D flat major key, 191–192
D major key, 166–169
D minor key, 178–179
D sharp minor key, 174–175
dampers, 72–73
Demidenko, Nikolai, 29
digital pianos, 6, 78–79
contrasted to acoustic, 79–81
recording of, 120–122
digital recording decks, 114–115
advantages/disadvantages of, 123–124

digital synthesizers, 83–84
diminished chords, 201, 250–251
diminuendo sign, 181
dominant sevenths chords, 240–241, 251
dominant/tonic relationship, 206–210
Domino, Fats, 20–21
dotted semitone, 163–164
dotted rhythm, 223–227, 263–266, 267
double bar line, 132

E
E flat major key, 183–187
E major key, 171–172
E minor key, 162–165, 206–208
effects units, for recording, 116–117
electric pianos, 6, 76
contrasted to acoustic, 76–77
recording of, 120–122
electronic keyboards, 6, 75
digital pianos, 78–81, 120–122
electric pianos, 76–77, 120–122
recording and, 120–122
songs using, 25
synthesizers, 81–85, 120–122
Ellington, Duke, 20

Ellis, Herb, 57
enharmonic equivalents, 192–193
escapement, of pianoforte, 2
exercises. *See* lessons

F

F major key, 178–179
F minor key, 188–190
F sharp minor key, 170–171
F sharp major key, 174–175
fall, of piano, 66
fifth scale degree. *See* dominant/tonic relationship
fingering. *See* lessons
first-inversion chords, 203
flat key signatures, 128, 177–194
  circle of fourths and, 178
  enharmonic equivalents and, 192–193
flyleaf, of piano, 67
forte, 144
fusion music, 52

G

G flat major key, 193
G major key, 161–165
G minor key, 180–183
G sharp minor key, 172–173
Gershwin, George, 20, 52

Giustini, Lodovico, 2

Gors & Kallmann pianos, 91
Gould, Glenn, 33–34
grand pianos, 65, 67, 89
Granz, Norman, 56–57
Grotrian pianos, 91
Guest of Honor, A (Joplin), 55

H

hammers
  in piano, 71–72
  in pianoforte, 2
  voicing of, 72, 98
Handel, George Fredric, 17
harmonic major sevenths chords, 239–240
harmonic minor scales, 205–208
harmonic tension, 206–210
harmonium, 6, 8
harmony, defined, 126, 196
harp (iron plate), of piano, 4–5, 71
harpsichord, 2–3, 6, 7
Haydn, Franz Joseph
  concertos of, 18
  sonatas of, 11–12, 28–29
headphones, 77, 79, 80
'Hey Jude' (Beatles), 23
home recording studios. *See* recording, equipment for

Hornsby, Bruce, 26
Horowitz, Vladimir, 39–40
humidity control, 96
hydraulis, 7
Hyman, Dick, 52

I

improvisation, 261
intervals
  defined, 157, 196
  of major chords, 196–198
  of minor chords, 198–199
iron frame/plate, of piano, 4–5, 71

J

Jando, Jeno, 28–29
Jarrett, Keith, 52
jazz/pop compositions, 19–26, 52
  Beatles and, 21–23, 24
  rock and roll and, 20–21
jazz/pop pianists, 51–62
Joel, Billy, 24, 59–61
John, Elton, 24, 61–62
Joplin, Scott, 54–55

K

Katin, Peter, 29
Kawai pianos, 92

Kemble pianos, 92
Kessel, Barney, 57
key signatures, defined, 126
  See also specific keys
keyboard instruments
  electronic, *see* electronic
    keyboards
  in popular music, 25, 59
  stringed, 6–7
  wind, 6, 7–8
keys, 66. *See also* notes
King, Carole, 24
Ktesibios, 7

L

learning to play. *See* lessons
LeCaine, Hugh, 82
ledger lines, defined, 126
left hand
  fingering lessons, 141–147
  four-note chords and, 222
  octaves, 146
  playing chords with, 211–215
Lennon, John, 22, 24, 62
Leschetizky, Theodor, 44
lessons
  flat key signatures, 177–194
  four-note chords, 219–231
  left-hand fingering, 141–147
  octaves, 136, 146
  playing with chords,
    257–276

right-hand fingering, 129–140
sharp key signatures,
  155–176
three-note chords, 195–215
two-hand fingering, 148–153
when to start, 102–103, 104
Leuschner, Michael, 29
Lewis, Jerry Lee, 21
lids, piano
  adjustable, 67
  recording and, 119
listening, 217–219
Liszt, Franz, 40–43
  Chopin and, 36–37
  concertos of, 18
  tone poem of, 17
Little Richard, 21
loud pedal, 4, 68, 72–73, 148
lyres, 69

M

'MacArthur Park' (Webb), 23
magnetic tape recorder,
  112–114
major chords. *See* chords,
  three-note
major keys
  A, 170–171
  A flat, 188–190
  B, 172–173
  B flat, 180–183, 185
  C, 156–159, 185, 199–203

D, 166–169
D flat, 191–192
E, 171–172
E flat, 183–187
F, 178–179
F sharp, 174–175
G, 161–165
G flat, 193
tone/semitone pattern of,
  161
major sevenths chord, 227,
  234–237
major thirds, 196
Manilow, Barry, 24
Martin, George, 21–23
McCartney, Paul, 22, 23, 24
melody, 196
  defined, 127
Mendelssohn, Felix, 17, 18
mezzo forte, 135
mezzo piano, 139
microphones, 115–116
middle C, 128–129
MIDI (Musical Instrument
  Digital Interface), 84
minim, 138
minim rest, 132, 138
minor chords
  intervals of, 198–199
  natural versus harmonic,
    204–210
minor keys
  A, 156–159, 185
  B, 166–169

B flat, 191–192
C, 183–187
C sharp, 171–172
D, 178–179
D sharp, 174–175
E harmonic, 162–165, 206–208
F, 188–190
F sharp, 170–171
G, 180–183
natural versus harmonic, 204–208
minor sevenths chords, 237–239
minor thirds, 196
mix-down deck, 118
mixing, 122–123
moderato, 134
Moody Blues, 24
Moog, Robert, 82
Mozart, Wolfgang Amadeus
concertos of, 17, 18
sonatas of, 12, 28
multitracking, 121–122
music stand, 66

N

natural minor keys. *See* minor keys
natural notes, 156
ninth chords, 245–249
notes
defined, 127
names of, 128–129
notes, value of, 127, 138
crotchet, 131, 138
minim, 138
quaver, 146–147, 229
semibreve, 138

O

octaves, 136, 146
open-position chords, 243
operas
of Elton John, 62
of Scott Joplin, 55
organs, 6, 7–8
Oscar Peterson Trio, 57
overdubbing, 121–122

P

Paderewski, Ignacy Jan, 43–47
political life of, 46
Paganini, Nicolò, 41
Pass, Joe, 58
pedals
loud, 4, 68, 72–73, 148
practice, 69
soft (damper), 3, 68, 148
sustain, 68, 73, 148
Pederson, Niels, 58
Perahia, Murray, 28
Perlman, Itzhak, 30–31
Peterson, Oscar, 55–58
pianists
classical, 27–34
jazz/pop, 51–62
romantic, 35–49
see also repertoires
piano
care of, 95–99
choosing of, 87–94
history of, 1–5
manufacturers of, 5–6, 90–93
parts of, 66–73
types of, 63–65, 74
see also electronic keyboards
pianoforte, 2
pin block, 73
pitch, defined, 127
playing by ear, 219
polyphony, 80
pop compositions. *See* jazz/pop compositions
posture, at piano, 107
practice, 101
concentration and, 106–107
habits and, 108
listening and, 218–219
pedal for, 69
posture for, 107
time needed for, 105–106
Prokofiev, Sergei, 17, 18
prop sticks, for piano lid, 67

Q

quavers, 146–147, 229

R

Rachmaninov, Sergei
  concertos of, 18
  Horowitz and, 39
ragtime music, 54–55
raised seventh chords. *See*
  harmonic sevenths chords
Ramone, Phil, 24, 60
Ramsey Lewis Trio, 20
Ravel, Maurice, 18
recording
  of acoustic piano, 119–120
  digital, 123–124
  equipment for, 110–119
  of non-acoustic piano, 120
  of practice, 106
  in professional studio, 110
  techniques for, 109, 121–123
reel-to-reel tape recorders,
  113–114
repair, of piano, 99
repeat sign, 135
repertoires
  classical, 9–18
  jazz/pop, 19–26
  see also pianists
resolutions, 266, 268, 269
restoration, of piano, 99
rests

crotchet, 132, 138
  defined, 127
  minim, 132, 138
  semibreve, 138
'Rhapsody in Blue'
  (Gershwin), 20
rhythm, defined, 127
rhythmic pattern, 136
right hand
  fingering techniques,
    129–135, 139–140
  four-note chords and,
    221–222
  playing chords with, 210–211
rock and roll music, 20–21
romantic compositions, 36
romantic pianists, 35–49
root position chords, 203
Rubinstein, Arthur, 47–48
Russell, Bob, 20

S

Saint-Saens, Camille, 18
Samick pianos, 92
sampler sound unit, 117
scale degrees. *See* circle of
  fifths; circle of fourths
Schimmel pianos, 92
Schubert, Franz Peter, 15
Schumann, Robert, 17
second-inversion chords, 203
Seiler pianos, 92

Serkin, Rudolph, 48–49
seventh chords
  dominant, 239–240
  harmonic major, 239–240
  inversions, 241–244
  major, 227, 234–237
  minor, 237–239
sharp key signatures, 155–176
  circle of fifths and, 160–161
  enharmonic equivalents
    and, 192–193
sharp sign, 161
Shostakovich, Dimitri, 17, 18
sight reading, 219
Silberman, Gottfried, 3
six-eight time, 229
Smith, Charlie, 57
soft (damper) pedal, 3, 68, 148
sonatas, 10–11, 15
soul music, 53
soundboard, of piano, 70
spinet, 6, 7
spinet pianos, 64, 89
square pianos, 3–4
staccato, 268, 270–271
stave, defined, 127
Steinmayer pianos, 92
Steinway & Sons pianos, 92
stems
  defined, 127
  placement of, 135
stride piano plying, 52
strings, 69, 99
studio piano, 64–65, 89

sunlight, 97
sus, 250
suspended chords, 250
suspensions, 266, 268, 269
sustain pedal, 68, 73, 148
syncopated rhythm, 272–275
synthesizers, 6, 81
    analog, 81–82
    contrasted to acoustic
        piano, 84–85
    digital, 83–84
    MIDI, 84
    recording of, 120–122
Szokolay, Balazs, 29

T

Tatum, Art, 58–59
    Peterson and, 56
Taupin, Bernie, 61–62
Tchaikovsky, Peter, 18
teachers
    for adults, 104–105
    for children, 103
tempo, 134
    defined, 127

thumb, moving around
    fingers, 150–151
tied rhythm, 223–227, 263–266,
    267
time signature, 134
    defined, 127
tone poem, 17
Toscanini, Arturo, 39–40
Treemonisha (Joplin), 55
triads. *See* chords, three-note
tuning, of piano
    after move, 90, 98
    importance of professional,
        98
    universal, 118
tuning pins, 73
two-hand fingering
    techniques, 148–153

U

upright pianos, 65, 89
used pianos
    buying, 93–94
    selling, 99–100

V

virginal, 6, 7
Vivaldi, Antonio, 17
voicing, of hammers, 72, 98

W

Waller, Fats, 52
Webb, Jimmy, 23
whole note, 138
whole rest, 138
Wonder, Stevie, 25
Wornum, Robert, 5

Y

Yamaha pianos, 91, 92
Young & Chang pianos, 92

Z

Zimmernam pianos, 92
Zumpe, Johannes, 4